Running & Philosophy
A Marathon for the Mind

To J. P., Scott, Doug, and Paul

Running & Philosophy
A Marathon for the Mind

Edited by
Michael W. Austin

Blackwell
Publishing

BLACKWELL PUBLISHING
350 Main Street, Malden, MA 02148-5020, USA
9600 Garsington Road, Oxford OX4 2DQ, UK
550 Swanston Street, Carlton, Victoria 3053, Australia

First published 2007 by Blackwell Publishing Ltd

1   2007

Library of Congress Cataloging-in-Publication Data

Running and philosophy : a marathon for the mind / edited by
Michael W. Austin.
        p. cm.
    Includes bibliographical references and index.
    ISBN 978-1-4051-7120-5 (hardcover : alk. paper) — ISBN 978-1-
4051-6797-0 (pbk. : alk. paper)   1. Running—Philosophy.
2. Runners (Sports)—Psychology.   3. Runners (Sports)—Conduct of life.   I. Austin,
Michael W.

    GV1061.R8344 2007
    613.7′172—dc22
                                                                            2007010758

A catalogue record for this title is available from the British Library.

Set in 10.5 on 13 pt Sabon
by SNP Best-set Typesetter Ltd., Hong Kong
Printed and bound in Singapore
by Markono Print Media Pte Ltd

For further information on
Blackwell Publishing, visit our website:
www.blackwellpublishing.com

Contents

Foreword

Amby Burfoot

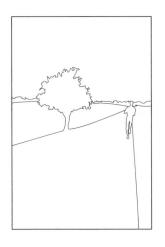

In my early running days, while still a high-school and college student in the 1960s, I didn't grasp the connection between running and philosophy. In fact, I thought they were polar opposites. Looking back, I think I missed the forest for the trees. Running was such an all-consuming passion for me then that I couldn't see beyond my next stride.

My college tried to set me straight. I was fortunate enough to attend one of those small Northeastern universities that still believed in the Great Books and the Great Thinkers. As freshmen, we were actually required to take a full two semesters of this stuff. I remember who we read, at least the names: Socrates, Plato, and Aristotle in the fall; and come spring, Kant, Schopenhauer, and Marx. But what were they trying to tell me? I'll be damned if I understood a word of it.

Truth is, my friends and I on the cross-country team railed against the whole tangled lot of them. Words, words, words. These guys suffered from mental constipation, we told each other. They were stuck in their heads – a lousy place to experience life to the fullest. We, on the other hand, were pushing the envelope. Sixty miles this week. Seventy next week. And more, sometimes much more, particularly in my case, since I was the most obsessed in my group.

I understood that mankind faced major problems. There was the War on Poverty, and the looming conflict in Vietnam. We were already concerned about the environment, and man's proper stewardship. Everyone was talking about the worldwide population crisis. But I was mostly wrestling with another issue: How could I cram more and better miles into a training week, and improve my marathon time?

Fortunately, through the years, I had some great teachers, and they lifted my vision. The most important of all was my longtime mentor John J. ("The Younger") Kelley, winner of the 1957 Boston Marathon and my first cross-country coach. Kelley read Henry David Thoreau and absorbed Bob Dylan, not a bad combination. He was an organic gardener before anyone else knew what that meant, and he ran or biked to his high-school teaching job rather than use the "infernal, internal combustion machine." He preached and lived the simple life, and his huge energy and intellect drew me in.

Shortly after I began working at *Runner's World*, I spent a day with Jim Fixx, whose *The Complete Book of Running* had made him the world's most unprepared millionaire. It also didn't change a single cell of his being. He lived casually and worked prodigiously, traits absorbed from a Quaker upbringing. Fixx considered his daily 10-miler through the seaside roads of Greenwich, Connecticut, the unassailable high point of his day. It was his reward, like a large scoop of ice cream. But he absolutely wouldn't allow himself the reward until late afternoon, following a long day of research and writing.

And then there was George Sheehan, MD, the guru-gnome-doctor-philosopher who will forever be the most popular writer to grace the pages of *Runner's World* magazine. Sheehan wrote often about the importance of "play," and this drew many readers to him. But even more flocked to another of his central messages – that we are all heroes in our own lives, and we'd better set a course full of appropriately heroic challenges.

Reading through *Running & Philosophy: A Marathon for the Mind*, a somewhat academic book after all, I was amazed that it didn't strike me that way. I expected it to be intimidating and off-putting, like my college philosophy semesters and those inscrutable Greeks and Germans. Instead, it read much more like Kelley and Fixx and Sheehan. And, dare I say this? It mirrored the thoughts and debates that have filtered through my own mind during more than 100,000 miles of running. Here, in one chapter, is a runner who needs a workout to let off steam after a fight with his spouse. Been there, done that (too often). Here's another who wonders if running is a sort of religion, and another trying to unravel the nature of happiness.

Others ask: Is pain instructive? How should we serve our community? Is running an art like other aesthetic pursuits?

Ohmigosh, I've wrestled with all these questions myself while running, sometimes in the company of training partners, more often by myself. Does that make me a philosopher? I'd certainly like to call myself one. But I don't think it matters. Here's what matters.

Running provides a great time and space for thinking. Non-runners believe the activity is a strenuous physical one, a strain on the heart and legs. But we runners know different. Once we're in shape, the heart and legs excuse themselves, and we become almost pure mind as we run. Away from our desks, monitors, keyboards, phones and meetings, we run on autopilot, and there's nothing else to do but . . . think.

Alan Turing invented the computer in the middle of a run. Musicians compose. Writers write. Actors rehearse. Physicists contemplate the Big Bang. And philosophers work on the even Bigger Questions, the ones that affect each of us every day of our lives.

We run, therefore we think. It's that simple. And the results can be surprisingly profound.

Preface
Warming Up Before the Race

Michael W. Austin

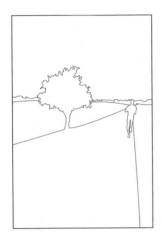

Running and philosophy, perhaps surprisingly, have a lot in common. Both are often difficult, and often rewarding. Each requires endurance and patience. Runners and philosophers often receive puzzled looks from non-runners and non-philosophers. Why would someone get out of bed on a cold, dark, winter morning in order to run five miles? And what in the world can you do with a degree in philosophy, anyway? Of course, most runners aren't professional runners. But it's also true that most philosophers aren't professional philosophers. We are all philosophers. We have beliefs about the nature of reality, the nature of human beings, what kind of life is the best life, and whether or not there is a God, to name just a few of our philosophical beliefs. And we often have reasons, hopefully good ones, for these beliefs.

Runners and philosophers have something else in common. They both want to get somewhere. *The Oxford Dictionary of Philosophy* notes that the term "discourse" is derived from a Latin word – *discursis* – which means "a running from one place to another."[1] In pursuit of answers to life's big questions, philosophers move from such questions – What can we know? What is real? Does God exist?

---

[1] Simon Blackburn, (ed.), *The Oxford Dictionary of Philosophy* (New York: Oxford University Press, 1996), p. 107. Thanks to Charles Taliaferro for bringing this to my attention.

How should I live? What is true happiness? – towards possible answers to those questions. Professional philosophers create and analyze discourses in pursuit, ultimately, of the truth. Sometimes we fall short of the goal, but we are generally happy to move from one place to another, if in that movement we arrive closer to the truth.

Runners want to get somewhere, too. Sometimes we simply want to make it to the end of a training run. In a race, some runners want to arrive at the finish line first and in record-setting time, while others are just happy to arrive there at all. But most runners seek more than the finish line, or the end of a training run. Many also take running to be an important way to arrive at some truth about themselves and the things in life that they care about. For many of us, running is a path to self-discovery, a part of our pursuit of happiness, and provides a time of solitude within which we are able to reflect on our lives and some of the bigger questions in life. And it is here that the goals of the runner and the philosopher overlap. Both running and philosophy, at their best, help us to learn something about ourselves, what is really valuable in life, and perhaps even something about the nature of reality itself. These are the kind of questions that human beings have wrestled with for ages, and they are the kind of questions considered in this book. Reading this book will not decisively answer all of life's big questions for you, any more than one good training run will enable you to set a new marathon PR. However, a good training run can get you one step closer to that new PR, and reading this book can get you closer to arriving at some good answers to some of life's big questions.

There's one more thing that running and this book have in common. Sometimes, the longer you go, the harder it gets. The last few chapters of this book are a little bit more challenging, much like the last few miles of a marathon. But much like finishing a marathon, thinking through the difficult issues in these final chapters – the human soul, human nature, and the role of emotions in our lives – is definitely worth the extra effort.

So before your next run, read a chapter. And even if you don't solve one of the great philosophical mysteries of human existence during your run, you'll at least have something to think about instead of that burning pain in your quads.

Acknowledgments

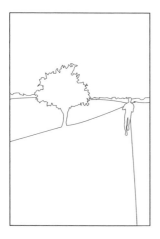

Thanks to each of the contributors for their hard and excellent work. Each of them helped make the process of editing this book an enjoyable one. Thanks also to Jeff Dean, Danielle Descoteaux, and Anna Oxbury at Blackwell for their enthusiasm, advice, and support. Bill Irwin deserves a special note of thanks for the guidance and editorial insight he provided from start to finish. Finally, I'd like to express my gratitude to Dawn for her patience, encouragement, and love.

Chapter 1
Long-Distance Running and the Will to Power

Raymond Angelo Belliotti

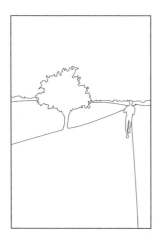

The 1984 version of the New York City Marathon was especially grueling. I toed the starting line with over 18,000 other participants. I was in my late thirties, an average long-distance runner, competing in my seventh marathon. My aspirations were modest: finish in around 3.5 hours with enough flair to sustain lies in later life about how good I once was. In my previous marathons, I had attained those goals. But on October 28, 1984, weather conditions were brutal for long-distance running, and I was struggling with internal demons. I wanted desperately to run valiantly, but my body was breaking down. Why not pack it in and regroup another day? But if I quit now, wouldn't it make quitting easier in the future? How badly did I want it? What was I willing to pay, physically and emotionally?

I was not alone. Thousands of other runners were waging their own internal wars. About one hour ahead of me was the frontrunner, a hitherto unknown Italian competitor named Orlando Pizzolato. Sportswriter Bryan Burwell captured the moment well:

The strength-sapping 74 degree heat and 96% humidity had been devastating enough, but now Orlando Pizzolato was hearing noises rattling around in his head, the kind of noises that demanded his attention . . . as his legs cramped and his stomach twisted in pain in those final six miles – familiar, old haunting voices that constantly whispered, *"Mi fermo? Mi fermo?* [Should I stop?]."[1]

Pizzolato, stalked by second-place finisher David Murphy, stopped eight times over the last six miles. Grabbing his stomach, contorted in pain, he looked over his shoulder to locate Murphy. Then each time he soldiered on.

> In the final miles, Pizzolato had to decide how he would be remembered . . . Would it be as a weather-worn quitter, whose brief moment of glory would slip away when his body surrendered to the elements before he could complete the race of his life? Or would he be remembered instead as a stubborn champion who battled his body, his mind, obscurity and Murphy all the way to the finish?[2]

Pizzolato refused to succumb to the sirens of comfort and won the race in 2:14:53. As the story of Pizzolato's stirring triumph filtered back through the pack of runners, I was desperate. Buoyed by the success of an Italian, I rationalized that this might be a special day for those blessed with Mediterranean genes. I called upon the spirits of my parents and grandparents. What would Joe DiMaggio do? (He would have been smart enough to stay home and drink coffee instead of running.) Giuseppe Garibaldi would not quit, would he? (Hey, he always had a horse under him. Probably did not run a mile in his entire life.)

Over 20 percent of those who started this race, including world-class runners such as Rod Dixon, did not finish. From miles 18 through 23, I remember virtually nothing except the humidity, the fog swirling about my head, and the conflicting voices in my psyche waging their ongoing debate. How would I remember myself on this day?

The better angels of my nature prevailed. (Would I have told a story in which I quit like a mutt?) I crossed the finish-line in 3:25:11, good for 1,764th place. Completing the race in the top 9 percent of starters was commendable for a plodder. More noteworthy, though, was my victory over the "dwarf" within me. And I had waxed 1983 New York City Marathon champ Rod Dixon!

---

[1] Bryan Burwell, "Pizzolato No. 1!", *New York Daily News, New York City Marathon/84*, October 29, 1984, pp. 1, 15.
[2] Burwell, "Pizzolato No. 1!", p. 15.

Although it did not occur to me at the time, the skirmishes waged within Pizzolato, me, and thousands of others that day reflect precisely the types of self-overcoming and personal transformation that animate the philosophy of Friedrich Nietzsche (1844–1900).

Amor Fati

Nietzsche insisted that inner conflict was inescapable. Human beings embody multiple drives, deep ambiguity and ambivalence, and internally mirror the ongoing flux of the cosmos. Refusing to accept what he took to be the false consolations of religion, Nietzsche was convinced that our world lacks inherent meaning and value. We can call this a belief in "cosmic meaninglessness." As such, the only meaning and value possible must be humanly constructed and fragile.

For Nietzsche, the lack of inherent cosmic meaning and purpose challenges us to respond positively: to accept our lives in their entireties and to fashion them in such a way that we luxuriate in our time on earth without the distractions of revenge and resentment. Nietzsche captures this response in his call for *amor fati* (love of fate):

> I do not want in the least that anything should become different than it is; I myself do not want to become different.[3]
> My formula for greatness in a human being is *amor fati*: that one wants nothing to be different, not forward, not backward, not in all eternity. Not merely bear what is necessary, still less conceal it – all idealism is mendaciousness in the face of what is necessary – but love it.[4]

Amor fati, then, captures Nietzsche's highest value: maximally affirming life with full understanding of its tragic dimensions. Suffering and adversity, instead of being avoided, should be crafted for practical advantage. Abundantly healthy spirits respect the order of rank based on merit, cherish opportunities for self-transformation through struggle and rich exertion, seek personal challenges from motives of joy and love of life, and scorn cowardly hopes for transcendental salvation. This life is my only life and if I confront it with aesthetic creativity and a full heart it will be quite enough.

---

[3] Friedrich Nietzsche, *Ecce Homo*, trans. Walter Kaufmann (New York: Random House, 1967), "Why I Am So Clever," sec. 9.
[4] Nietzsche, *Ecce Homo*, sec. 10.

Runners, typically, take up their sport to improve fitness levels and to test their capabilities. The adage is true: Everyone can be a winner in a marathon. In principle, all runners can attain personal best performances or achieve their individual goals regardless of where they place. Long-distance runners try to do their best against their own internal weaknesses, forces of nature such as weather, and the allure of the easy life.

They must nurture some of Nietzsche's more important subsidiary values: discipline, hardness, and risk-taking.

A marathon runner of average ability who aims for a reasonable time, say to finish around four hours, must put in weeks of training. A world-class competitor shooting for victory must put in months of more intense training. In each case, discipline is required. Training runs must become part of a runner's daily routine, not merely negotiable possibilities. Often, runners must overcome their own inclination to laziness – part of what Nietzsche called the "dwarf" within us – to ensure training is completed. A hardness of spirit results wherein higher levels of physical fitness beget more challenging routines. Runners must take risks along the way.

At first blush, Nietzsche is an unlikely candidate for long-distance running. His frail constitution and physical awkwardness invariably rose up to embarrass him when he ventured into the world. Yet the loneliness of the distance runner resonates in Nietzsche's solitary struggles to forge a worthy self, to construct an interesting life narrative. Training for and running a marathon require uncommon discipline, the overcoming of serious obstacles, the refusal to yield, undertaking physical and psychological risks, high energy, extraordinary exertion, and pursuit of a lofty goal that lacks a transcendental imprimatur. Marathoners battle the fiercest of foes: their own psyches. They must resist the dwarf within each of them, with full knowledge that they cannot vanquish the dwarf once and forever. And during their self-transforming, enthusiastic contests, as countless endorphins flow giddily within them, marathoners can bay "*amor fati*" at the skies. We can imagine Nietzsche laughing.

The Will to Power

The will to power, taken as the fundamental drive of all living things, is the impulse to dominate one's environment and extend one's influence. In human beings, the will to power sometimes manifests itself as brute force, but more frequently requires creativity, boldness, and innovation. The will to power connotes a process, not a fixed entity, which has growth, expansion, and accumulation at its core.

Not all manifestations of the will to power have equal value for Nietzsche. Life-affirming power flows from psychological abundance. Having forged a unity out of multiple, often conflicting, drives, the healthy will to power has the clear direction of self-overcoming. Moderation arises from joy in restraint, it transforms suffering and hardship into creative opportunities, it sublimates and spiritualizes cruel impulses into cultural advantages, and it finds joy in confronting the ambiguity of the world of Becoming.

Nietzsche claims that the typical catalog of human desires – for love, friendship, respect, procreation, biological nourishment, competitive glory, and so on – are all manifestations of the will to power. Accordingly, underlying the greatest altruistic and cultural values such as justice, truth, beauty, self-sacrifice, and art is the natural impulse to command and dominate.

The will to power is a "primitive" for Nietzsche: it is life and life is a complex struggle within and outside the human psyche. The will to power is the name Nietzsche gives to the recurring struggle among closely interrelated entities in the world. Power does not mean anything when taken abstractly; instead, it requires the mutual resistance of linked, living things. More subtly, will to power underwrites the struggles among the multiple drives we embody. These multiple drives, as well as the impulse for self-overcoming, are merely different manifestations of the same instinctual drive. Sublimation, self-perfection, and self-overcoming within the individual, and influence, domination, and command over others and the world, all fall under the rubric of will to power.

The philosophical subtext of Nietzsche's invocation of will to power is clear: our forms of knowledge, morality, truth, logic, and religion – all the alleged foundations of our institutions and theoretical enterprises – are the consequences of power struggles which themselves lack rational justification. While these alleged foundations present themselves as neutral exemplars of the persuasiveness of better rational arguments, undeniable metaphysical grounding, and glimpses of a natural order embedded in the universe, they are in fact nothing more than the effects of the will to power.

The will to power of long-distance runners centers on overcoming their limitations, pushing to reach close to 100 percent of their capabilities, and finishing their projects. Probably the most bizarre marathon ever run was the 1908 Olympic marathon in London. This race began what was later to become the standard distance of 26 miles and 385 yards (42,195 meters). The standard had previously varied from 40,000 to 41,860 meters. The race consisted of a 26-mile route from Windsor Castle to the Olympic Stadium, but 385 yards around the stadium track were added so that the finish-line would be directly in front of Queen Alexandra's royal box. We can blame Phidippides, the messenger who supposedly carried the news of the Greek victory over the Persians at the Battle of Marathon in 490 BC, for the first 26 miles. But I have often cursed, with good reason, Queen Alexandra while laboring over the final 385 yards.

The will to power of marathon runners has never been illustrated more keenly than by Charles Hefferon of South Africa, Dorando Pietri of Italy, and John Hayes of the United States, the fiercest competitors in the 1908 Olympic marathon. The British runners, hyped by patriotic zeal, set too fast a pace and faded. By the 18-mile mark, Hefferon led Pietri by over three minutes. By the 20-mile mark, Hefferon's lead was almost four minutes. Pietri then made his move. Still leading around the 24-mile mark, Hefferon began to tire badly. He then pulled a rock of Grady Little proportions.[5] He accepted a celebratory drink of champagne from a bystander. Predictably, he soon became dizzy and developed stomach cramps.

If that was not enough, spectators began slapping Hefferon vigorously on the back as gestures of well-intentioned but ill-advised support. A half-mile from the stadium entrance, Hefferon was passed by Pietri. But wait! The Queen Alexandra-inspired extra 385 yards proved decisive. Pietri was dazed and staggered about the track in the wrong direction. Olympic officials scurried to his aid and pointed him toward the finish-line. (Thankfully, they did not pour him an Amaretto.) After traveling a few feet, Pietri collapsed on the track. Medical personnel and track officials, fearing the Italian might perish,

---

[5] Grady Little was the manager of the Boston Red Sox in 2003. Against all evidence, he left his starting pitcher, Pedro Martinez, in too long in the deciding game of the American League Championship Series. As a result, the Red Sox lost a pennant to the New York Yankees that seemed well in hand. In reaction to fan outrage and media ridicule, Little was, mercifully, fired.

Raymond Angelo Belliotti

helped Pietri to his feet. But down goes Dorando! Officials again helped him to his feet. Down goes Dorando! The scene repeated several times.

Eventually, another runner, John Hayes of the United States, appeared in the stadium. After Pietri's fifth collapse, the chief race official caught him and carried him across the finish-line in victory. Although Dorando Pietri was initially declared the winner, American officials filed a successful protest and Hayes was awarded the gold medal. Pietri, seemingly flirting with death, survived.

The race, though, turned out to be a good career move for Dorando Pietri and John Hayes. Spurred by the high drama, promoters offered both competitors impressive money to turn professional. They ran dozens of races over the next few years, earning much more money than they could otherwise have garnered. Their most famous battles were two match races in New York City in 1908 and 1909, both won by Pietri. (I don't know whether Hefferon, who was awarded the Olympic silver medal upon Pietri's disqualification, received endorsement offers for Mimosas.) Moral of the story: Never underestimate the will to power of a marathon runner.

The Last Man

Nietzsche reserves special contempt for that most despicable human type, which he calls the "last man." The last man shrivels before the thought that the cosmos lacks inherent value and meaning. In their search for security, contentment, and minimal exertion last men lead shallow lives of timid conformity and superficial happiness. They take solace in a narrow egalitarianism that severs them from the highest human possibilities: intense love, grand creation, deep longing, passionate exertion, and adventure in pursuit of excellence.

> "We have invented happiness," say the last men, and they blink. They have left the regions where it was hard to live, for one needs warmth. One still loves one's neighbor and rubs against him, for one needs warmth. Becoming sick and harboring suspicion are sinful to them: one proceeds carefully. A fool, whoever still stumbles over stones or human beings! A little poison now and then: that makes for agreeable dreams. And much poison in the end, for an agreeable death. One still works, for work is a form of entertainment. But one is careful lest the entertainment be too harrowing. One no longer becomes poor or rich:

both require too much exertion. Who still wants to rule? Who obey? Both require too much exertion . . . everybody wants the same, everybody is the same . . . "We have invented happiness," say the last men, and they blink.[6]

The highest ambitions of last men are comfort and security. They are the extreme case of the herd mentality: habit, custom, indolence, self-preservation, and muted will to power prevail. Last men embody none of the inner tensions and conflicts that spur transformative action: they take no risks, lack convictions, avoid experimentation, and seek only bland survival. They invent "happiness" as the brutish accumulation of pleasure and avoidance of suffering. They "blink" to hide themselves from reality. They ingest "poison" now and then in the form of religious indoctrination focused on a supposedly blissful afterlife. Last men lack the vigor and exalted will to power that can view this world as it is, yet maximally affirm it. Nietzsche was not describing the middle-class mentality of his day, but rather the banality of the possible classless society of the future.

Like cockroaches after a nuclear explosion, last men live the longest. Nietzsche understands that higher human types are more fragile, more likely to squander their abundant passions in acts of self-overcoming than last men who are concerned narrowly with species survival. Expanding one's influence and discharging one's strength often jeopardize self-preservation. For Nietzsche, the quality, intensity, and authenticity of a life are higher values than its duration.

Long-distance runners pursue their goals from a sense of fullness, from a zest for life that is revealed and nurtured by vigorous activity. Their quest for authenticity – understanding and celebrating life in all its dimensions; freely choosing and pursuing projects that require creativity and result in self-transformation; taking full responsibility for the persons they are becoming – scorns the values of last men. Nietzsche would applaud the justified self-pride that envelops a marathon runner after crossing the finish-line. Accepting a challenge most people would avoid, demanding a discipline from self that remains uncommon, enduring internal conflicts that last men would deny, and forging a unity of character out of their inherently multiple drives,

---

[6] Friedrich Nietzsche, *Thus Spoke Zarathustra*, in *The Portable Nietzsche*, trans. Walter Kaufmann (New York: Viking Press, 1954), pt 1, "Zarathustra's Prologue," sec. 5.

the joyful marathoner brightly illustrates Nietzsche's most cherished values.

But no project, however successful, can complete the self. Our lives, instructs Nietzsche, are processes that end only with death or from that moment when we lose the basic human capabilities required for self-making. Until then, we should view ourselves as elegant artists whose greatest creations are the selves we continue to refine.

For long-distance runners that means today's psychological and physical triumph cannot guarantee tomorrow's success. Each race is run anew. Each challenge is met afresh. Always, those noises and voices will rattle around in the long-distance runner's head.

Add one more crooner to the chorus: The spirit of Nietzsche reminds us that our resolutions of these internal, psychological wars will manifest the persons we are and influence the persons we might become.

Chapter 2

Chasing Happiness Together

Running and Aristotle's Philosophy of Friendship

Michael W. Austin

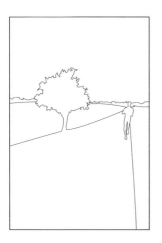

Why? This is a question that runners and philosophy majors are both used to hearing. "Why major in philosophy – what kind of job will that get you?" "Why on earth would you run five miles before breakfast?" Philosophers, who are rarely at a loss for words when asked this question, may give the questioner more of an answer than she bargained for. Runners, too, often have ready answers to those who wonder about the sanity of their sport:

A lot of people run a race to see who is fastest. I run to see who has the most guts.

Steve Prefontaine

I always loved running . . . it was something you could do by yourself, and under your own power. You could go in any direction, fast or slow as you wanted, fighting the wind if you felt like it, seeking out new sights just on the strength of your feet and the courage of your lungs.

Jesse Owens

I'm going to go out a winner if I have to find a high school race to win my last race.

Johnny Gray

There are as many reasons for running as there are days in the year, years in my life. But mostly I run because I am an animal and a child, an artist and a saint. So, too, are you. Find your own play, your own self-renewing compulsion, and you will become the person you are meant to be.

George Sheehan

Steve Prefontaine ran to see who had the most guts. Jesse Owens ran to experience independence. Johnny Gray ran to win. And George Sheehan told us to run so that we can find and be our true selves. Millions of others run for many other reasons, including physical and psychological health, to face and overcome a challenge, and even for the sheer enjoyment running can provide. What many Olympians and average runners have in common is that for them, running is a crucial part of the good life. Running helps make them happy.

But what does any of this have to do with philosophy? The nature of and means to happiness have been issues of perennial concern to philosophers. For example, the notion of human happiness plays a central role in Aristotle's ethical theory. As Aristotle (384–322 BC) puts it, happiness is "activity of soul in accordance with virtue" (1098a15).[1] Happiness is not merely feeling good. It isn't mere emotion, but something deeper. If I am happy, for Aristotle this means that I am flourishing as a human being. A happy person is doing well, and is deeply fulfilled because of who she is and how she lives. For Aristotle, we must be virtuous in order to be truly happy. We need to be courageous, honest, friendly, just, and good critical thinkers (among other things) in order to be happy. We know that running can lead to health for the body. Aristotle's view is that possessing and practicing the virtues leads to and constitutes health of the soul.

If being virtuous is a requirement for being truly happy, then the natural question to ask is how do we become virtuous? There is a lot to say about Aristotle's answer to this question, but here I want to focus on one aspect of that answer. Aristotle argues that in order to be virtuous, we need friendships in our lives. But not just any type of friendship will do. We must be involved in a particular type of friendship, friendship that is based on virtue. The friendships of runners often illustrate Aristotle's understanding of this highest form of friendship, as well as friendship in its lower forms. And as we shall see, running is well suited for fostering the type of friendship that Aristotle thinks is necessary for being happy.

---

[1] Unless otherwise noted, this and all subsequent quotations are from Aristotle's *Nicomachean Ethics*, trans. W. D. Ross (Oxford: Oxford University Press, 1980). Available online at http://classics.mit.edu/Aristotle/nicomachaen.html.

Why We Do What We Do

In his *Nicomachean Ethics*, Aristotle says that "... all knowledge and every pursuit aims at some good" (1095a15). All of our endeavors aim at some good that serves as their purpose. For example, Aristotle says that the purpose of the study and practice of medicine is health; the purpose of shipbuilding is a ship; and the purpose of economics is wealth. But in a human life properly lived, there is a chief good, a final goal at which all of our endeavors ultimately aim. The chief good that all human action strives for is happiness, according to Aristotle. Everything that we do is ultimately for the sake of happiness. Recall that Aristotle understands happiness as something deeper than merely getting what we want or feeling good about our circumstances. Happiness refers to well-being, proper and full human functioning, fulfillment, and inner peace.[2] On an Aristotelian understanding of the good life for human beings, we desire physical health and material wealth because they can help us to achieve our ultimate aim – happiness. They do not, in and of themselves, make us happy. This is true for everything else that we do. Whether we're pursuing knowledge, a career, a relationship, or even a new PR in the marathon, we are ultimately chasing after happiness. Happiness is our ultimate goal because it is, in a sense, our desired final destination. We do what we do because we believe that it will help us to be happy.

The Wrong Equipment

One of the great things about running is that you don't need a lot of equipment to participate in the sport. Some suitable clothes and a decent pair of shoes, and you're ready to hit the road or trail. But if you don't have the proper equipment, you'll suffer the consequences. Several years back I began having pain in my shins. It had been a while since I'd run consistently, and I was just starting up again, but the pain was familiar. I had shin splints. I'd been training on concrete sidewalks in shoes meant either for racing or for very efficient runners, neither of which applied to me. I was using the wrong equipment.

---

[2]   See Kelly James Clark and Anne Poortenga, *The Story of Ethics: Fulfilling Our Human Nature* (Upper Saddle River, NJ: Prentice Hall, 2003), pp. 23–9.

After changing to a suitable pair of cushioned training shoes, my shin splints disappeared.

How does friendship fit into all of this? We know that being virtuous is difficult. There are many barriers to living a courageous, just, temperate, and honest life. Aristotle is aware of this, and so he gives us some practical guidance in our pursuit of a good life. He tells us that "... it is impossible, or not easy, to do noble acts without the proper equipment" (1099a30). We need the proper equipment to overcome the difficulties that arise when we try to live good lives. This is where friendship comes into play. Aristotle believes that friendship is part of the equipment we need to live a virtuous life and so be truly happy. Just as a runner needs the proper equipment to excel in the sport, so all of us need the proper equipment to excel at life. A crucial piece of that equipment is friendship. If a person is to be happy, that person will need friends.

However, not just any kind of friendship will do. Aristotle argues that there are two types of friendship that won't help us in our quest for virtue and happiness:

> Now those who love each other for their utility do not love each other for themselves but in virtue of some good which they get from each other. So too with those who love for the sake of pleasure; it is not for their character that men love ready-witted people, but because they find them pleasant. Therefore those who love for the sake of utility love for the sake of what is good for themselves, and those who love for the sake of pleasure do so for the sake of what is pleasant to themselves, and not in so far as the other is the person loved but in so far as he is useful or pleasant ... Such friendships ... are easily dissolved, if the parties do not remain like themselves; for if the one party is no longer pleasant or useful the other ceases to love him (1156a10–20).

The first kind of friendship that Aristotle refers to is friendship based on utility. In this kind of friendship, the parties involved are only in the relationship because of what the other party can do for them. I've had this sort of friendship with other runners. As a cross-country runner in high school, some of the relationships I had with my fellow teammates were built solely on our ability to make each other better runners. (Admittedly, I usually got the better part of the deal, because I usually had more room to improve). These relationships were based on utility – the mutual benefit we provided one another – because we were merely helping each other train harder and run faster, so that we could perform better on race day. Aristotle contends that this type of friendship is inadequate as a means to acquiring virtue and achieving happiness.

But is this really the case? Someone might object (as we philosophers love to do) that running helps one to develop discipline and self-control, which are both valuable character traits that are conducive to happiness. Given this, it's plausible to think that the friendships I had with some of my fellow runners in high school, though based on utility, still helped equip me for happiness. In one sense, this is true. However, whatever moral benefit I received did not come from my friends, but from the activity of running itself. More to the point, if I valued my teammates only because they were useful to me in helping me achieve my running goals, and not for *their* sake, then there is something missing as far as the pursuit of virtue and happiness is concerned. To qualify as a friendship of the highest sort, of the kind that will equip us for happiness, something more is required.

Before we look at what else is required for the highest form of friendship, we need to look at the other kind of friendship that is inadequate for the task of building a truly happy life. This is friendship that is based on pleasure, in which I care about my friend only insofar as he provides me with some pleasure. Perhaps he's funny, and I enjoy his company because of this. But if I value my friend only because he's funny, or for some other reason is pleasant to be with, then the friendship will fall short in aiding me in my pursuit of happiness.

The point is not that all friendships based on utility or pleasure are somehow morally problematic, though many are, but rather that these friendships will not help us acquire virtue and be happy. We need something more in order to achieve these goals.

The Proper Equipment

Friendship based on virtue is what we need. Just like I needed a pair of cushioned trainers to help keep my shins healthy, we need friendships based on virtue to help us develop virtue and be happy.

In this type of friendship, which Aristotle refers to as "perfect friendship," both friends are virtuous. They possess and exercise the virtues, and help each other to be good and live good lives. It is this mutual assistance in living a virtuous life, focusing on the good of the other, that characterizes perfect friendship. Perfect friendship is not based on utility or pleasure, though it is useful and pleasant, in the right way. It is based on virtue and a selfless regard for one's friend. Aristotle claims that this type of friendship endures, unlike friendship in its other forms. In the other types of friendship, if my friend is no longer useful or pleasant, the relationship ends. Friendship based on virtue endures, however, because genuine goodness endures. And endurance is a good thing, both on the roads and in our closest relationships.

Aristotle tells us that perfect friendship requires many things, including "trust and the feeling that 'he would never wrong me'" (1157a20). The friends must be good, and they must deeply trust one another. Perfect friendship requires time, familiarity, mutual good will, and mutual sacrifice. Each friend has a genuine concern for the well-being of the other, and cares for the other because of his or her good character. Each assists the other in living a good life, a life of virtue and happiness. Since we are often prone to self-deception, or at least inaccurate assessments of our own characters, we need good friends who can help us see ourselves as we really are, and then help us make progress towards virtue and happiness.

Friendship Between Runners: Faster Times and a Better Life

Running with friends is an excellent way to help you improve your PR at a given distance, enhance the quality of your training, and simply enjoy running more. These types of friendships with other runners exemplify friendship based on utility and friendship based on pleasure. Running books and magazines often advise runners to incorporate group runs and runs with friends into their training schedules for these reasons. But another reason to run with friends is that running provides a context that is well suited for developing perfect friendship.

As we've seen, Aristotle says that developing a friendship based on virtue requires time, familiarity, trust, mutual good will, and mutual sacrifice. Running provides an excellent setting in which these requirements can be met. Running with the same person gives you the chance to spend time with them. Of course, merely spending time with someone doesn't necessarily lead to friendship, much less the type of friendship Aristotle argues is necessary for living a good life. But running together, because it involves meeting challenges together, and being with your running partner away from computers, cell phones, and televisions frees you up to develop a deeper friendship. Running five miles with someone on a regular basis provides ample opportunity for familiarity, trust, mutual good will, and mutual sacrifice to develop.

My own experience, and the experience of other runners, testify to this. When I was in graduate school at the University of Colorado, a fellow graduate student and I would meet weekly for a five-mile run around the Boulder Reservoir. Some mornings we'd do nothing but run, because it was dark, cold, and very windy along the Front Range of the Colorado Rocky Mountains. Other times, though, we'd talk about our childhoods, philosophy, fatherhood, and our families. Knowing that Brett was waiting for me helped me get out of bed on those cold winter mornings, when it was very tempting to skip my run. So our friendship helped me as a runner. But the time spent together on the trail enabled us to get to know each other in deeper ways, and encourage each other in our other pursuits.

In the May 2005 issue of *Runner's World*, John Bingham, a.k.a. "the Penguin," reflects on the nature of the friendships of runners. Bingham quotes the German philosopher Friedrich Nietzsche, who said that "Exhaustion is the shortest way to equality and fraternity."[3] Expanding on this idea, Bingham observes that the types of friendships you develop with your running buddies enable you to "go past age, gender, ethnicity, social status, and all of the initial criteria we normally use to judge people." There is something to this. On the road, your socio-economic status won't help you run faster. Older runners are able to challenge younger ones. Women outrun men. But it's not all about speed (especially for the Penguin!). Bingham contends that one reason many runners run slower is that they want the social interaction that running provides. They would rather not run eight miles gasping for breath the whole way, when they could run slower and use that time to connect with another person.

The value of friendships developed and experienced in the context of running can also be seen in the experiences of Kristin Armstrong, the former wife of all-world cyclist Lance Armstrong. Armstrong

[3] Friedrich Nietzsche, *Human, All Too Human: A Book for Free Spirits*, ed. R. J. Hollingdale (New York: Cambridge University Press, 1996), p. 263.

talks about the value of running and the friendships she experienced with her training partners during her divorce while she was training for and completing her first marathon:

> The conversations you have on a long run are unlike what you have when you're chasing toddlers, refilling sippy cups, or retrieving pacifiers. I now got to hear and tell stories in detail, broken only by the occasional need to run single file. There is something to sharing a private burden or relating a painful experience while chugging down the road. It's less about advice or validation. The wisdom, tears, and laughter we shared gave me an insight and appreciation for my friends that I have not had since I was in college. . . . It was more than a novice athletic achievement, it was a journey of friendship, the healing power of sport, and the confidence of achieving a goal I once considered reserved for those with more talent and resolve. It was a reminder that with good company and hard work, regular people can do something special. And it was special.[4]

Armstrong's friendships with her running partners illustrate another important idea of Aristotle's – the common good.[5] In the May 2005 issue of *Runner's World*, Armstrong shares about her involvement with Fertile Hope, an organization that helps cancer patients faced with infertility. Her own children were born as a result of using her husband's frozen sperm and in-vitro fertilization, necessitated by the infertility that resulted from Lance's chemotherapy in his fight against cancer. Kristin Armstrong and her friend Paige Alam organize and host the Fertile Hope 5k in Austin, Texas. In the third annual running of the race, Armstrong and Alam helped raise over $100,000. Armstrong and Alam worked together for the common good, helping make society a better place, especially for those suffering from infertility.

Runners and friends can work together for the common good, which is another important aspect of the good life. Many races are designed to raise money for charities, such as children's hospitals, the Susan G. Komen Breast Cancer Foundation's Race for the Cure, and organizations that provide sports wheelchairs for disabled children and young people. The Leukemia and Lymphoma Society's Team In Training program provides runners with a personalized training program and a personal website for online fundraising, enabling them to raise funds for leukemia, lymphoma, and myeloma research and

---

[4] Kristin Armstrong, "The Next Big Step," *Runner's World*, August 2004, pp. 58–9.
[5] See Aristotle, *Politics*, trans. Benjamin Jowett (Mineola, NY: Dover Publications, 2000). Available online at http://classics.mit.edu/Aristotle/politics.html.

patient services.[6] The Team in Training program has raised over $595 million since its formation in 1988. By integrating friendship and running and working together for the common good in these ways, we are able to personally experience and help foster in others the type of happiness that is desirable for all human beings. We're able to chase happiness – together.

The Finish

We must have and use the necessary equipment in order to achieve true happiness. Physical health is one aspect of this, insofar as physical fitness contributes to our overall well-being. Given this, running can contribute to a happy life. Aristotle would remind us, however, that the soul must also be healthy if we are to be happy. We must possess and consistently exercise the virtues if we want to successfully reach the goal of happiness over the course of our lives. To be a good runner, one must practice. And to be a good person, one must practice the virtues. In order to do this, we need to have friendships that are based on virtue, in which we pursue good lives together.

Aristotle concludes his discussion of friendship in his *Nicomachean Ethics* as follows:

> ... whatever it is for whose sake [men] value life, in that they wish to occupy themselves with their friends; and so some drink together, others dice together, others join in athletic exercises and hunting, or in the study of philosophy, each class spending their days together in whatever they love most in life; for since they wish to live with their friends, they do and share in those things which give them the sense of living together. Thus the friendship of bad men turns out an evil thing (for because of their instability they unite in bad pursuits, and besides they become evil by becoming like each other), while the friendship of good men is good, being augmented by their companionship; and they are thought to become better too by their activities and by improving each other (1172a1–15).

Aristotle would advise you to go out for a run, if that is something that you love to do. And while you're at it, he would say, take a *good* friend with you.[7]

[6] http://www.teamintraining.org
[7] I would like to thank Dawn Austin, Bill Irwin, Dan Lucht, and Ron Messerich for their comments on earlier versions of this chapter. For more on what philosophers have had to say about friendship, see Michael Pakaluk (ed.), *Other Selves: Philosophers on Friendship* (Indianapolis, IN: Hackett Publishing, 1991).

Chapter 3
Running with the Seven Cs of Success

Gregory Bassham

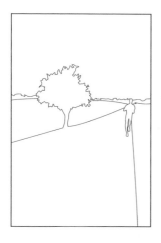

Prologue: September 12, 2005

I'm a 46-year-old philosophy professor, and in seven weeks I'll run my fourth marathon and make my second serious attempt to qualify for the world's greatest road race: the Boston Marathon. My quest to run Boston has been by far the hardest thing I have ever done. If I succeed, it will be the culmination of four years of sweat, pain, and frustration, but also of joy, self-discovery, and renewal. Throughout this process, I have drawn inspiration not only from running experts like George Sheehan, Jeff Galloway, and Bob Glover, but also from many philosophers, including one of America's leading public philosophers, Tom Morris. A former philosophy professor at the University of Notre Dame, Morris is the author of 18 books, including *True Success, If Aristotle Ran General Motors, The Art of Achievement, The Stoic Art of Living,* and *Philosophy for Dummies.* Today he is one of the most active business speakers in America, with clients that include many of America's largest corporations. In his talks around the country and in his many books, Morris often speaks of "the Seven Cs of Success," a simple but universal framework for achieving excellence in business, academics, sports, leadership, or any challenging endeavor. Although I first encountered Morris's Seven Cs more than a decade ago when I was his teaching assistant at Notre Dame, it wasn't until I began running that I realized how relevant and powerfully motivational they were not only to my running goals but to my personal and professional life as well. In this essay, I explain how Morris's Seven Cs of Success can help any runner achieve his or her fitness and competitive goals.

Condition One: We Need a Clear Conception of what We Want, a Vivid Vision, a Goal Clearly Imagined

Let all your effort be directed toward some object, let it always keep some goal in view!

Seneca (4 BC–AD 65)

"The quest for success," Morris writes, "always begins with a target. We need something to aim at, something to shoot for."[1] To be successful in any challenging, worthwhile endeavor, we need goals both to *motivate* and to *guide* us.

Runners, of course, run for lots of different reasons. Non-competitive runners may run to get fit, lose weight, reduce stress, enjoy nature, or just to relish some time alone or with good friends (human and otherwise). Competitive runners run for all these reasons, plus others (testing themselves, meeting challenges, winning awards, lowering their blood pressure, whipping their boss's ass in a 5k). But whatever their reasons for running, all runners understand the importance of motivation.

Nearly all runners enjoy running. For some, it's even addictive. But for serious runners there are many, many times when running *isn't* enjoyable. Times when the voice of temptation – "It's too cold," "I'm too sore," "I'm too busy," "My girlfriend said she'd dump me if I ran a marathon on her birthday" – becomes loud and insistent. Goals keep us focused on the prize and motivate us to stay the course. As University of Louisville basketball coach Rick Pitino notes, goals "give us a vision of a better future. They nourish our spirit; they represent possibility even when we are dragged down by reality. They keep us going."[2]

---

[1] Tom Morris, *True Success: A New Philosophy of Excellence* (New York: Berkeley Books, 1994), p. 35. Hereafter "Morris."
[2] Rick Pitino, *Success Is a Choice: Ten Steps to Overachieving in Business and Life* (New York: Broadway Books, 1997), p. 45.

Goals not only motivate us to aim high and to persevere, they also keep us on track and guide our progress along the way. As Morris points out, "vague goals can't motivate specific behavior" (Morris, p. 37). That's why we need clear, specific short-term goals as well as lofty long-term ambitions. Specific short-term goals – logging 45 miles this week, running three races this month, starting my kick a quarter-mile earlier – keep us focused and disciplined, challenge us to improve, and help mark our progress along the way. As George Sheehan notes, "we must keep our eye on the goal, keep looking at the hills."[3] But it's also important to remember to take the hills one at a time.

Most of us are capable of achieving far more than we think we can. Only by setting high, demanding goals can we maximize our potential. Of course, it's also important not to deceive yourself and set wildly unrealistic goals. That only leads to frustration and wasted energy – and sometimes embarrassment. Case in point: The guy who crowed, "I've been waiting to do this for three years" as he passed 59-year-old George Sheehan halfway through a six-mile race. He riled the wrong competitor. A mile down the road Sheehan passed him back.[4]

Condition Two: We Need a Strong Confidence that We can Achieve our Goal

Self-trust is the first secret of success.
                            Ralph Waldo Emerson (1803–82)

"Our life," said the Roman emperor and philosopher Marcus Aurelius (AD 121–80), "is what our thoughts make it." This is a point on which philosophers, running coaches, and successful people in all walks of life agree: Winners believe in themselves. They are confident, enthusiastic, and consistently positive. As the extraordinarily successful University of Tennessee women's basketball coach Pat Summit remarks:

[3] George Sheehan, *This Running Life* (New York: Simon and Schuster, 1980), p. 280. Hereafter "Sheehan."
[4] George Sheehan, *Running and Being: The Total Experience* (Red Bank, NJ: Second Wind II, 1998), p. 187.

No one ever got anywhere, accomplished anything, or survived any amount of ill luck, by being negative. . . . Attitude is a choice. What you think you can do, whether positive or negative, confident or scared, will most likely happen. When you doubt, you create a negative. . . . How many times have you watched someone fail, because they were full of self-doubt? Afterward, what do they say? "I knew it."[5]

Confidence is important in many areas of life, but it's absolutely vital in running. Confidence gives us the courage to set high goals and launch out boldly to achieve them. It keeps us going when we encounter defeat, disappointment, or discouragement. And confidence is contagious: by acting and being confident we create a climate of positive thinking and feeling that gives everyone in our running circles a lift, including ourselves.

Bob Glover, longtime director of the running classes for the New York Road Runners Club, tells the story of a woman who badly wanted to make the Greater New York Racing Team but felt she wasn't good enough to meet the time standards necessary for membership. Glover had seen her progress in speed sessions and believed she was not performing to her ability due to lack of confidence. He gave her a series of challenging but realistic time goals and asked her to visualize achieving them. "But do you really think I can run that fast?" she asked nervously. "I don't think you can, I know you can," Glover replied. A short time later she ran a personal best and qualified for the team.[6]

Condition Three: We Need a Focused Concentration on What It Takes to Reach that Goal

We should work hard with all the courage we can muster, ignoring any distractions, and struggle with a single purpose.

Seneca

It's not enough to have a goal and to be confident of achieving it. Like about 50 million other kids around the world, my 10-year-old

---

[5] Pat Summit, *Reach for the Summit: The Definite Dozen for Succeeding at Whatever You Do* (New York: Broadway Books, 1998), p. 181.
[6] Bob Glover and Shelly-lynn Florence Glover, *The Competitive Runner's Handbook*, 3rd rev. edn. (New York: Penguin Books, 1999), p. 300.

son hopes someday to play major league baseball and is confident he will do so. Clearly, however, the odds are stacked against him. Those few kids who will fulfill their dream of playing in the Bigs will need luck, talent, and an intense focus on achieving their goal.

Meeting challenging running goals requires dedication, planning, and sacrifice. Many novice runners start out like a ball of fire, but like the people in Jesus' parable of the sower and the four soils, fall victim to distraction, adversity, or the "worries and riches and pleasures of life" (Luke 8:14). To get from A to B to C to D, where D is some performance at the very top of our powers, requires an uncommon singleness of purpose. Those who succeed prioritize their running in ways that others may find difficult to understand. They keep their eyes steadily on the prize.

The price of losing focus can be high, as Australian runner Ron Clarke learned at the 1964 Tokyo Olympics. Clarke, the world-record holder at nine distances, was the overwhelming favorite to win the 10,000-meter run. Three days before the finals, he jogged onto the track to begin his last easy workout. Caught up in the moment, he began to run faster and faster. He blazed past 5,000 meters in world-class time. His time at four miles was an unofficial world record. A half-mile later, yielding to the pleas of fellow Australian runners, Clarke slowed down and ended his workout. The damage, however, was done. In the finals he finished a disappointing third.[7] Losing his focus meant losing the contest.

Condition Four: We Need a Stubborn Consistency in Pursuing Our Vision, a Determined Persistence to Achieve Our Goal

He who would arrive at the appointed end must follow a single road and not wander through many ways.

Seneca

We all love to take credit for our successes while blaming external, uncontrollable factors for our failures. It's never our fault that we lost; it's always _____ [fill in the blank with the appropriate excuse].

[7] Allan Lawrence and Mark Scheid, *The Self-Coached Runner* (Boston: Little, Brown, 1984), p. 3.

Runners are no different. You almost never hear disappointed runners after a race say, "I wasn't in shape" or "I didn't put out." It's always: "the weather was bad," "the course was hilly," "my ankle was hurting," or "the course seemed long."

The truth is, most of the time *we're* to blame for our lack of success. As Morris remarks, "one of the single most widespread and powerful sources of failure nowadays is a form of self-sabotage – self-destructive behavior" (Morris, p. 143). We yield to temptation, backslide, act inconsistently with our own goals and values. If only we stayed the course, we would succeed. But time and again, we don't. We lack what philosopher Francis Bacon (1561–1626) calls "the foundation of virtues." We lack consistency.

In running, as in any challenging endeavor, consistency requires *tenacity*. Tenacity, as Olympic bronze medalist Allan Lawrence notes, is the distance runner's "stock-in-trade." "Tenacity is what drives him on to finish the race when he wants to quit, what makes him pick up the pace when he is about to be passed, what makes him go out in the cold rain for the long training run he knows he needs."[8] The history of running is full of stories of extraordinary tenacity, from Phidippides' three-day, 260-mile run to seek help from the Spartans in 490 BC, to Guy Gertsch's amazing feat of running the 1982 Boston Marathon in 2:47, despite having snapped his right femur at the five-mile mark. But my favorite example of runners' tenacity is a true story featured in the 1984 film *Chariots of Fire*.

As most readers of this book will recall, the film centers on the exploits of two British runners, Harold Abrahams and Eric Liddell, both of whom defied long odds to win gold medals at the 1924 Paris Olympics. Liddell, a sprinter whose best distance was 100 meters, set a world record in the Olympic 400-meter finals, an event he ran only because he refused to compete in the 100 meters since the heats were held on Sunday. But Liddell's gutsiest race may have been a year earlier, in July 1923, when he won a 440-yard race in Stoke-on-Trent to qualify for the British Olympic team. Fifteen yards into the race, Liddell was cut off and knocked over the wooden railing by J. J. Gillies, who was favored to win the race. After rolling over two times on the grass, Liddell got up, vaulted over the railing, and began chasing the other runners, all of whom were now at least 20 yards

---

[8] Lawrence and Scheid, *The Self-Coached Runner*, pp. 6–7.

ahead of him. Throwing back his head in his patented, unorthodox style, Liddell sprinted all-out to win the race by two yards.[9]

Tenacity, however, is a two-edged sword for runners, because it's easy to injure yourself through overtraining. This is a problem I've run into repeatedly during my short running career. I began running four years ago, at age 42, as a way to get fit and to work toward challenging goals. The first year I ran I had one problem after another – blisters, blackened toenails, muscle pulls, sore knees, and repeated cases of tendonitis. The second year was better, but as I increased my mileage in preparation for my first marathon, I hurt my knee, had to cut way back on my training, and ran the Harrisburg Marathon in a disappointing 3:59. Ditto for my third year, when I began regularly to medal in my age group, but over-trained and developed severe tendonitis in my right ankle four weeks before I hobbled through the Scranton Steamtown Marathon in 4:11. This year, finally, I've been injury-free, and I feel like I have a good shot at qualifying for Boston. My times in races have been good (three miles in 18:15, a five-miler at a 6:25 pace, a half-marathon in 1:37); but this year I've deliberately sacrificed mileage in order to avoid injuries. To qualify for Boston I need to run a marathon in 3:30:59 or less (an 8:02 pace). Marathon experts generally recommend a 20-week base of 40–60 miles weekly before running a competitive marathon. Over the past 20 weeks I've probably averaged 25–35 miles per week, with five or six medium-long training runs (13–18 miles), and one very painful marathon run in 82-degree heat, which I finished in 3:43. Whether this relatively light training schedule will be enough to get me to Boston remains to be seen. But it seems to be the best way for me to avoid injury, and in line with the best philosophical advice on success, I'm sticking to it consistently.

Condition Five: We Need an Emotional Commitment to the Importance of What We're Doing

> To succeed at anything, you need passion.
>
> George Sheehan

"Nothing great was ever achieved without enthusiasm," said philosopher Ralph Waldo Emerson. In running, as in life, we need *passion*

---

[9] Ellen Caughey, *Eric Liddell: Olympian and Missionary* (Uhrichville, OH: Barbour, 2000), pp. 5–9.

– a robust sense of the value of what we are doing – to energize us, to motivate us to overcome challenges and disappointments, to prod us to dig deeper, and to give us the courage to take risks.

No one has written more eloquently about the physical, emotional, and spiritual benefits of running than physician-philosopher George Sheehan. A respected New Jersey cardiologist, Sheehan began running in his mid-forties, and quickly established himself as both a standout runner (at age 50, he ran a mile in 4:48, for example) and as a popular writer and lecturer. An avid reader of philosophy who frequently quoted Plato, Nietzsche, and William James in his weekly columns for *Runner's World* magazine, Sheehan found running to be "a path to maturity, a growth process" that continually challenged him "to go further, to grow more, to become a more complete human being" (Sheehan, p. 244). More than this, running became for Sheehan a *spiritual* experience, a path to self-awareness and transcendence. He writes:

> When running becomes for me, as my poet friend put it, "a totally entered experience," it becomes a religious experience. I give it my body. I give it my mind. I give it the yearnings of my heart, the further reaches of my soul. From the act of running – now an act of awareness, of love, of stretching myself – comes whatever wholeness, whatever certitude I possess then for the rest of the day. . . . When I run . . . the body and spirit become one. Running becomes prayer and praise and applause for me and my Creator. (Sheehan, p. 274)

Clearly, philosophy deepened Sheehan's experience of running, and running enriched his philosophy.

As a great philosopher once said (or was it my friend Sal, the salesman of erectile dysfunction treatment?), sustained excellence requires sustained passion. This can be difficult, however. Running races is like eating pizza: it's hard to feel as passionate about the fifth slice as you felt about the first.[10] So how can a runner sustain enthusiasm and commitment over the long haul?

There are two keys to keeping our emotional commitment high. The first is imagination. The most passionate people tend to use their imaginations well. They envision vividly some new challenge, or the

---

[10] A married, middle-aged running buddy of mine once told me that he took up running when it finally sank in that he was never going to have sex with any woman other than his wife *ever again*. Now at least he gets to work up a sweat with new people at every race. And, unlike at home, if he's able to finish, he gets a free t-shirt.

best results of whatever activity they're passionate about, or even put themselves into a compellingly interesting fantasy in their mind's eye. Think of my son imagining his triumphant day at bat in a major league ballgame, with the game on the line and the crowd roaring. As Sal and all the great thinkers of the past have noted, imagination fuels passion.

The second key to renewed emotional commitment is to continually set new goals. Think of another sport that often generates sustained, avid commitment: golf. Why do so many golfers enjoy the game just as much at age 70 as they enjoyed it at age 40? Yes, it still gets them out of the house, but mainly it's because they're continually setting new goals. As they get older, the goals may get lowered (breaking 80 after age 60, breaking 85 after age 70), but with the changes of age, the new goals can be just as challenging as the old goals were. A goal is never fully defined by just one number. The number is always set in a context, and it's the overall context that endows the number with its true value. This is true in running as well: at a certain point every runner has to face the fact that he or she will never again run a total personal best. But as long as there are new and interesting goals to be met in each year, at each season of life, mountains to be climbed, and dreams to be dreamed, a runner's passion can be sustained.

Condition Six: We Need a Good Character to Guide Us and Keep Us on a Proper Course

Character is destiny.

Heraclitus (c. 530–470 BC)

Is a good ethical character necessary for success? No. Sometimes, as the Psalmist laments, the wicked do prosper. Scoundrels do sometimes rise to positions of great wealth, power, or fame. Nevertheless, there are two important connections between goodness and success, Morris argues. First, a good character may not be necessary for worldly or material success, but it is essential for what Morris (following Aristotle) maintains is "true success:" "success that is deeply satisfying, that involves making the most of our potential, and that is sustainable over the long run, the sort of success that contributes to all forms of health and human flourishing" (Morris, p. 221). Second, in most cases a good character is either necessary or at least helpful in achieving long-term worldly success. Unethical people tend to make enemies, create distrust, and engage in patterns of unethical or illegal conduct that, when discovered, lead to their downfall. Moreover, unethical people tend to lack virtues such as hard work, integrity, fairness, sensitivity, and trustworthiness that often contribute to long-term success. By contrast, good people cultivate the virtues necessary for real achievement, and attract to themselves the people who can help them make good things happen. Few people want to help a jerk. By contrast, lots of people will rally around you and offer their assistance if they see you as a genuinely good person. And this is very relevant to real-world success. Rarely is anything of great value accomplished alone, even when it comes to the solitary-looking pursuit of running.

Certain qualities of character are absolutely essential to running success. Without virtues such as commitment, courage, self-discipline, drive, resiliency, toughness, consistency, hopefulness, and persistence no one can achieve their potential as a runner. Through practice and habit, running can help us to develop these virtues. What's more, running can teach us important lessons about life. He who can muster the self-discipline to run in rain and snow, fight back against adversities and disappointments, and dig deep to discover his own inner strengths and resources – he is the one most likely to be what A. P. Cullen calls "a true sportsman in the greater game of life."[11] A person who has cultivated ethical self-discipline in other aspects of his life is also more likely to be able to muster the self-discipline that is needed here. An ethical foundation can facilitate sporting success, as well as the sportsmanship that makes for true success in the realm of any athletic endeavor.

Condition Seven: We Need a Capacity to Enjoy the Process along the Way

Life must be lived as play.

Plato (427–347 BC)

Some kinds of goods, Plato reminds us, are both desirable for their own sake and also desirable as means to other ends.[12] Happiness is

[11] Quoted in Caughey, *Eric Liddell*, p. 121.
[12] Plato, *Republic*, book 2, 357a–b.

such a good. Happiness is an intrinsic good, something we want for its own sake. But it is also an instrumental good, a means to other goods, including true and durable success. By cultivating a capacity to enjoy the process along the way, we can learn to kick back and savor the fruits of our hard work. But we can also find in such moments the motivation and refreshment for pushing on to even greater successes.[13]

Most runners don't run to lose weight or get fit, they run because they enjoy it. It becomes a huge part of their life, of who they are. It was only in running that George Sheehan felt "whole and true and living at the peak of my being" (Sheehan, p. 135). And as Morris notes, such moments of peak contentment are usually times of what poet Donald Hall calls "absorbedness."[14]

People are absorbed when they are totally into what they're doing, totally engrossed in the present task and the present moment. George Sheehan experienced such a moment when, at age 54, he ran a sub-11:00 indoor two-miler:

> I was for those minutes completely and utterly relaxed, unconcerned about the outcome, yet completely absorbed in what I was doing. I was in what has been described as a cocoon of concentration, absolutely involved, fully engaged in running. Not racing or winning but simply running. Everything was harmony and grace. Everything was pure. Effort had become effortless.[15]

The feeling of contentment that often accompanies moments of absorbedness illustrates a fundamental insight about happiness that

---

[13] Speaking of refreshment, it should be noted that running is one of the few sports in which performance can actually be enhanced by (moderate) beer drinking. As George Sheehan notes (*This Running Life*, p. 90), sports physiologists have found that many runners actually run better following a night of beer drinking. To running-history buffs, the performance-enhancing effect of beer is hardly news. On January 2, 1884, after downing either 26 or 27 beers the night before, Harry Hutchens ran 300 yards on a curved track in 30 seconds flat. And in 1816, after three days and nights of drinking, the legendary Abraham Wood bet that in an hour he could: catch a duck on the turnpike road, pluck it, roast it, eat it, then run a five-minute mile. He won the bet. After eating the duck (washed down with a quart of ale), he ran a mile in 4:56, all in less than an hour. And just last year, after no more than about a dozen beers, I believe I was able to run to the closest men's room in near-record time. For beer-fueled accomplishments other than my own impressive dash, see Edward S. Sears, *Running Through the Ages* (Jefferson, NC: McFarland and Co., 2001), pp. 89, 56.
[14] Tom Morris, *The Art of Achievement* (Kansas City, MO: Andrews McMeel, 2002), p. 163.
[15] Sheehan, *Running and Being*, p. 174.

philosophers call "the hedonistic paradox." The paradox is this: Usually the happiest people are not those who pursue happiness directly, who make happiness their goal. Rather, the happiest people tend to be those who experience happiness as a *by-product* of other things they value and enjoy, such as loving relationships and engaging in challenging and rewarding work. As Morris writes:

> The best way to enjoy your life is to have something to focus on other than enjoyment. And something bigger to focus on than just your life. Cultivate enjoyment, look for pleasure in what you do, adopt a spirit of playfulness in as many ways as you can, but always have in your life an overall structure of goals that are worthy in themselves to pursue, goals other than pleasure or enjoyment, toward which you can work. And always have goals that go beyond the confines of your own immediate self-interest. Only that can bring the deepest enjoyments.[16]

Runners understand the hedonistic paradox because they live it daily. They find happiness through sweat, sacrifice, and struggle. To most non-runners this is a complete enigma. Cars pass a lonely runner on a solitary road – lungs burning, knees aching – and the passengers shake their heads. Why would anyone want to do that, they wonder. The runner, in turn, barely notices the car. For her, reality is this road, this moment, this feeling. Soon she will be back in the world of deadlines, piano practices, and endless loads of laundry. But for the moment there is nothing but this road, this feeling of wholeness, this Zen-like effortless effort. For her, journey and destination have fused. Success is *now*.

Epilogue: December 18, 2005

Conquer yourself rather than the world.
René Descartes (1596–1650),
as paraphrased by Jean-Paul Sartre

November 6, the day of the New York Marathon, dawned warm and sunny. Much *too* warm and sunny, in fact. The forecast high was 70 degrees Fahrenheit, a record for that date in New York City (plus 97

---

[16] Morris, *The Art of Achievement*, p. 177.

percent humidity at the start). According to exercise physiologists, runners slow an average of one second per mile for every degree over 60. I knew that New York was already a notoriously slow and congested marathon course. All the information I had read had cautioned that runners should expect to run 5–10 minutes slower than they would in most other marathons. Now, if the exercise physiologists were right, I could expect to lose another four minutes and 20 seconds due to the heat.

Minutes after the race began I knew I was in serious trouble. With 37,000 runners crammed onto the Verrazanno Bridge, the pace was agonizingly slow. At 10 k I was four minutes behind my projected race pace. Most frustratingly, with a nearly solid mass of slow-moving runners constantly in front in me, it was impossible to speed up for more than a few seconds at a time, and even that was possible only by constant zigzagging across the course. At the halfway mark my time was 1:45:52, more than seven minutes slower than my half-marathon time at the Erie Marathon seven weeks earlier. In my previous three marathons, I had never run the second half of the race in less than two hours and five minutes. Now I would need to run 20 minutes faster than that to qualify for Boston.

As impossible as this seemed, I knew I had one thing going for me: In the seven weeks prior to the marathon I had thrown caution to the wind and trained hard, including frequent two-a-days, speed-work, and several long runs of up to 22 miles. At mile 16, as we entered Manhattan, the sea of runners ahead of me finally began to thin a bit, and I picked up the pace.

At mile 20 my time was 2:40:49, just slightly off pace. Yet I knew that this was the point in all my previous marathons when I had hit "the Wall" and slowed to a crawl.

At mile 21, just slightly later than usual, I did hit the Wall. But this time, whether because of my training or the extra adrenaline provided by the cheering crowds, I ran through it. My legs felt like 150-pound sacks of hamburger meat and my kidneys were killing me, but I knew that Central Park was less than three miles away. I began passing other runners right and left.

Then, as I got into the Park, my heart sank. The narrow streets and paths of the Park funneled runners into a tightly congested pedestrian version of rush hour in Manhattan. I frantically zigzagged right and left, squeezing past slower runners whenever there was the slightest opening, hearing curses in a polyglot of languages as I brushed people's shoulders and nearly tripped a couple of runners. At mile 25, I saw "Team Bassham," friends and family who were there to cheer me on. I choked up as my son Dylan, the major-league wannabe, ran beside me for half a mile. With 50 yards to go, a slight opening appeared in the sea of runners, and I sprinted to the finish. The time on the race clock was 3:33:05, but I knew that what mattered was the "chip time," the time it took me to go from the start to the finish as recorded by the computer chip I had attached to my shoe. I looked at the time on my watch, which I knew would vary at most a few seconds from my chip time. My watch read 3:31:08. I had missed qualifying for Boston by *nine seconds*!

As trite as it sounds, I tried to be "philosophical" about this bitter disappointment, but it wasn't easy. But even before I had received my finishers' medal, I had resolved to try again.

Two days later, I was out pounding the pavement in my blistered feet. Soon I was running two-a-days again, usually in the dark, and frequently on snow and ice as an early winter hit Northeastern Pennsylvania where I live. Six weeks after New York, I boarded a plane in Philadelphia to run the Jacksonville Marathon.

During my weeks of training for Jacksonville, Morris's Seven Cs of Success had kept me focused and determined. Yet as I stood in a cold rain on the starting line in Jacksonville, I felt like all "philosophy" was behind me. My only thought was: "You came here to do this. Now do it."

Three hours, 20 minutes and 40 seconds later I crossed the finish line, more than 10 minutes faster than I needed to qualify for Boston. I did it. I attained my goal.

Now I have some new goals and I face four months of winter training to get ready for Boston, which is in mid-April. I doubt, though, that I'll worry too much about running a good time there. That will be a time to remember Morris's Seventh C: a capacity to enjoy the process along the way. Whether I run a good time or not, I now know I will have a very good time indeed![17]

---

[17] Greg completed the 2006 Boston Marathon in 3:22:24. In September 2006 he ran the Harrisburg Half-Marathon in 1:29:28, qualifying for the New York Marathon.

Chapter 4
The Phenomenology of Becoming a Runner

J. Jeremy Wisnewski

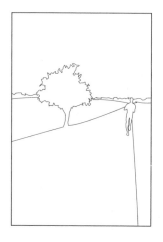

Consciousness is in the first place not a matter of "I think that" but of "I can."

Maurice Merleau-Ponty

Running an Experiment / Running: An Experiment

When I began thinking about this chapter, I was not a runner. I was, like many philosophers, a secret despiser of the body: I wanted to be pure mind. The idea of eating, walking, sweating, and all of those other indelicacies stopped me cold. I not only wanted to *avoid* running – I also wanted to *not be able to do it at all*. To run, I must have secretly surmised, was to acknowledge my physicality – and to do that was to concede that I wasn't simply a mind going to work on tough philosophical questions.

Ironically, though, I have always been *intellectually* interested in questions concerning the body: What exactly is the relation of the body to our understanding of the world? What is the role of the body in perception? I have long recognized that the way I encounter the world is deeply indebted to my bodily condition. When I am exhausted the world reveals itself to me differently than when I am full of energy; when I am hungry particular elements in my visual field leap to my attention.

In beginning to contemplate (as pure minds do) my initial aversion to running, I began to see that my aversion had more to do with my own understanding of the activity – and of my body – than anything else. I conceived running as a burden on my body that would yield unpleasant results: I would be tired. I would sweat. I wouldn't be able to go very far.

These are not the issues of a pure mind: they are issues of one who encounters the world through one's bodily existence. This idea – that the way we understand things is conditioned by our bodily states – is an idea that permeates the writings of Maurice Merleau-Ponty (1908–61). Merleau-Ponty maintained that traditional philosophy has misunderstood the body by regarding it as one object among many. The body, however, is *not* an object. It is, as he puts it, our expression in the world. It is that which enables us to understand things as we do.

And it was this contemplation that led me to a running hypothesis: if I altered my *body*, I would also alter my experience of the world. If I enabled my body to *learn to run*, the world would reveal itself to me in a different way. If Merleau-Ponty is correct, I surmised, I would experience a Gestalt change in my experience of the world. That is, I would experience a radical shift in my perception and understanding of the world. In fact, if Merleau-Ponty is correct, a running experiment would enable me to *see* the world differently. As I trained my body to comport itself differently to distance, exhaustion, and the like, I would also *encounter the world itself* in a different manner.

Testing my running hypothesis thus required doing some good old-fashioned phenomenology. Phenomenology is the branch of philosophy that deals with *phenomena* – with the way things appear to us in the world. The task of phenomenology is careful description: the aim of the phenomenologist is to capture the way things reveal themselves to us in everyday life, and to capture this *despite* our propensity to oversimplify. To investigate Merleau-Ponty's view, I would attempt to capture the phenomenology of learning to run.

This, then, was the running experiment: I would become a runner, and I would test the view that the way we experience things is intimately connected to our bodily existence. What follows is an account of my experiment – and, I think, a partial vindication of Merleau-Ponty.

Running on Empty: The First Weeks

Determination is the most crucial component to becoming a runner. I found that I needed it at every turn, literal and otherwise: getting out of bed at (or, more honestly, around) 6:20 each morning, sticking to a schedule, not cutting corners during my run. Those first weeks are a blur of determination, bargaining, disappointment, anger, and exhaustion – emotional stages that in some ways resemble the stages one goes through when mourning. And these are not isolated emotions. They run together, overlap, reveal things in ways that are often surprising and sometimes troubling.

On the first day of my running experiment, my emotions ran the gamut. I arose at 6:20 a.m., excited at the prospect of becoming a runner. I stretched for a few minutes, not really knowing what I was doing, and then headed out. Excitement quickly gave way to worry. I had decided to run for 20 minutes, but by the time I reached the beginning of my cul-de-sac, a mere three minutes had passed, and I was running out of steam. I began to bargain with myself. "Perhaps today I will only go 10 minutes," "I should ease myself into this," "I'll run longer tomorrow," and so on. And as I bargained, I remembered to keep moving.

On that first day, I must have spent most of the time in self-debate – arguing with myself about what I ought to do. My body moved forward despite my protestations – not quite convinced that there would be a resolution to the then-current melee: my desire to stop competing against my commitment to move forward, my ability to bargain competing against my pride. Somehow, I made it 20 minutes.

In the days following the commencement of my running experiment, I was daunted (but not stopped) by: sore muscles, a blister, a cold, an angry dog, rain, and the inertia of the non-runner. As I had anticipated, the world *did* reveal itself differently in those first weeks, though not in the way that I expected.

First, the minor phenomenological differences during the run: I noticed that, with only a little concentration, one could watch the horizon bob up and down as one moved forward. The world could lose perceptual constancy – something achieved in the first months of life. I could imagine that it was the horizon moving, and not me.

I also noticed that I measured the world I encountered in terms of minutes and distance. As I developed a route, I began to experience one particular turn as halfway, another as near-completion. The way I experienced the last long stretch of road before stopping, too, was decidedly unpleasant: it was "that which separated me from rest;"

"that which blocked my path to bodily peace." I can best summarize my phenomenology in the early weeks as simply the phenomenology of obstacles. Running itself seemed to me an obstacle. Each time I ran I thought of myself as pushing through one more thing that stood in the way of vindicating Merleau-Ponty.

But the first weeks also brought a major phenomenological surprise – one that I found bothersome. In those first weeks, I felt decidedly *distinct* from my body. Indeed, it seemed to stand in the way of my goals. To achieve my goals, I attempted, as often as possible, to simply *forget that I had a body*. As odd as it might initially sound, I tried in those first weeks to think mostly of Aristotle as I ran. I realized that the more I could occupy myself with Aristotle (or other matters), the easier it was to forget what my body was doing – and hence the easier it was to continue to run. If I could occupy my mind with such things as Aristotle, and not with the movements of my body, I found I could effectively *let my body run* while I did something else.

This was troublesome because it suggested to me something entirely at odds with the view I had set out to vindicate. It suggested that there might be a difference between mind and body. Indeed, I was immediately reminded of one of Plato's famous arguments: one thing, Plato claimed, cannot do two opposite things at the same time. Thus, if it appears that an object (such as person) is doing two things at the same time (both standing still and moving), it must be the case that the object has different *parts* engaging in the different behaviors (a person stands still, but his arms move about wildly).[1]

How could I think of Aristotle and run at the same time? It looked like, if Plato was right, different parts of me had to be doing the two different things: my mind thought, while my body ran. But if this were true, then Merleau-Ponty's view was in serious trouble. Merleau-Ponty contends, after all, that we are our living bodies; we are *not* two distinct things (mind and body) that somehow causally interact. I began to worry about my thesis, but I continued to run.

---

[1] See Plato, *Republic*, book 4, 436b–c: "It is clear that the same thing cannot do or undergo opposite things; not, at any rate, in the same respect, in relation to the same thing, at the same time. So, if we ever find that happening here, we will know that we are not dealing with one and the same thing, but with many."

Philosophical Interlude: Mind, Body, and Embodied Mind

In the first weeks of my running experiment, I was led to the view that *perhaps* "letting my body run" amounted to showing that my mind and body were not, after all, identical. But to claim that thinking while running indicates a separation of mind and body is surely an intellectual leap – one that it is natural to make, perhaps, but a leap nonetheless. Merleau-Ponty helps us to see this.

Merleau-Ponty claims that the very idea that there are *two* things – mind and body – is a faulty point of departure if we want to understand what it means to exist as we do in the world. Beginning with the opposition between two things (in this case mind and body) characterizes what Merleau-Ponty calls "objectivist thinking." Objectivist thinking, Merleau-Ponty claims, "knows only alternative notions; starting from actual experience, it defines pure concepts which are mutually exclusive" (p. 57).[2] These include subject/object, mind/matter, reason/cause, and so on – in short, all of the binary oppositions of traditional philosophy.

But to give up the opposition between mind and body is *not* merely to say that the two are identical. Indeed, this way of putting things is not the best way to express Merleau-Ponty's view. The view is better expressed by saying that the categories of "mind" and "body" systematically mislead us when we attempt to understand and describe our experience of the world (and hence also my experience of running). When we begin with these categories, we are led to make *mistakes* about the world. For example, "I regard my body, which is my point of view on the world, as one of the objects of that world" (p. 81) – an object that is distinct from my mind and, in most cases, controlled by it.

But our own body is not an object. Our body is our perspective on the world (p. 81). An object can be put down, walked around, investigated from multiple perspectives. We cannot "put down" our bodies, or walk around them, or leave them in the closet while we run errands. To think of ourselves as minds that control bodies is to make the mistake of thinking that our living bodies are objects like any others.

---

[2] All citations are from Maurice Merleau-Ponty, *Phenomenology of Perception*, trans. Colin Smith, (London: Routledge Press, 2002).

And it is precisely this mistake that is so tempting when I claim that I *let my body run*. The expression assumes, at the outset, that there are two *kinds* of things – minds and bodies – and this assumption will certainly color anything that follows.

So, how are we to characterize my experience in those first weeks? What will enable us to describe my ongoing self-debate, or the fact that I often tried to *trick* my body into running by simply concentrating on other things? And how exactly do we respond to Plato's argument?

My attempts to "trick" my body (by thinking of other things while running) can actually be regarded as *evidence* for Merleau-Ponty's view of things: I found it immensely difficult to run when I was thinking about running. When I set myself the task of concentrating on my movements, deliberating about my body as it moved, and thinking about how much more needed to be done, running did not come easy. When, however, I simply allowed my body to operate – when I stopped trying to control the body or over-think my activity – the running came much more easily.

In thinking about running while we run, it is easy to regard our bodies as objects that are meant to be controlled. But our awareness when running is not ideally an awareness of exerting control over some object – forcing that object to conform to some set of rules. To regard the body in this way is to make the very mistake that Merleau-Ponty warns against. The body is central to our existence; it is not an object.

As Merleau-Ponty famously claims, "consciousness is in the first place not a matter of 'I think that' but of 'I can'" (p. 159). So too we can say of running: being able to run – and to run more fluidly – is not a matter of *thinking* at all. In fact, thinking about running while doing it can actually *impede* running. When I started thinking about Aristotle during those first weeks, this evidenced not the distinction between mind and body, but the way in which perception *runs through* the body. To put this another way, we might say that we are neither mind nor body; we are embodied mind. My thinking about Aristotle enabled me to *live* my body rather than attempt to control it with thought. And when I stopped trying to control my bodily movement with thought and concentration, I found that I was able to run freely, and, moreover, to *think* freely – unimpeded by worries of how much more I would need to go before I could finally stop. My thinking did not allow me to run; my running allowed me to think.

I was not, of course, always successful in this. In fact, I often failed. I often found myself concentrating on distance and minutes; on exhaustion and sweat. But we should not regard this as a mind and a body at odds with one another. In every instance I was a unified being, expressing my agency in the world in a way that reflected the state of my body, just as Merleau-Ponty would have predicted. It is only when we think of our minds as distinct from our bodies that we allow ourselves to believe that running and thinking are opposite. These activities *are not* opposite. They both express my living body as it copes with and tries to understand the world around it.[3]

As I continued to run, I came to see that my initial worry was ungrounded. Merleau-Ponty could still be vindicated. Although I had not had a Gestalt switch even after two months of running, I did begin to notice many differences. Perhaps the primary difference was that there were moments when I ran and thought about nothing other than running. I could say goodbye to Aristotle as well as to my desire to treat my body as an object. In those moments, I first glimpsed what the goal of my running was. I was to attain a style of freedom – to be free from worries about distance and time, and free to let my thoughts roam over the same landscape my body did.

Keeping Track: Concluding Reflections on an Ongoing Experiment

The summer in North Carolina is not the friend of the novice runner. I was running in the early morning, but in temperature and humidity that was almost unbearable. It was this that led me indoors, and it was indoors where I turned a proverbial corner. It had been two months since I began the experiment, and I was beginning to worry that I would never attain what I had initially expected: an epiphany in which I suddenly simply *was* a runner.

Fortunately, my failure to have such an epiphany led me to rethink my initial assumptions. I had expected the change in my experience of running to be instantaneous – a Gestalt switch that suddenly

---

[3] And it here that we see why Plato's argument does not find footing: in order to postulate two separate things, we must be confronted by opposite activities. So long as we do not make the mistake of thinking that we are bodies plus minds (as opposed to being embodied minds), we will not be led to the view that thinking and running are opposite.

transformed the world into something it had not been before. I imagined that I would have the sort of ah-ha experience that altered the way I understood my activity. I thought, moreover, that I would instantly be able to understand the altered significance the world had for me in my sudden emergence as a "runner." I was wrong on all counts.

One does not become a runner instantly. The understanding of things that accompanies a runner, the way the ease of movement emerges – even when that movement is difficult – is something that develops organically over time, and perhaps never completely. In this respect, running is more like a skill that is practiced than a goal that is achieved. My initial mistake was to believe that becoming a runner amounted to entering a particular *state*, rather than being one that practiced a particular skill. Running is not like a high school diploma: it is not something that you get and which stays with you for the remainder of your days. It is, rather, an *ability* that can wane from the lack of use, or express itself with greater grace the more one engages with it. Again, I had not paid enough attention to Merleau-Ponty: our consciousness is more a product of what we do than what we think. Our abilities can improve, and our perceptions of things alter with our abilities.

As an ability that develops over time, running is much like other ways in which we employ our bodies to express ourselves in the world. Carpentry, sex, language-use, cooking, and most other skills can be developed to astounding degrees, and the degree to which these are developed will determine the way in which we experience the world around us. A gourmet cook will notice flavors I simply cannot; a master carpenter will appreciate workmanship that I would pass over in an instant. So too with a runner: the runner will experience things in a way that reflects the abilities of the runner. As these abilities are bodily in nature, we can see immediately why the body is essential to our perception of the world: we develop skills by developing our bodies, and these embodied skills enable us to see things that we would otherwise fail to see.

The skills we have and the projects in which we engage express what the philosopher Martin Heidegger (1889–1976) calls our "being-in-the-world". Our "world" – in the sense common to phenomenology – is that which matters to us; that which has significance to those projects that make sense of our lives.[4] Merleau-Ponty's main

---

[4] When we speak of the "business world" or the "world of fashion" we are using the term in this way: the term picks out an area defined by a distinct set of concerns.

contribution to the notion of being-in-the-world is that the body is a constitutive element of our existence within our world: it makes sense of everything that we do and are. Without understanding the body, we cannot understand perception, ethics, art, love, death, or anything else. We must also understand the body to understand running.

But to say that understanding the body is essential to understanding running is *not* simply to say that we could not run without a body (a true, but uninformative claim). It *is* to say that part of what it means to understand what runners do is to understand how their bodies express themselves in the world – and how their bodies intermingle with the world around them. As Merleau-Ponty claims, the body "is a nexus of living meanings" (p. 175). To be a runner is to *be your body* in a particular way – and hence to experience things in a particular way.

A runner *is* her body in a particular way. She is her body in a way that enables the world to present itself in a way that a non-runner does not yet see. As I continued to run, I came to realize that becoming a runner involved inhabiting a different world. My body ceased (in my best instances) to be an obstacle to my goals; it became instead an enabler. I stopped thinking of it as a tool. Indeed, I stopped thinking about it at all. In my finest moments, my body was absorbed into its environment. And it was here – and perhaps only here – that *I* was truly running, rather than simply employing my body to run. It is this, I think, that separates the novice from the advanced runner. The advanced runner is absorbed in the runner's world; the novice is simply trying to run. While I am not yet an advanced runner (will the experiment ever end?), I occasionally have glimpses of what it means to be a runner – and these glimpses are longer than they used to be. And what I see when in those moments is a world I did not formerly know, through a body that I did not formerly have.

Does this vindicate Merleau-Ponty? Certainly not entirely. It does, however, help to show how his work can contribute to our understanding of what is involved in becoming a runner: to become a runner one must learn to live in a runner's world. For myself, I straddle two worlds. And so I will continue the experiment – sometimes truly in the runner's world, and sometimes eagerly trying to be in it.

Chapter 5
In Praise of the Jogger

Raymond J. VanArragon

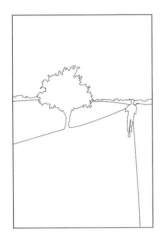

It's common practice at wedding receptions for a video camera operator to solicit best wishes for the bride and groom. It can be disconcerting for the unfortunate guest, minding his own business, to find himself trapped in front of a camera and expected on the spot to come up with something profound or touching or witty. At my own wedding, one friend actually managed to say something that was truly memorable for me. He had been a teammate of mine on our college cross-country and track teams, and like most members of those teams he took running quite seriously. In his remarks he warned me sternly not to become a "jogger." "I want you to be a runner," he said. "I don't want you to become a jogger, doing it just for fitness. I don't want to see that happen."

Obviously my friend thought that for a competitive runner to become a jogger would be a significant and even shameful comedown. At the time, I agreed with him and felt a bit insulted by his unspoken suggestion that I was, in fact, already becoming a jogger. But later I got to thinking. What's so bad about being a jogger? Why is it so much better to be a runner? And what's the difference anyway? Reflecting on all this has led me to think that my friend and I had been wrong. Becoming a jogger would not be a comedown for a runner. In fact, there are good reasons for adults who run to strive to be joggers rather than runners. Consider this chapter a belated response to my friend's admonition, a response from one who is not in fact a jogger but would love to become one.

The Runner and the Jogger

So, what's the difference between a runner and a jogger? That's a difficult question, in part because the words "runner" and "jogger" are used in different ways by different people. But I'm going to draw out a common understanding of them, the sort that I think my friend intended. It's worth noting that in his warning he didn't refer at all to *speed* – he didn't say, "I don't want you to become a jogger, plodding through 10-minute miles on a good day." Instead, he referred to *motive*: the jogger runs "just for fitness." In doing so, I think my friend hit the nail on the head. It's true that joggers are often slower than runners, but that is not their defining feature. Essential to runners and joggers are their motives, the fundamental reasons why they get out regularly and go running, rather than lying on the couch and watching television. The runner and jogger run in pursuit of different goals, and that's what makes them what they are.

What are those goals? What defines a runner, in my view, is that his primary motivation for running is competitive: he runs to win, or to get faster, or to place higher than before. The primary goal of the jogger, on the other hand, is fitness. And "fitness" here must be understood broadly: the jogger runs because of the contribution running makes to her physical and mental health. She runs because doing so makes her more fit to live a good and productive life. Fitness thus understood is without qualification a splendid motive for running, and I am filled with admiration for those who find that motive sufficient to get them out the door consistently. At the same time, I also admire many runners and recognize the value of many of their goals. My concern with the runner is that pursuing those goals and being solely motivated by them can lead to all sorts of problems, some of which can be quite significant for adults with families and careers to attend to. With that in mind let's first consider the perils of the runner before turning to praise of the jogger.

Different Kinds of Runners

The runner, as I have suggested, is primarily motivated to run by the desire for competitive goods. But there are different kinds of competitive goods and correspondingly different kinds of runners. There are two kinds of runners I'm especially familiar with. I'll call them *Prize Runners* and *Challenge Runners*.

The Prize Runner, as you may have guessed, is motivated to run primarily by the lure of medals, trophies, and perhaps money, as well as the admiration and glory that come with winning or placing highly in races. Of course, unlike some of the benefits of running, these ones are scarce and can only be acquired by a few. While everyone in a race can enjoy the thrill of competition, which is certainly valuable, only one runner can win, only a few runners can get the glory that comes with being first on a team, and so on. Pursuit of these goods keeps the Prize Runner running. If it weren't for them, he wouldn't bother.

There are quite a few Prize Runners out there, I think. One way to tell whether a person really is a Prize Runner is to see what happens when he realizes that the prizes and glory are no longer within his reach. Many Prize Runners under those conditions show their true colors: they lose interest and hang up their shoes. In my experience, this is quite a common occurrence on college cross-country teams. It can be extremely discouraging for a high school champion to come to college and discover that he's not even the fastest freshman on his own team, and more discouraging still when the teammates ahead of him include people he regularly trounced in high school. (That too is quite common: some runners who won races in high school matured early and have less room for improvement in college than those who took their time developing. As a late bloomer myself, I came to appreciate how all that worked out.) Some Prize Runners under those circumstances stick it out, motivated perhaps by the desire to retain an athletic scholarship. Others reorient themselves and come to be motivated by team goals or goals that don't require such elusive individual success. But many reveal their true colors by quitting.

In pointing this out, I do not mean to denigrate Prize Runners, even ones who quit. I do not blame young runners who are accustomed to winning for having "the prize" be their primary motivation. Winning is great fun, after all. Still, it is often regrettable when disillusioned Prize Runners quit, regrettable both for the teams that they leave behind and for themselves insofar as they end up missing out on all the other benefits of running.

The second kind of runner is the Challenge Runner. Like the Prize Runner, she pursues goods that revolve around competitive running, but hers are usually more widely available and depend less on competition with others and more on competition with self. So a Challenge Runner may be motivated by the desire to set a personal record or to finish higher in a race than she did last year, for example.

There is much to admire about Challenge Runners. Many of them set high goals for themselves and then overcome obstacles and display remarkable determination in the pursuit of them. A vivid example of this involves Rob, a college teammate of mine, who was involved in a jet-ski accident the summer after his freshman year and suffered extensive muscle damage and a badly broken leg. Upon visiting him in the hospital afterwards, my friends and I concluded that his running career was over. It would have been for us. And yet rather than packing it in, Rob resolved to do the training necessary to get back to where he was before the accident. By the time he was a senior, he was actually faster than he had been as a freshman. What he did was more impressive than the achievements of many Olympic runners, in my opinion.

I expect that a good number of people who run are actually Challenge Runners, including many of those members of high school and collegiate cross-country teams who are not especially talented and yet keep plugging away. Members of the non-running public tend to view Challenge Runners, especially the slower ones, with a mixture of admiration and bemusement: admiration because of the inspirational sort of self-motivation that they display, and bemusement because of how much misery they put themselves through for what appears to be such an insignificant payoff. But the payoff can be of enormous significance to the Challenge Runner, and the desire for it can keep her running even if she never comes close to winning anything.

Perils of the Prize Runner

We have already seen how the goods the Prize Runner pursues are scarce and available only to a few. But note that not only are those goods scarce, they are also *fleeting*, so that even those who can win them for a time can't do so for long. High school champions often find that they can't win in college, and many who win in college find that they can't win significant races afterwards. Of course, it is easier for the Prize Runner to win if he attempts to dominate the local road-racing scene rather than seeking after Olympic glory. Some runners do find success in local 5ks to be sufficiently meaningful and motivating; but for others, winning those events does not provide nearly the satisfaction that winning collegiate races did. (And neither does winning one's age group. I know this from experience, having recently captured first prize in my age group in a race so thin that everyone who entered won a trophy.) But no matter what prizes a Prize Runner pursues, there comes a time when winning them is no longer possible for him: he encounters competition that is too strong or he slows down with age and is overtaken by the next generation of racers. If a person is motivated only by those prizes, he could quit running long before his body stops him, and in doing so would forgo all the other benefits that a lifetime of regular running can yield.

It's worth considering, in this regard, the career of Bob Kennedy, an enormously successful American distance runner. Kennedy won numerous collegiate and open national titles in cross-country and in track, and became the first American to break 13 minutes in the 5,000 meters. But even he reached his limit. He has been unable to win a medal at the Olympics or World Track and Field Championships due to the extraordinary level of competition at those events. Kennedy has nonetheless enjoyed a long career in competitive running. His longevity may be due, interestingly enough, to the fact that he is *not* a Prize Runner. The magazine *Running Times* suggests instead that Kennedy's aim in running is to find out how good he can be. "It's a healthy way of approaching it because if I say I want to win an Olympic medal, it may or may not happen," he is quoted as saying. "It's such a difficult thing to do . . . but if I have the attitude of finding out how good I can be, then if I'm the best ever, great, but if I'm no better than I am now, I can live with that too, because all you can expect from yourself is what you're capable of."[1] So it sounds like he's a Challenge Runner. Perhaps if he were a Prize Runner, motivated only by the desire for Olympic glory, his career wouldn't have lasted so long and wouldn't have been so satisfying for him.

A second worry about the Prize Runner is that he is especially prone to certain kinds of vices. One is pride. A person who runs solely for the sake of acquiring prizes and glory may at heart be motivated by the desire to cultivate an attitude of superiority and confirm the feeling that he is more valuable and significant than other people.[2]

---

[1] Chris Lear, "Return of the King," *Running Times*, July/August, 2004. You can find this story at http://www.runningtimes.com/issues/04julyaug/kennedy.htm.

[2] In fairness to the Prize Runner, pride is a vice that very many of us have in some form or other. My contention is that the Prize Runner's goals – both being motivated by them and fulfilling them – make him especially susceptible to this vice.

Another vice the Prize Runner is prone to is a certain kind of dishonesty. The problem here is that he doesn't need to be an honest competitor to achieve his goals: cheating will do just as well, and maybe better. Of course, athletes in many sports can be corrupted by the lust for glory and success – consider the recent troubles of major league baseball. But this corruption is certainly present among runners as well, even if distance runners have not been subject to the spectacular doping scandals that have plagued some of the world's top sprinters. Because of his goals and the difficulty of attaining them, the Prize Runner may be unusually inclined toward this sort of corruption.[3]

These concerns about the Prize Runner are significant ones. There is nothing wrong with running to win, but I think it would be better to be motivated by something less fleeting, and with less of a tendency to promote vice, than the prizes and glory that motivate the Prize Runner.

Perils of the Challenge Runner

The first concern I will mention about the Challenge Runner is that she, like the Prize Runner, may have goals that she is simply unable to achieve. Setting high goals and pushing oneself to achieve them can be a very good thing, of course; but goals set too high can produce frustration and disappointment when they aren't met.

Runners, of course, frequently overestimate their own potential and, as a result, are frequently disappointed with themselves. I coached college cross-country for a time, and while it was a wonderful job in many ways, one of the things I found hard to take was seeing a runner deeply unhappy with a performance that I considered quite in line with her capabilities. Unrealistic expectations can also cause problems after college, even more so because people inevitably slow down as they age. Several years ago I ran a race where afterwards the winner was just disgusted with how he had run. (He made

---

[3] This may become even more of a temptation later in the life of the Prize Runner who struggles to stay at the top. Two outstanding American distance runners, Mary Decker Slaney and Regina Jacobs, were suspended late in their careers as a result of failed drug tests, though Slaney's test remains controversial.

that quite clear, too, apparently unaware that those whom he had vanquished might feel put out by his complaints about how poorly he had done.) He mentioned to me later that he had run about two minutes faster in college – which was almost 20 years earlier. His situation was really unfortunate: even though he won handily and ran exceptionally well for a man over 40, there was no hint of joy or satisfaction in what he had achieved.

Not all Challenge Runners are like that, of course. Many thrive as they move from one challenge to another; and when they find themselves unable to run as fast as they used to, they adjust their goals accordingly, using their slowdown as a source of humor rather than anguish and taking pride in what they are able to accomplish. Still, the problem cases highlight a real challenge for Challenge Runners: they need to perform the delicate balancing act of keeping their goals high enough to motivate them and low enough to be realistic. If the goals aren't high enough, they lack the power to motivate; if they're too high, the runner pursuing them can get discouraged; and with each extreme the runner might quit, which, as we have said many times, would be a bad result.

A second problem that Challenge Runners face is a tendency to overtrain (a problem for Prize Runners, too). This tendency is sometimes the result of unrealistic goal-setting, but sometimes not. In general, the source of this problem seems to be that running is a sport where it appears, on the face of it, that if you only do more you will get faster and if you want to get faster you have to do more. This impression is encouraged by stories of world-class runners who achieved their status by running miles and workouts that are unfathomable to most of us. The story about Bob Kennedy in the *Running Times*, for example, mentions how in the mid-90s he began training in London with a number of elite Kenyan runners whose workouts were legendary, a change that led to significant improvements in his race times. Highly motivated Challenge Runners struggling to meet their goals can be inspired by such stories to crank up their training beyond what their bodies can handle.[4] And doing that is entirely

---

[4] In a very good book called *Daniels' Running Formula*, (Champaign, IL: Human Kinetics, 1998) Dr. Jack Daniels labels low-ability, highly motivated runners, many of whom are what I've called Challenge Runners, as "potential over-trainers." He also cautions against overtraining and offers guidance for setting up a training program appropriate to one's abilities.

counterproductive, almost inevitably resulting in the sort of nagging injuries that leave runners miserable and unable to train. (A friend of mine would try to push the limits with his training and avoid injury at the same time by engaging in the questionable practice of loading up on as many as 20 ibuprofen pills every day to fight off his aches and pains. I'm not sure I would recommend that course of action.)

A final concern for Challenge Runners is that running can develop for them into an unhealthy obsession. There may be nothing wrong with a life dominated by the drive to run as fast as one can – for people who have space in their lives for it. High school and collegiate runners are prime examples of such people, but other adults are similarly blessed.[5] And wholehearted immersion in an activity like competitive running can be of great benefit to the person who does it. Still, an obsession with running can have deleterious effects. It can prevent one from spending adequate time on other essentials, such as schoolwork and family activities. In addition, the single-minded pursuit of his goals can make the Challenge Runner cranky and downright difficult to live with, especially when he fails to meet them. I know this from experience, and, unfortunately, my college room-mates do too.

These problems for the Challenge Runner can be serious for anyone, but especially for those of us with families and careers to attend to. For us, it would be a bad thing if running became an obsession, and even worse if it also became a regular source of frustration and disappointment. In short, for most of us our obligations to our spouses, children, and employers trump whatever obligation we may have to find out how fast we can run.[6] A Challenge Runner who spends little time with his children because he wants to take five minutes off his marathon time ought to stop and re-examine his priorities.

The perils of the runner, then, provide some reason for those of us who run to seek to be motivated by other goals – like perhaps the goals of the jogger.

---

[5] Some runners flaunt their obsession. I've seen high school and collegiate runners wearing team shirts with the slogans, "Running is my boyfriend" and "Running is my girlfriend."

[6] Professional runners like Bob Kennedy are exceptions to this rule, since running *is* their career.

In Praise of the Jogger

We saw earlier that the jogger's primary reason for running is fitness, broadly understood. The average jogger is not interested only in a trim physique.[7] Instead, she is motivated to run regularly by the desire to cultivate virtuous habits and promote her own mental and physical health. And she does so because the health and virtue that running promotes help her to do her work well and be a benefit to those with whom she has contact. In short, joggers run because of the way that running helps them to live a good life, and I can't think of a better reason to run than that.

It should be easy to see that many of the perils of the runner do not similarly afflict the jogger. The running goals of the jogger are flexible insofar as fitness in different periods of life requires different amounts of physical activity. The jogger is not inclined to cheat or train too much in order to get faster, since getting faster is not her aim and the cheating or overtraining in fact prevent her from achieving her primary goals. Neither is an obsession with running a problem for the jogger. She understands the reason for which she runs, and if she sees that she has become too single-minded she takes steps to rectify it.

Finally, the goals of the jogger are not fleeting. We saw that the Prize Runner eventually reaches a point when there are no more races he can win. But this is just a special case of a more general problem for those who run solely in pursuit of goals that can be definitively achieved. Those who run in order to break 20 minutes in a 5k, for instance, or three hours in the marathon, or for that matter those who run to lose 10 pounds – when their goals are achieved (or prove unattainable) that can cause their desire for running to wane. The goals of the jogger are different: there is never a point at which the jogger's goals are finally achieved. Staying fit and healthy is a process that the jogger is engaged in indefinitely, and so long as running can effectively contribute to that process, she has all the motivation she needs to stick with it.

Before you conclude that the running life of the jogger is drab and devoid of challenge, consider that joggers *can* participate in races;

---

[7] Those who run primarily for the sake of a trim physique may also properly be called joggers, since they are not motivated by the competitive goods of the runner. But they are not the sort of joggers I'll focus on in the text.

they *can* train extra hard from time to time in order to run fast times; and so on. So joggers may look for all the world like runners. But the jogger is different from the runner in virtue of the fact that those things merely add variety to her running. They are not her fundamental motivation for running. When there is no race to train for and no challenges to meet – other than the constant challenge of living a good life – she gets out there and runs anyway. And when she does for a time pursue those challenges, she keeps them in perspective, recognizing the overall purpose for which she runs and not getting unduly wrapped up in those secondary (and temporary) goals that she has set for herself.

Still, the jogger's goals are never definitively achieved, which makes it profoundly difficult to be motivated by them. It is much easier to be motivated by the sort of concrete goals that the runner pursues. Being a jogger requires an enormous amount of discipline and virtue, and I daresay that not many of us have it. But the unquestionable value of the jogger's goals together with the difficulty of pursuing them makes the jogger all the more worthy of our admiration and praise.

For my part, though I admire joggers, I should repeat that I'm not one myself. Indeed, I am acquainted firsthand with the difficulty of becoming a jogger, and similarly acquainted with some of the perils of the runner. As a collegiate runner, I was the beneficiary of superb coaching, excellent teammates, and a little natural talent; and so I experienced some success. It's true that I was altogether obsessed with running during those years, but that was probably a necessary part of the experience and for the most part it did me and those around me no harm. (There was one exception: in a moment of sheer lunacy I broke up with my girlfriend because I thought our relationship was having a negative impact on my running. She and I are now approaching our 10-year wedding anniversary, and I still haven't lived that down.) Running was a source of great joy for me during my college career, and I am filled with gratitude when I think back on it.

After graduation, however, the problems crept up. I had trained solely because of the challenge of racing, but after my final collegiate track season ended, I found that the races that I could compete in were not meaningful enough to keep me going. As a result, I lost interest and simply faded out of running. Since then, I have on a few occasions started up again in order to train for a local road race; but after each race I have lapsed, running so infrequently that each time out has been an unpleasant struggle. I long to become a jogger, but so far I haven't managed to do so.

And yet I have not given up on that dream. My hope right now is that if I train from race to race, enjoying the benefits of running and making it again a regular (but non-dominant) part of my life, eventually I won't need the races to motivate me anymore. There is no guarantee that I will succeed. But you can see in this discussion how far we've come. My friend, in his videotaped admonition, suggested that for a runner it would be a real comedown to become a jogger. I now hope, to the contrary, that being a runner can serve for me as a stepping stone to becoming a jogger. Far from a comedown, that would be a truly magnificent achievement.[8]

[8] I would like to thank Matt Davidson, Mike Austin, and Paul Reasoner for helpful comments on earlier drafts of this essay, as well as Jason Washler, whose comments at my wedding inspired it.

Chapter 6
Running Religiously

Jeffrey P. Fry

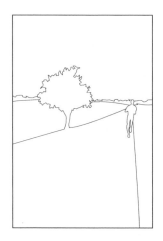

I run religiously. At the time of writing this chapter I've just surpassed four consecutive years without a day missed.[1] As running streaks go, however, mine is relatively modest.[2] I attribute it to numerous factors, including a good deal of luck, stubbornness, a fragile ego, my personal vision of a good life, and, significantly, the cooperation and support of others. Long-distance running is my forte, and it's not always a graceful activity. Grace may be more aptly associated with gliding athletes and spiraling spheroids, while some of the greatest distance runners of all time have exhibited awkward styles that can be uncomfortable to watch. Distance running is, after all, closely allied with pain and suffering, as is discernible from the contorted expressions of runners of all ages, body types, and levels of expertise.

[1] In the interest of full disclosure, during this streak I have set as my target a minimum of two miles a day, but I have typically run farther. In February 2005 I contracted a virulent form of apparent food poisoning, which landed me in the local hospital's emergency room. The following day I only made it around the block once before I was reduced to walking. The friends I consulted advised me to count this day! In my rather arcane way of reckoning, to count as a consecutive day of running, I do not have to complete the run within 24 hours of the previous day's run. Thus, I may run one day at 8 a.m. and on the following day at 4:30 p.m. The streak includes runs on two continents and in six different countries.
[2] Former world champion triathlete Scott Tinley once informed me that he has an acquaintance who reports a streak of some 18 years.

Those of us who are devotees of running have identities shaped by this activity. We attend to our daily ritual with "near-religious seriousness."[3] This ritual may end with a feeling of restoration – both of body and soul – but typically only after a period of discomfort. It's the religious-like quality of the running experience that I want to highlight and explore. In what ways is it apt to speak of *running religiously*? Is running actually a religion? What are some religious-like qualities and religious uses of running? Finally, might the suffering that frequently accompanies running signal an intriguing connection between religion and running? These are important questions, particularly in an age in which running maintains a high degree of popularity and many individuals who no longer find institutional religion satisfying continue to seek spiritual fulfillment. Could there be a conjunction between these two phenomena?[4] Some scholars equate expressions of contemporary sport with religion. Others see fundamental differences between sport and religion. In looking closely at running, however, I think that it's possible to find some middle ground. Let's begin our inquiry with the possible identity of running and religion.[5]

Is Running a Religion?

Should running actually be considered a religion? Perhaps the issue strikes the reader as a non-starter. But it is merely a more focused form of a question that has intrigued numerous scholars: Should sport, *in general*, be classified as religion? Both sides of the issue find proponents with well-articulated positions.

The Catholic theologian Michael Novak writes of sports in general:

> Sports are religious in the sense that they are organized institutions, disciplines, liturgies; and also in the sense that they teach religious qualities of heart and soul. In particular, they recreate symbols of

---

[3] I borrow this felicitous phrase from Patricia Westfall, "The Second Self," *Savvy*, December 1984, p. 99.

[4] I am indebted to Elizabeth N. Agnew for the observation and suggestion.

[5] Note that I am using the word "identity" here in a somewhat loose sense. I'm not employing a more technical sense of "identity" whereby if you are running you are being religious *and* if you are being religious, you must be engaging in running.

cosmic struggle, in which human survival and moral courage are not assured. To this extent, they are not mere games, diversions, pastimes. Their power to exhilarate or depress is far greater than that.[6]

Note that Novak displays a bit of reticence. Sports represent religion in some sense, but not exactly in the way that, say, Methodism or Catholicism do (Novak, p. 129). Charles Prebish, however, bites the bullet. He writes:

> For me, it is not just a parallel that is emerging between sport and religion, but rather a *complete identity*. *Sport is religion* for growing numbers of Americans, and this is no product of simply facile reasoning or wishful thinking. Further, for many, sport religion has become a more appropriate expression of personal religiosity than Christianity, Judaism, or any of the traditional religions.[7]

This is not easy terrain to negotiate. First of all, attempts to grasp the essence of religion have proved notoriously slippery (some would say insuperably difficult), as demonstrated by the conflicting accounts of numerous nineteenth- and twentieth-century Western scholars who sought to capture it. Is the essence of religion located in our inner lives, or is religion perhaps exemplified in externalities such as rituals? Is either aspect a necessary or sufficient condition for the existence of religion? What is religion's proximate aim? Is it the attainment of enlightenment, the possession of a transforming faith in a god, or perhaps appeasement of fickle powers ruling the cosmos in order to secure protection or the ongoing rhythm of agricultural processes? The complexities in detailed descriptions of religious traditions are legion.

Defining sport proves also to be no easy task, as illustrated by scholarly debates over the "tricky triad" of sport, games, and play.[8]

---

[6] Michael Novak, "The Natural Religion," in *Sport and Religion*, ed. Shirl J. Hoffman (Champaign, IL: Human Kinetics, 1992), p. 36.

[7] Charles Prebish, "'Heavenly Father, Divine Goalie': Sport and Religion," in *Sport and Religion*, ed. Shirl J. Hoffman, p. 48. Prebish is not claiming that all sport is religion. He states that "the whole issue of sport as religion turns on the premise that sport is a religion only insofar as it brings its adherents to an experience of ultimate reality, radically alters their lives as a result of the experience of ultimacy, and then channels their positive gains back into society in a generally viable and useful fashion" (pp. 50–51). As will become apparent, my own view has some similarity to Prebish's claim that there is a contingent connection between sport and religion. Although we both posit a connection, I do not believe that I equate the two in precisely the way that Prebish does at times.

[8] See for example, Bernard Suits, "Tricky Triad: Games, Play, and Sport," in *Philosophy of Sport and Other Essays: Critical Readings, Crucial Issues*, ed. M. Andrew Holowchak (Upper Saddle River, NJ: Prentice Hall, 2002), pp. 29–37.

The outcomes of these debates are serious, since they are fraught with political implications. In some cases, such as in the allocation of green spaces, being a sport may provide a degree of clout not afforded to a "mere" game.[9] In reality, it seems that most of us live with a certain amount of vagueness with respect to understandings of both religion and sport. Thus, any attempt to capture and compare essences of religion and sport may be overreaching.

So, what is left to do? It is still possible to take elements that are paradigmatically, if not essentially, associated with religion, and see whether sport features these same elements. There are indeed interesting *structural* and *functional* parallels between religion and sport, regardless of whether these similarities ultimately prove sufficient to qualify sport as religion. We are focusing specifically on running, so let's look for structural and functional parallels between running and religion. While the following account is necessarily oversimplified, it may nonetheless illuminate our assessment of the religious-like qualities of running as a particular expression of sport.

Religious-Like Qualities of Running

In many widely recognized religious traditions we find a potent combination of myth and ritual.[10] These two can work hand in hand. Myths interpret rituals, and rituals enact myths.[11] The myths may be accounts of origins, or responses to other ultimate questions. While the rituals enliven the myths by enacting them, they are also performative in another sense. The prescribed rituals are thought to effect inner transformations and, in some traditions, to influence the workings of the cosmos. Religious traditions also celebrate heroic figures, if not indeed gods. The deeds of these figures, along with other myths and accounts of prescribed rituals, are transmitted through oral traditions and sacred texts.

---

[9] On this point and other political implications of being or not being accorded the status of a sport, see Jay Coakley, *Sport in Society: Issues and Controversies*, 6th edn. (Boston: McGraw-Hill, 1998), pp. 22–3.

[10] Note that in the academic study of religion, to employ the term "myth" does not necessarily indicate that a story is untrue. Indeed, one can speak of levels of truth, including, as one former teacher of mine put it, "the truth that hits you."

[11] I am indebted to my former teacher James Samuel Preus for this helpful understanding of the relationship between myth and ritual.

Jeffrey P. Fry

Sport exhibits many structural similarities to religion. It too has myths and rituals, and it recounts the exploits of heroic figures. Although the case could be made for many individual sports, our focus is on running, which is nothing if not ritualistic. In fact, it's exemplary in this regard. Consider the ritualistic, even meditative discipline of stretching, the choice of familiar running paths and meeting places with friends, and pre-race traditions. Of course, organized races are themselves replete with pomp, circumstance, and rituals, including the awarding of medals, which have little monetary but much symbolic value. Even the donning, removal, and *strategic placing* of our sweaty running gear are ritualistic acts.

Runners also have their personal myths. There are stories of "rave runs" that were aesthetic delights, of torturous hills and epic workouts. Running lore recounts the deeds of legendary figures, whose accomplishments seem almost supernatural. There are even shrines, such as the hallowed spot in Oregon where gifted and legendary runner Steve Prefontaine was killed in an automobile crash. The running diary in which we track our daily progress may not be a sacred book, or a liturgical calendar, but it is important to us as a record of the course of our running lives. These examples illustrate a number of intriguing structural parallels between running and religion. In addition, there are noteworthy parallels with respect to the functions of running and religion.

Religion has multiple intended *functions*, some of which have already been underscored. These range from maintaining the order of the cosmos (for example, by fertility rites thought to ensure agricultural processes) to providing mechanisms for protection, self-realization, and salvation. The practice of religion may also bring about an altered state of consciousness, or even a state of ecstasy, through which the religious devotee stands outside of or transcends his or her mundane self. Religion thus transforms both inner and outer space into sacred space and also converts ordinary time into sacred time.[12]

Running also has functional parallels to religion. Regular running helps bring a sense of order to one's life. The activity is restorative for the body and the spirit, and contributes to a sense of self-realization. Running also brings about altered and even heightened states

---

[12] See Mircea Eliade's classic work on the study of religion, *The Sacred and the Profane: The Nature of Religion*, trans. Willard R. Trask (San Diego: Harcourt Brace & Company, 1987).

of consciousness. On occasion, runners even experience a state of self-transcendence or ecstasy.

Finally, there is the issue of commitment, which is sometimes taken to be a hallmark of religious expression. According to the theologian Paul Tillich, religious faith exhibits "ultimate concern."[13] The spirit of dedication exhibited by serious runners approximates this characteristic. Of course, some might say that running creates a false religion, a form of idolatry, and that significant relationships are sometimes sacrificed on the altar of running. One must be candid here. No doubt running can be a form of escapism, or of literally running away from one's problems or responsibilities. Such considerations suggest that an adequate assessment of the relationship between running and religion must give careful attention to *the subjectivity of the runner*. I'll return to this shortly.

How are we ultimately to interpret these intriguing parallels between religion and running? What significance should we attribute to them, bearing in mind that some of the points made about running could also apply to other sports? Do the structural and functional similarities suffice to show that when we speak of running religiously we are actually equating running with religion? If so, should runners sprint to their local Internal Revenue Service agent to explore the various benefits conferred by a tax-exempt status?

Not so fast, according to Joan Chandler, who holds that sport and religion are "fundamentally different phenomena."[14] What marks the religious *as* religious? She claims that religions, unlike sports,

> provide detailed explanations of the origin and purpose of the world, clear statements about questions of ultimate concern (what many would call the "supernatural"), and continuing attempts to explain and cope with the existence of pain (Chandler, p. 56).

Chandler holds that sport has no special relationship to religion that makes it unique from a number of other activities. She writes:

> The parallels that have been drawn between sport and religion can equally well be drawn between opera and religion, theater and religion, and indeed between any institutionalized activity and a devoted

---

[13] Paul Tillich, *Dynamics of Faith* (New York: Harper Perennial Modern Classics, 2001).

[14] Joan M. Chandler, "Sport is Not a Religion," in *Sport and Religion*, ed. Shirl J. Hoffman, p. 55. Hereafter, "Chandler."

audience watching and/or interacting with trained participants (Chandler, p. 56).

The problem is that if we classify *all* of these activities as religious, then to designate an activity as religious is virtually meaningless.

Chandler seems to lay out necessary conditions for the presence of religion. Is she offering an *a priori*, prescriptive account of religion, or a descriptive account?[15] If she's simply stipulating what *she* means by "religion," then fair enough, but need we adopt her account? On the other hand, if she's making an empirical claim, then she assumes a burden of proof. Chandler's account of religion is arguably a selective, intellectualistic account of what religion does. It's in the detailed descriptions of religious traditions that we learn to appreciate their distinctive characters. And surely this is true with respect to individual sports as well.

Maybe running is not religion in and of itself. But at the very least it seems that there are intriguing parallels that make running religion-like. Furthermore, in some established religious traditions running is prescribed or utilized to facilitate the attainment of religious goals. Here religious adherents run for explicitly religious purposes, so that running has at times a fruitful, if contingent, relationship to religion.

Religious Uses of Running

The 2004 Summer Olympic Games returned to its ancestral home, Athens, Greece. The ancient Games, which featured races of varying distances, were religious as well as athletic festivals. Running, and sport in general, was placed in the service of religion by way of honoring the Greek gods. There was a conjunction, if not an identification, of running and religious *practice*.[16] The modern Olympic Games are ostensibly secular in nature. Still, organizers of the recent Games in Athens, by utilizing pageantry portraying Greek gods, gave

---

[15] By an "*a priori* account" I mean an account that doesn't take its cue from experience.

[16] There have been several recent publications on the ancient Olympic Games, no doubt due in part to the return of the Olympic Games to Athens. For one illuminating and highly entertaining account see Tony Perrottet, *The Naked Olympics: The True Story of the Ancient Games* (New York: Random House, 2004).

symbolic homage to the ancient practice of infusing the Games with religious significance.

When we examine other religious traditions, we find running employed as an aspect of spiritual practice. Native Americans utilized running messengers who were capable of prodigious athletic feats. To be sure, running in this context had a functional significance. But since for these indigenous peoples everyday life was saturated with the sacred, their running, which could be ceremonial in nature, also no doubt basked in a religious aura.[17] Halfway around the globe, Tibetan *lamas* known as *lung-gom-pas* runners are reported to have accomplished similarly astounding running endeavors while in a trance-like state.[18] But for illustrative purposes let's focus on another group of individuals who have fused running and religious practice.

The so-called "marathon monks," who reside on Mount Hiei in the area of Kyoto, Japan, practice a form of Tendai Buddhism that utilizes running in the quest to attain enlightenment in this life.[19] Indeed, those monks who complete the most arduous of the running regimens are held to have become living Buddhas. The most dedicated of the devotees undertake endeavors of several years duration. The 1000-day marathon is spread out over seven years, and involves for the most part 100–200 days per year of daily 30–60 kilometer jaunts. The seventh year, which consists of two 100-day terms, entails a yet higher degree of commitment and effort. The first term of the seventh year is the most demanding. It consists of 100 consecutive days of running 84 kilometers (52.5 miles) each day, which is equivalent to two marathons *per day!* The seriousness of this undertaking by the marathon monks is reflected in the fact that, traditionally, a participant who proved unable to fulfill his vow was obligated to kill himself.[20]

The prodigious athletic feats of the marathon monks involve walking, running, and making ritual offerings, all while in a meditative state and under conditions of sleep deprivation and meager food intake. This spiritual practice entails extreme discipline and a transformation of consciousness. In the case of the marathon monks,

---

[17] See Peter Nabokov, *Indian Running: Native American History and Tradition* (Santa Fe, NM: Ancient City Press, 1981).

[18] See Alexandra David-Neel, *Magic and Mystery in Tibet* (New York: Dover Publications, 1971), chapter 6, "Psychic Sports," pp. 199–241.

[19] See John Stevens, *The Marathon Monks of Mount Hiei* (Boston: Shambhala, 1988).

[20] I am unaware of any of the monks having taken these measures in recent history.

running is a central part of their religious quest and experience. The running is perhaps best viewed as both a test of their religious commitment, and as a facilitator of religious awakening. But why? Why should running be viewed as a particularly suitable discipline in service of attaining the goal of enlightenment?

Buddhist origins and teachings feature a concern about suffering, which is intimately connected to our attachment to the world as we perceive it in our naïve understanding. Buddhists attempt to reach an enlightened state of non-attachment, which entails the "confinement" of desires.[21] When our desires are "confined" or "tamed" we no longer crave the impermanent things to which we become attached, including our impermanent, illusory selves. Non-attachment results in a lessening of suffering or dissatisfaction, and ultimately to an end of rebirths into the world of suffering. In their quest to attain enlightenment, the marathon monks of Mount Hiei embrace and transform their suffering. Indeed, the monks magnify their suffering through a physical and spiritual exercise that ultimately helps them transcend suffering, all in the quest to attain an enlightened state in this very lifetime. Might there be other considerations that link religion and running through suffering?

Pain, Suffering, and Running Religiously

According to sociologist Peter Berger, religion helps us maintain a meaningful world, in part by providing legitimations for experiences that are highly resistant to attempts to render them meaningful. These experiences include pain, suffering, and death. According to Berger, religion is "the audacious attempt to conceive of the entire universe as being humanly significant." [22] Religion spreads a "sacred canopy" of meaning over our often chaotic lives. Thus, there is a close connection between religion and suffering, in that, according to Berger, religion tries to make sense of suffering.

The connection between religion and suffering is complex, however. Particularly noteworthy is the fact, aptly shown by Ariel Glucklich

[21] The word *nirodha* is variously translated. I follow here David Brazier, *The Feeling Buddha* (New York: Fromm International, 2000), p. 89. See also the entirety of chapter 24, "Taming the Fire."

[22] Peter Berger, *The Sacred Canopy: Elements of a Sociological Theory of Religion* (New York: Anchor Books, 1990), p. 28.

in his book *Sacred Pain: Hurting the Body for the Sake of the Soul*, that religion attaches positive significance to pain and suffering in numerous ways.[23] This positive appraisal flies in the face of a modern medical model that sees pain and suffering as signs of "personal disintegration."[24] It also stands in contrast to Elaine Scarry's claim that pain "unmakes" the world.[25]

Glucklich identifies numerous "religious ways of hurting" by examining interpretive models of pain in religious contexts. These include juridical models, medical models, military models, athletic models, magical models, models involving shared pain, and psychotropic and ecstatic models.[26] These various models operate in different ways to assign positive significance to pain. Thus, pain may be conceived as a form of divine punishment (juridical model) that will have beneficial effects, or as having a preventive or curative function (medical model) that is conducive to spiritual health. Of particular interest is the athletic model. As Glucklich notes, sport, like religion, is an arena of life in which positive significance is still attached to pain and suffering. The mantra "no pain, no gain" is one evident example. Because of its association with pain and suffering, the sporting life proves useful in helping illuminate religious life and experience.

In his book *Evil and the God of Love*, the philosopher John Hick recounts two approaches to the problem of suffering within the Christian tradition. One view, which can be traced to the theologian and philosopher St Augustine (AD 354–430), portrays suffering as a result of the catastrophic Fall of humanity. Suffering is punitive in nature, even if it may have corrective functions. The other view, which Hick locates in an incipient form in the thought of St Irenaeus (AD c.130–c.200), focuses on redemptive possibilities offered by suffering. Suffering provides an occasion for exemplifying and developing positive character traits such as compassion, generosity, and courage. Hence, suffering can become an occasion for "soul making."[27]

---

[23] Ariel Glucklich, *Sacred Pain: Hurting the Body for the Sake of the Soul* (Oxford and New York: Oxford University Press, 2001).

[24] Glucklich, *Sacred Pain: Hurting the Body for the Sake of the Soul*, p. 7.

[25] Elaine Scarry, *The Body in Pain: The Making and Unmaking of the World* (Oxford and New York: Oxford University Press, 1985).

[26] Glucklich, *Sacred Pain: Hurting the Body for the Sake of the Soul*, chapter 1, "Religious Ways of Hurting," pp. 11–39.

[27] John Hick, *Evil and the God of Love*, rev. edn. (San Francisco: Harper & Row, 1978).

Earlier I noted that running, and in particular distance running, is closely associated with discomfort. It is not always easy to characterize this experience. At times it may seem less than precise to describe this experience as a painful one, although running can readily become a painful experience, particularly when injuries develop. Running can also easily develop into a form of misery or *suffering*, and for this reason some coaches deal out running in punitive doses.

But for those of us who are dedicated to the sport, running is a voluntary form of ritual suffering. If it's not *religious* suffering per se, it shares affinities with religious suffering. Indeed, as already noted, religious thinkers have concluded that sport helpfully illuminates the nature of religious suffering. Suffering through running may be particularly apt in this regard, because it shares features of numerous models which are used to illuminate religious life. For example, running certainly has an educational element. We can learn much about ourselves through disciplined running. Running may also have preventive and curative functions with respect to our physical, mental, and emotional health. Indeed, runners may attribute a sense of spiritual well-being in part to their running.

Running, like religion, sometimes involves vicarious suffering, such as when individuals who wish to identify with the suffering of relatives or friends enter races or fun runs whose purpose is to raise money for charitable causes, including research into debilitating and deadly diseases. Running guru George Sheehan has suggested that runners may identify with the suffering of other runners to the extent that they attain "the consciousness the Buddhists call *metta*, the absolute identification with another suffering human being."[28]

These considerations indicate that the suffering experienced through running need not be equated in an Augustinian mode with punishment, and in particular, self-punishment. Rather, the suffering that accompanies running may, on occasion, be redemptive in nature and contribute to "soul making."

But given all of these useful applications, is suffering while running *religious* suffering? I would argue that the key is the *intention* of the runner. One can *make* the experience of running a component of

[28] George Sheehan, *Running and Being: The Total Experience* (New York: Simon and Schuster, 1978), p. 217.

religious practice and experience.[29] More broadly, almost any experience can take on a religious quality, depending on how one *approaches* it. So, even if running is not an intrinsically religious experience, it can be infused with religious significance. The particular religious frame of reference that one brings to the experience will determine *how* one views the pain and suffering of running, and how one utilizes the experience for religious purposes.

While not unique in being a helpful vehicle for religious expression, running can be useful for a variety of religious approaches. Thus, running can function as a form of religious offering, serve as a means of facilitating communion with nature, or be incorporated into a kind of prayerful meditation. Running as a meaningful exercise is, in any case, an activity whose significance is informed by the runner's intentions and purposes.

The Heart of Running Religiously

George Sheehan once flirted with the idea that running was religion. But on a trip to Alaska, where he was to give a lecture on running, he came to a different conclusion. Running was, he decided, best construed in a metaphorical way as a "place." It was like a monastery that one could fill with various objects and activities, including religious devotion.[30] But, if upon reflection, Sheehan decided that running was not religion per se, why did he compare running to a monastery, which seems to attribute a religious-like quality to running? Was it the case that, ultimately, Sheehan could not escape positing a tight connection between running and religion, even if he could not identify running as a form of religion? I would argue that Sheehan occupies the middle ground, to which I alluded in my introduction. In doing so, he is drawn towards adopting a religious framework

---

[29] For the insight that intentionality is key, I draw on Roger D. Joslin, *Running the Spiritual Path: A Runner's Guide to Breathing, Meditating, and Exploring the Prayerful Dimension of Sport* (New York: St Martin's Griffin, 2003). Note that I am not offering here any appraisal, explicit or implicit, about the truth of metaphysical claims that may be advanced by any particular religious tradition. Christianity exists as a religious tradition (actually it houses numerous traditions), whether its metaphysical claims – its claims about the ultimate nature of reality – are true or not.

[30] For Sheehan's essay "Is Running a Religion?" go to http://www.georgesheehan.com/essays/essay46.html.

to inform his understanding of the significance of the running experience.

I too feel this pull. In positing a middle ground, I have argued that running has religious-like qualities, many of which are shared in common with other sports, though this feature is perhaps not sufficient to qualify running in particular, or sport in general, as religion. Running is also employed in religion, and the association of running and religion is apt, because of the close association of each with suffering, which holds potentially redemptive qualities. Finally, I have claimed that even if running per se is not religion, running can become religious, and not merely in the sense of exemplifying devotion. Rather, running becomes religious in a robust sense when one infuses the experience – not unnaturally – with religious meaning and purpose.[31]

[31] I would like to thank Elizabeth N. Agnew for helpful comments on various drafts of this chapter.

Chapter 7
Hash Runners and Hellenistic Philosophers

Richard DeWitt

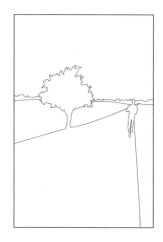

If you have half a mind to hash, that's more than enough . . .

So there we were, my wife and I, passing through Paris on vacation, and joining up for an afternoon run with the Paris version (actually, one of three in Paris) of the Hash House Harriers. Although we had hashed for some years, this was our first time doing a hash run in Paris. It started off as great fun, and really, it never ceased to be great fun. We were strangers to the group, but we were treated, as always at hashes, as welcome guests.

The run started off uneventfully, and we were getting a really great, lightning quick tour of some of the highlights of Paris. But about a half hour into the run, events took an unusual turn. Our pack of about 20 or 25 hashers found ourselves with our backs against a tall stone wall surrounding what we would later discover was the Italian embassy. Forcing us into this position were 20 or 25 machine-gun toting French *gendarmes* (the French police, who carry some serious weapons). They were unsure who we were and what our intentions were, and they seemed not in the mood to take chances. We in turn were not sure of their intentions, though we were quite sure they were better armed than we. Faced with more weaponry than most of us ever expected to see at one time in our lifetimes, and certainly never expecting to see such weapons pointed at us, we did what a typical hash group would do. We looked at each other, collectively shrugged our shoulders, and said, in an unworried way, "It's a hash."

This sort of shoulder-shrugging, unworried, unperturbed approach to events, even events that would otherwise seem rather perturbing, is common among hashers. Most hash runs are relatively uneventful, but given the nature of these runs (more on this below), there is the occasional unusual event. Hash packs have been known to have to dangle from the underside of a tall railway trestle when, during an attempted crossing of a ravine via the railway trestle, they were caught by the unexpected appearance of an oncoming train. Hashers occasionally lose the trail and have to be rescued, often out of the woods, sometimes late at night. And while there are thousands of hash groups (more officially known as Hash House Harriers) scattered around the world, each with its own personality, one trait that most hashers tend to develop is the sort of unworried, unperturbed approach to events, best summarized by the unworried "It's a hash" phrase.

As it turns out, the sort of unworried attitude one finds among hash runners bears a striking similarity to the attitude cultivated by the major philosophical schools of the period typically referred to as the "Hellenistic period." In the pages to follow, I want to use hash runs as a means of illustrating the most important philosophical schools of the period (the Hellenistic period) that followed the heyday of the big three Greek philosophers Socrates, Plato, and Aristotle. We'll of course need to explore a number of items, since the details of much of what I've mentioned so far will likely not be familiar. For example, who are the Hash House Harriers, and what exactly is a hash run, or just "hashing?" When was the Hellenistic period, and what philosophies were common during that period? And, of course, what do modern hashing and Hellenistic philosophy have to do with one another? Let's take a brief tour of these questions.

The Hash House Harriers

Hashing is a type of cooperative, rather than competitive, run, whose origins date back to the 1930s. At that time, a group of Brits living in the Malaysian country of Kuala Lumpur decided to spice up their frequent meetings at the local eatery and watering hole (which they had nicknamed the Hash House) by doing a modified version of a game played in their youths. The basic idea was that one person, the hare, would be given a head start, and would use bits of paper to mark a running trail. Where the trail went would be unknown to the rest of the group, and might include an occasional false trail. The rest of the group (the pack, or harriers) would attempt to follow the hare's trail and, if possible, catch the hare. However the chase turned out, the eventual outcome of the event was a social get-together, usually with food and always with refreshing beverages.

The group came to be known as the Hash House Harriers, and over the years, groups of Hash House Harriers sprang up in cities all over the world. Currently there are almost 2,000 active hash groups, and chances are there is one near you. Modern hash runs have not strayed appreciably from the central aspects of the first hash. The hare still marks the trail in advance (some hash group groups prefer a "live" hash, where the hare gets only a short head start; other hashes tend to have the hare set the trail hours in advance). The preferred marking method now is with flour. That is, the hare typically takes out a two- or three-pound bag of white flour, and uses the flour to periodically mark trees, the ground, whatever. (Following September 11, 2001, with the increased concern over mysterious white powder, many groups have taken to avoiding flour in populated areas, instead going back to the traditional paper or sometimes using chalk when setting trails in populated areas.)

Usually, the hare will set the trail in such a way as to keep as many of the runners – fast, slow, and in between – as together as possible. One technique for this is the use of "checks." Here's how this works. Suppose you're running along, following the trail of flour. You come to a flour "X" on the ground (referred to as a "check"). This means there will be multiple flour trails going off in different directions from this point, only one of which will be the true trail (the others, not surprisingly, are known as false trails). The job of the fastest runners is to decipher which is the true trail, and in the time it takes them to do this, the rest of the pack will have caught up.

In keeping with the cooperative aspect of the hash, a standard vocabulary has arisen that allows the members of the pack to communicate with each other. For example, a call of "on-on" means the person is on the true trail and you should follow him or her; "looking" means the person is not on trail but is rather looking for a mark; "checking" means the person is checking one of the multiple trails at a check but does not yet know whether he or she is on the true trail, and so on. In a good hash run, and again, in keeping with the cooperative nature of the run, the entire pack – young, old, fast, slow – come in more or less together.

Although there are a lot of similarities among the many hash groups around the world, it is not surprising that various hashes will have somewhat different personalities. For example, some groups tend to run exclusively on roads, some almost exclusively on trails, some prefer mostly off-trail bushwhacking, some emphasize the socializing and refreshing-beverage aspect of the hash (such a hash group is often referred to as a drinking club with a running problem), and so on.

But one trait that is common to almost every hash group is the unworried, "It's a hash" sort of mentality, and it is that attitude that I want to focus on in discussing the ties between hashing and philosophy.

In Praise of (the Right Sort of) Apathy

We tend to think of apathy as a negative trait, and we almost always view apathy as a trait to be criticized. Not so for the type of apathy I want to discuss here, which had its origins in the popular philosophies of the Hellenistic period. And it is also this sort of apathy – the right sort of apathy – that is today probably best exemplified by the unworried "It's a hash" sort of mentality typical of hash runs.

As you might guess, I want to use this section to make some ties between (the right sort of) apathy, Hellenistic philosophy, and hashing. But before delving into apathy, some background material on Hellenistic philosophy might be useful. Around 300 BC, Alexander the Great (356–323 BC) conquered an enormous area around the Mediterranean, including much of what is now Greece, Turkey, Iraq, Iran, Syria, Pakistan, Afghanistan, and India. Notably, Alexander's teacher was Aristotle (384–322 BC). Aristotle's teacher was Plato (428–348 BC), and Plato's teacher was Socrates (469–399 BC). The upshot was that Alexander was very much influenced by Greek philosophy and Greek ideals, and his conquest of the region around the Mediterranean spread that Greek influence much more widely than ever before.

Think of the term "Hellenistic" as meaning more or less "Greek-ish," and think of the "Hellenistic period" as this period just discussed, in which Greek philosophy and culture were spread, largely via the conquests of Alexander, around a large area surrounding the Mediterranean. The Hellenistic period is generally viewed as running from about 300 BC to about 150 BC (at which time the Roman culture began to dominate, although some of the Hellenistic philosophies would continue to be popular for several more centuries).

As hinted earlier, a certain type of apathy played a central role in the philosophies of the Hellenistic period, and something similar to that Hellenistic concept is currently found in the mind set of most hash runners (at least, those who have hashed long enough to develop this particular sort of apathy). Importantly, the Hellenistic (and hashers') concept of apathy, and the concept usually associated these days with the term, are very different.

Our modern word "apathy" derives from the Greek *apathia*. Notice the structure of the word: *a* (that is, non) plus *pathia* (that is, pathos or passion). So parsed literally, *apathia* is a lack of pathos, a lack of passion. While this might sound like the usual current concept of apathy, the "I don't give a s***" sort of apathy, it really is not. In the Hellenistic concept, one does not merely have apathy; rather, one acquires it. And acquiring *apathia* can be a long, involved process. And importantly, one cannot acquire *apathia* without first having pathos, that is, without first being passionate. One must work, and work passionately, to understand the universe and to understand one's place in that universe, and this might (depending on the particular philosophy in question) include serious study of logic, physics, ethics, and other disciplines. But the key general idea behind the Hellenistic philosophies is that if you are passionate about such study, you will come to understand the universe and your place in that universe. And it is this deep understanding of the universe, and your place in that universe, that leads to peace of mind, to mental tranquility, mental unperturbedness. In short, a passionate study of philosophy (possibly including the fields mentioned earlier, that is, logic, physics, and ethics – philosophy used to include just about all inquiries into knowledge) will lead one to an unworried, tranquil state of mind. That is, one's passion will eventually lead to *apathia*, the right sort of apathy.

Now, I am not about to suggest that hash running involves serious study of physics, logic, ethics, and the like. But I do think that the sort of unworriedness reflected in the "It's a hash" phrase is quite similar to the unworried state that was the goal of all the schools of the Hellenistic period. And as in that period, this is not an attitude that comes naturally to most. It must be developed (and not surprisingly, some hashers never do develop it, as was no doubt the case with the Hellenistic schools as well, that is, no doubt there were many members of the schools who never achieved the goal of *apathia*).

It is worth mentioning that, much as different hash groups have different personalities, and different hashers have different means of coming to have the right sort of "It's a hash" type of apathy, so too the various schools of the Hellenistic period differed on how best to attain this state of mind. Let's take a minute to look briefly at the four main schools of the Hellenistic period, and each school's approach to achieving *apathia*. (By the way, I should mention that *apathia* is not the only term used by the Hellenistic schools to describe the unworried state of mind they were seeking. *Ataraxia* is another common term, also indicating an unworried, unperturbed state of mind. For this overview of Hellenistic philosophy, I'll use *apathia* as a sort of generic term reflecting the main goal of all the Hellenistic schools.)

Purported Paths to (the Right Sort of) Apathy

The four main schools of the Hellenistic period were Cynicism, Stoicism, Epicureanism, and a brand of skepticism that is often termed "Pyrrhonian Skepticism" or simply "Pyrrhonism." By the way, our modern terms "cynic," "stoic," "Epicurean," and "skeptic" do indeed derive from these Hellenistic schools. But as with *apathia*, the modern meaning of these terms has diverged markedly from their original meanings.

Of the four main schools, the Cynics are the least complex school, and so are the easiest to describe. The Cynics are probably the least philosophically sophisticated, and they seem to have been the least popular of the four main schools of the period. In a nutshell, for a Cynic, the route to an unworried, unperturbed state of mind was through the recognition that nothing natural is bad, and that one ought to live according to one's natural urges. (I can think of a number of hashers, and even entire hash groups, that seem to take more or less this approach to achieving an unworried state of mind.) By all accounts, the Cynics took this "nothing natural is bad" view quite literally. Are you a good Cynic? Are you feeling horny? That's a perfectly natural urge. Have a willing partner? So what if you're in the middle of a crowded place. No problem – clear a space and go at it. Remember, nothing natural is bad, and you should live according to your natures. Cultivating this approach to life will lead you to an unworried, tranquil state of mind.

Again, the goal here is to achieve an unworried, unperturbed state of mind by recognizing and acting on your natural urges, and recognizing that no such natural urges are bad. The Cynics were also big on avoiding anything that might turn out to be a hindrance (again, because such hindrances would not be conducive to an unperturbed state of mind). This would include avoiding work; not worrying about social customs, values, and norms; avoiding marriage and children; steering clear of religion, neglecting hygiene – you name it. If it might prove to be a burden or obligation, no matter how small, a good Cynic would avoid it.

While the Cynics are the easiest of the four schools to describe, in contrast, the views of the Stoics were probably the most complex of the four schools, and it was this school that involved the most detailed work on logic, physics, and ethics. Stoicism was, for quite some time, enormously popular. As it lasted for some time, Stoicism also went through a variety of stages. But throughout, the goal again was *apathia*, that sort of mental unworriedness, unperturbedness, peace of mind.

As suggested, although the goal of the Stoics is not difficult to state, the path to that goal is rather complex. In broad brushstrokes, though, the key idea is that through a study of interrelated fields including logic, physics, and ethics, one would come to understand the workings of the universe. In particular, we eventually come to understand that there is a pervading rational order, or *logos*, to the universe. And as part of that universe, we are part of that overarching rational order. Roughly speaking, if we are successful in our studies we come to understand that whatever our situation in life, all is as it should be, and this understanding results in peace of mind, that is, in the desired state of *apathia*.

Now, no doubt the Stoics had a much more complex and detailed path to *apathia* than do most modern hashers. But the general story is the same. Cynics, Stoics, and various hash groups – and the two Hellenistic schools we will discuss in a moment – have different ideas on how best to cultivate an unworried state of mind, but the general goal – the state of mind referred to by the term *apathia* – is roughly the same, whether we are speaking of any of the Hellenistic schools or of modern hash runners.

Turning now to a brief description of the Epicureans, this group likewise sought peace of mind. For us, the term "Epicurean" suggests someone seeking immediate bodily pleasure, usually involving extravagant dining. For the original Epicureans of the Hellenistic period, immediate bodily pleasure was not at all the goal. In fact, such short-term pleasures were largely to be avoided, as such pleasures would often lead to one becoming dependent on passing pleasures that are largely not under one's control. Instead, one should strive for long-term pleasure, largely through a simple lifestyle (which avoids bodily unpleasantness) and a study of philosophy, especially physics. An understanding of physics, the Epicureans maintained, would lead one to understand that there is nothing to fear in the cosmos. In particular, two of the most pervasive concerns, the fear of the gods and the fear of death, are not to be feared. For the Epicureans, physics tells us that the gods not only did not create the universe, but also can have no influence on the universe and hence no influence on us. Thus we come to recognize that there is nothing to fear from the gods. Likewise, we can learn through physics that there is no afterlife. But our lack of existence after death should in no way be frightening or worrisome. After all, when we contemplate the time before we were born, we do not find our lack of existence then to be frightening or worrisome. Likewise, with proper study, we come to realize that our lack of existence after death is also not frightening or worrisome.

The last school of the Hellenistic period is the Skeptics. As suggested earlier, here I will mainly have in mind what are sometimes referred to as the "Pyrrhonists" or "Pyrrhonian Skeptics," in contrast to the "Academic Skeptics" associated with Plato's school (after his death). Once again, the goal of the Pyrrhonian Skeptics was peace of mind, *apathia*. The general idea of the Pyrrhonists is easy to understand: we are all faced with issues, decisions, questions, and so on for which we do not have full information. Will I be happiest pursuing a life in medicine? A scholarly life? A life in the business world? A life dedicated to charity? Should I believe this, or that? Am I ready for marriage, or would it be best to wait? And is this the right person – will we be happy together? Should I go directly into a career, or should I take time off to travel? Should I remain in my current job, or start off on a new career?

The Pyrrhonists recognized – and here they are almost certainly correct – that for any issue or question or decision, there always seem to be reasons supporting each of the various options, and reasons against each. It seems we can never hope to achieve certainty on any question. Such uncertainty often leads people to a worried, perturbed state of mind. But for the Skeptics, instead of getting ourselves worked up over such issues, and worrying and losing sleep, and becoming perturbed, we should just recognize that there are reasons and arguments for and against each option, and thus we are best off suspending judgment on all such issues.

We should not think of the Pyrrhonian Skeptics as making any positive assertions, such as "nothing is certain" or "we ought not to believe one thing rather than another." Rather, in response to any question, picture a good Pyrrhonian as giving a sort of non-committal shoulder-shrug. Will I be better off going to medical school or devoting my life to charitable work? (Shoulder shrug.) Should I enter a career immediately or wait? (Shoulder shrug.) Am I ready for marriage? (Shoulder shrug.)

This sort of shoulder shrugging response from a good Pyrrhonian Skeptic is reminiscent of the shoulder-shrugging "It's a hash" reaction of a typical hasher when faced with an unusual situation. Whether hashers are surrounded by machine-gun toting *gendarmes*, or forced to hang from a high railway trestle due to an unexpected train arriving during a bridge crossing, or losing the trail and having to wait until midnight for a deep woods rescue by fellow hashers, the shoulder-shrugging "It's a hash" attitude reminds one of the shoulder-shrugging Pyrrhonists of the Hellenistic era.

One question that arises in connection with Pyrrhonian Skepticism is this: if one suspends judgment on all matters in this sort of shoulder-shrugging way, how is one to act? After all, a philosophy that suspends judgment on whether you are better off having cornflakes or rat poison for breakfast seems an unlikely candidate for a rewarding, day-to-day philosophy. At first glance, it also seems difficult to imagine how such a philosophy could lead to peace of mind.

The key here, for the Pyrrhonians, is to act according to what seems most natural. That is, suspend judgment on every matter, and then act by what seems natural. Don't spend time fretting over whether you'll be happier with medical school or a life of charitable work. Suspend judgment, don't worry about it, and take whatever course of action seems most natural. Cultivating this approach to life will lead you not to worry about anything. And that is the Skeptics' recipe for peace of mind, that is, for *apathia*.

Once again, notice that although the details of the approach to life taken by the Pyrrhonian Skeptics differs from the approach taken by the other Hellenistic schools, and differs from the approach taken by modern hashers, we find that the ultimate goal of the schools of the Hellenistic period, and of modern hashers, is much the same: peace of mind, unperturbedness, unworriedness, mental tranquility. In a word, *apathia*, the right sort of apathy.

Life's a Hash

I hope, in these brief pages, to have provided a quick look at a somewhat unusual, though growing, style of running, and to have used that style of running as a way to illustrate a collection of philosophical schools that played prominent roles in our history. As with the members of those schools, hashers tend to develop an unworried approach to hash runs in particular and to life in general. The well-seasoned hasher tends to strive for what the Hellenistic schools strove for, that being a sort of unworried, unperturbed state of mind. And in a way reminiscent of the Hellenistic schools, it is not unusual for hashers to extend this approach to issues that arise not only during hash runs, but in life in general. Or, to modify slightly the usual phrase, Life's a hash.

Richard DeWitt

Chapter 8
What Motivates an Early Morning Runner?

Kevin Kinghorn

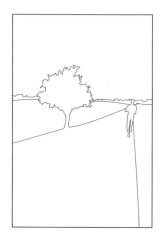

In the spirit of honesty, I have to say at the outset that my wife is the runner in our family. An injury to my knee during college meant that I'd get my future exercise from cycling, not from running. I'd like to be able to tell you that, if not for my knee injury, I'd currently be posting good times along with my wife in such events as the London Marathon (her most recent race). But the truth is that although I was a pretty decent sprinter, I was always mediocre at anything over 200 meters. Besides, if I were to train with my wife, I'd have to join her in getting up before work to run at 6:00 a.m. And that has always struck me as cruel and unusual punishment.

Confessions of a Night Owl

I have a certain kind of curiosity about any runner who gets out of bed to go on a run in the early hours of the morning (I think the description "middle of the night" is more accurate, but never mind). You see, I occasionally formulate a grand plan to wake up early and get my daily exercise in before starting the rest of the day. But I'm somehow never able to follow through with this grand plan for more than a few days.

Here's what typically happens. On about the third or fourth day, I get as far as putting on my workout clothes. Sometimes I even start exercising for a few minutes. But then I make some excuse like: "I feel extra tired this morning. Maybe I have a slight cold coming on, so the prudent thing is probably just to go back to bed. I'll have a good workout tomorrow." But when tomorrow comes, and the alarm clock goes off at 5:30 a.m., my grand plans have lost their momentum. I mutter to myself, "What *was* I thinking?", and I roll over and go back to sleep. My early morning exercise plans never last more than a week.

My wife never seems these days to have any such difficulty going for an early morning run. She made a decision some weeks ago to train every day for an upcoming marathon. And when the alarm clock sounds each day, she's out of bed and into her routine in a flash. She never seems to struggle with a decision about whether she should go running that day. She never seems prone to making lame excuses like: "Maybe I have a slight cold coming on." It's as if her body is on autopilot and she simply does by rote what she's in the habit of doing.

If early morning exercise can be described as a series of struggles for me, and if it can be described as no struggle at all for my wife, then my uncle falls somewhere in between the two of us. He's retired now, but still regularly goes on an early morning run. He's been doing so for decades. Although he does usually meet his mileage goal each week, he no longer runs every day. Some days when he wakes up, he simply says to himself, "I don't feel like going out today." (Hey, he's retired; he's earned the right!) Unlike me, however, he never seems to lose his overall momentum to exercise early in the morning. He still manages to get up and run three or four days a week.

So there seem to me to be three types of early morning runners. First, there are people like me who, when they get up early in the morning, wrestle every step of the way with the temptation to stop what they're doing and go back to bed. Second, there are people like my uncle who wake up and decide whether to go running – but once they make their initial decision, they follow through with it easily and unhesitatingly. Third, there are people like my wife for whom the whole process occurs out of habit and without any real thought that they might actually choose *not* to go running that day.

Philosophically, these three types of runners are interesting because they can help us understand the distinction between *decisions* and *intentional actions*. Philosophers who study human action make use of this distinction in explaining the different sources of our actions.

　　　　　　　Kevin Kinghorn

And when we've come to understand this distinction – which we'll explore by looking at our three types of runners – we'll be in a position to describe in some detail the thought processes of the early morning runner.

Group 1: The Constant Struggler

As I've already confessed, I'm a member of our first group of runners, whom I'll call the "constant strugglers." The constant struggler wrestles with a series of decisions every time the alarm clock goes off. Does he get up or hit the snooze button? (Often, this decision ends up being made a number of times in the course of a morning!) Once he's sitting up, does he go ahead and get dressed or does he lie back down? Once he's dressed, does he go out the door or stay at home and read the paper? Once he's out the door and onto the street, does he start running or keep walking? At the end of each street corner (or, for track runners, at the end of each lap), he must wrestle with the decision to stop or keep going. Thus, what is characteristic of this first group of runners, the constant strugglers, is that they must make a whole series of decisions if they are to complete their morning run.

Of course, not *every* move they make will qualify as an actual *decision*. When running, a runner doesn't *decide* to put his left foot here, then his right foot there, and so on. It would be mentally exhausting if we had to concentrate on each step and actually make a decision as to whether our foot should go, for example, *here* or six inches to the right. Instead, what happens is this: We make a decision to run to the next corner, or to run another lap. And our bodies simply "carry out" our intention without much, if any, additional conscious thought. This point becomes quite important as we turn to consider our second kind of runner.

Group 2: The Single Decision Maker

You'll remember my earlier comment that my uncle only makes one initial decision each morning about running that day. Once that decision is made, everything else follows. This kind of scenario really is not that unusual.

Imagine that you're in bed one evening, unable to sleep, and you remember the leftover pizza in the refrigerator. You decide to go downstairs and help yourself to a slice or two – maybe even pour yourself a glass of beer to wash it down. (Even elite athletes have to carbo-load, you tell yourself.) By the time you've sat down at the kitchen table with your food, how many decisions have you made? Probably, the answer will be: one. You don't decide to get out of bed and then, once out of bed, weigh your options about how to get downstairs before *deciding* to head toward the stairs. Once downstairs, you don't map out different floor-plans for getting to the kitchen and then *decide* to walk through the living room, then *decide* to open the fridge, then *decide* to get out the pizza, then *decide* to put it on a plate. All these subsequent "decisions" are really just different aspects of the single decision to get some pizza instead of continuing to lie in bed.

Similarly, runners like my uncle make the single decision to go running. Everything else simply follows and there are no further actual *decisions* made. But what should we call these further actions? After all, when my uncle takes an individual step during his run, it's not as if the raising of his legs is a reflex action (like when a doctor hits your knee with a rubber hammer to test your reflexes). So how should we characterize these actions that follow from his initial decision?

Philosophers who analyze human actions typically refer to these subsequent steps as "intentional actions." Our modern understanding of intentional actions owes much to the work of Elizabeth Anscombe (1919–2001). Anscombe emphasized that intentional actions are those actions of ours about which we can give our own reasons as to why we perform them. Thus, an intentional action can be contrasted with things like the reflex action of raising your leg when it's struck by a doctor's rubber hammer. To give an explanation of why your leg jumps, Anscombe explained, you would need to include your observation of what the doctor is doing to your leg. You wouldn't simply be able to give *your* own reasons for initiating this action.

One example of an intentional action is your action of holding this book right now. You might be holding it with your left hand, or with your right hand, or perhaps with both hands. You might be holding the book two feet from your eyes, or six inches from your eyes, or somewhere in between. Are you currently conscious of any *decision* you made to hold the book this way instead of some other way? Probably not. But this action of holding the book a certain way is still an intentional action. If someone asked you why you're holding

Kevin Kinghorn

the book as you are, you would be able to explain that the reason is that it's a comfortable way of positioning the book so your eyes can easily focus on the words of the page. Thus, your intentional actions don't always have to be actual *decisions*. In everyday life, our intentional actions greatly outnumber the conscious decisions we make.

Let's return to the case of your decision to eat pizza late at night. In this case you make only one decision: the decision to get some pizza instead of continuing to lie in bed. But all the actions that follow from this decision – the actions of walking down the stairs, opening the fridge, and so forth – are not decisions, but are instead *intentional actions*. Similarly, runners like my uncle make the single decision on any given day to go running. Once that decision is made, all the actions that follow from it – the actions of putting on running shoes, going out the front door, and so forth – are intentional actions. But, unlike with our previous group of the constant strugglers, these actions are not instances of actual decisions. Thus, this second group of runners is aptly termed the "single decision makers."

Group 3: Running by Rote

Let's move now to our third group of runners, of which my wife is a member. My wife made the decision some weeks ago to get in race shape for an upcoming marathon. The running she now does each morning is done in virtue of this earlier decision. Our third group of runners, then, are those people who have made an earlier decision – such as the decision to get in shape for a race, or to lose weight, or to lead a healthy lifestyle. Running each morning has become a habit and stems from this earlier decision. Members of this third group perform *intentional actions* when they go on their daily run; but they don't make daily *decisions* to run.

So, our third group of runners is in a similar situation to our previous group, the "single decision makers." One decision is made, and then everything that subsequently takes place occurs as a natural consequence. The only difference is that, for the third group, the actual decision to run occurs at some point in the past. And because this third group makes no daily decision to run, we might say that their running each day is done by rote.

There's a side issue worth mentioning at this point. In saying that my wife runs each day "by rote," I'm not suggesting that she mindlessly trains each morning, oblivious to any benefits from running other than better fitness for a pending marathon. Runners in the third group enjoy the early morning air on their daily runs. They enjoy communing with nature. They enjoy having accomplished something before most people are even awake. They enjoy jump-starting their day so as to feel vitalized as they begin work.

In view of these facts, it may seem wholly inadequate to describe my wife's early morning run as simply an act of getting in shape for a marathon. In some ways, it seems more natural to describe her run as an act of discipline, or an act of physical accomplishment, or perhaps even an act of communing with nature.

The good news is that we are not forced to describe the third group's early morning runs as *either* an act of communing with nature *or* an act of getting in shape. Rather, we can describe these early morning runs as *both*. Actions often can have multiple descriptions. Philosophers sometimes point to the example of shooting a gun. Should we describe this action as a person squeezing his finger? Or pulling the trigger of a gun? Or firing a bullet? Or shooting a man? Or killing an adversary? Well, the answer is that these are *all* legitimate descriptions of the action in question. A single action can have multiple descriptions.

So for my wife, there is no problem with explaining her daily run as an intentional action that follows automatically from a decision she made sometime in the past to get in shape for a marathon. *Explaining why* her act of running occurs does not prevent us from *describing* this act in any number of legitimate ways.

If the early morning runner really is like my wife, then he will not actually make a daily decision whether to perform an act of discipline that day, or an act of physical accomplishment, or an act of communing with nature. He won't actually be making any daily *decision* whatsoever. Still, his act of running – which, again, will be an intentional action and not an actual decision – can be accurately described as all of these things. And this is because, as we have seen, a single action can have a number of legitimate descriptions.

What's in the Mind of a Runner?

We're now in a position to summarize the thought processes of our three groups of early morning runners. In the first group, the "constant strugglers," options are weighed and decisions are made at every turn. No wonder constant strugglers often abandon their task. There are so many decisions that have to turn out the right way in order for a single run to be completed! The second group, the "single decision makers," don't face the same struggle. But they do face one struggle: the decision either to stay in bed or get up and go running. Happily, once the decision to run is made, there are no more struggles about the run that day. They still must perform a number of *intentional actions* if they are to complete their run; but they need not make any more *decisions*. Best of all is the third group: those who run by rote. None of their intentional actions on a given day of running amount to actual decisions. And without having to weigh options and make decisions, there is no struggle.

How does a person become a member of this third group, if he or she is not there already? The most common way into the third group is by means of habit. The more you perform a difficult action, the more you become naturally inclined to do that action – without hesitation and without struggle. For example, by forcing yourself to tell the truth when it is difficult, you get in the habit of telling the truth. And you eventually find yourself naturally inclined to tell the truth – without giving the matter any real thought. Aristotle (384–322 BC) made this point in remarking that "a state of character results from the repetition of similar activities." He observed, "We become just by doing just actions, temperate by doing temperate actions, brave by doing brave actions."[1] Adding to Aristotle's list, we could say that a person becomes a habitual early morning runner by running early in the morning!

If someone lacks the willpower to make consistently disciplined decisions over time until running becomes a natural habit, might there be other ways to become a member of the third group? Well, the answer is that it is at least *possible*. Sometimes an experience will be so emotionally significant for us that it has a dramatic and lasting effect on our motivations. For instance, a teenager who has just taken up smoking, and who then has a parent die from an emphysema attack before his very eyes, may be permanently affected by the experience and never able to bring himself to smoke again. And it is possible that some momentous event might so increase a person's

---

[1] Aristotle, *Nicomachean Ethics*, trans. Terence Irwin (Indianapolis, IN: Hackett Publishing, 1999), p. 19.

motivation to run every day that he jumps immediately into our third group of runners. For example, a person might be told by a heart specialist that, unless he takes up daily exercise, he won't live more than six months. Or, a youngster might be so inspired after watching a dramatic race at the Olympics that he determines there and then to someday become an Olympian himself.

In these cases, a single event may so greatly increase the person's motivation to run every day that he never subsequently has to wrestle with any real decisions whether to run. Still, although it is *possible* that one's motivation can be dramatically and permanently changed like this in an instant, surely this is an uncommon occurrence. The impact of even momentous events tends to wear off over time. It is far more likely that, if a person wants to move into the third group of runners, he will need to do so gradually over time by making disciplined running a natural habit.

I used to have hopes of making my early morning routine enough of a habit that I at least joined my uncle in the second group of early morning exercisers. But I know myself too well. Once I lose momentum from sleeping late a time or two, I lose the plot. I think my only chance is to psyche myself up, and then make a momentous decision on the spot that permanently changes my motivation. This will allow me to jump from the first group of constant strugglers right up to the third group. So, today I make solemn declaration of my decision to join my wife every day for early morning exercise! It'll just immediately become a habit which I'm never even tempted to break! (But wish me luck. My wife – who knows me pretty well – is already snickering as she's reading this.)

Chapter 9
A Runner's Pain

Chris Kelly

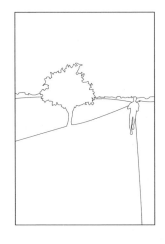

A Case History: A Run Up
La Concha

My Madrileñan girlfriend and I had bickered the whole four-hour drive down to the sea; and, so, as we pulled onto her parents' macadam driveway, I immediately shoehorned on my Asics with a popsicle stick. A lonely mountain peak (named *La Concha* or The Shell) loomed over the seaside town, and I was going to run up it. "Be back in a bit," I snapped, and ran off, the same silly arguments repeating under my breath in a loop. I was in what one might call *mental pain*. Running is much better than Advil for this kind of suffering, and so I hurried toward the mountain above Marbella.

I set a torrid, anger-goosed pace on the flat through the resort town's suburbia and up the couple-mile incline to the mountain's base. The heat of my run melted my muttering into a kind of submission, and my thoughts calmed. I reached the end of concrete and slowly zigzagged upwards through a sparse, pathless spread of pine and scrub brush. This was good running, low impact, lots of strength work, a continual sweat, a heavy, relaxed breathing, a good effort with no pain. I felt so wonderful and the mountain peak seemed so close, that I labored upward even as the terrain turned into a pebbly scree and the sun slowly sank against the ridge above me. Near the top of the ridge, my legs were burning intensely in the thighs and glutes. Tight little marbles of muscle knotted into my calves. My breath was whistling in the back of my throat, and my ears ached as if someone were firmly pressing her thumbs into the flesh of my neck beneath my earlobes. My gums throbbed for the lack of oxygen (*La Concha* was one mile high). The sweat slipped down my body.

All in all, I felt *great*.

There was pain, yes, but it was a *good* pain if that is possible: no nausea, no joint pain, just an overall heat that had ignited to burning in several areas. I was maxing out precisely when I wanted to. I summited just as the sun began to set beyond the florid expanse of the Mediterranean. Africa was revealed as a hazy moustache on the lip of the horizon and I found the rock of Gibraltar off in the distance. I felt effusively vital.

Then the sun disappeared with a visual *plop*, and it was past time to go down.

Unfortunately, my path down was not built for safe mountain running. Just below the peak was a long scree slope. Under the right conditions, scree can be skied in slalom fashion. Unfortunately, this scree was intermixed with bigger rocks and boulders, so every 10 feet of sliding would bring a bigger rock down behind me. After being hit by a couple of 10- to 20-pounders – once on the back of the knee and once on my tailbone – I proceeded more slowly in long ambling traverses. My bruised calf throbbed and there was a scraped exposed pain on my tailbone. I ignored these sensations; nothing I could do now would make them better or worse.

Things went from sad to morose. First, I caught a bad case of cottonmouth and couldn't swallow. I had stopped sweating and my skin had a cool clammy feel. As the light continued to fade, I started shivering and feeling ill. I hate nausea, and wanted to lie down, but I had to get off the mountain. I realized I was dehydrated. The world was darkening. There was no moon. What happened next is predictable. I found myself pressed against a rock wall in the dark. I jumped down toward a barely visible patch of dirt and landed half on, half off a rock. There was a tiny pain, the snap of a walnut shell, in the side of my knee. I took a few steps, and each one brought a thin needle of pain just under my kneecap. It was not an overwhelming pain, a train whistle in the far distance, but it was a *bad* pain. I felt *hurt*. Nausea, chills, bruises, burning legs, tight chest, sore feet, an inability to swallow had not stopped me from running, but this squeal from the knee sat me down. I didn't want to spend the night there, but I couldn't keep going in the dark with a bum knee. Besides, it had gotten to the point where at any moment I might step off a cliff. I was severely dehydrated. It was getting cold. I was in a foreign country, in a foreign town. I wondered what Anabel and her parents were thinking. I was worried: mental pain again.

So that's the beginning of my story. It's a simple story, all about pain and pleasure, suffering and enjoyment: mental pain (frustration), and pain mixed with pleasure, and bruising pain (calf, tailbone), cold (shivering), the unpleasantness of nausea and cottonmouth, and, finally, joint pain.

I suggest that the runner's intimacy with the varieties of physical suffering allows her an insight into what makes life valuable. More specifically, I suggest that the runner is connected with an ancient philosophy of living: that a good life is determined much less by the particular sensations that make it up and much more by our attitude toward those sensations, by the meaning we take those sensations to have.

Intrinsic Value versus Instrumental Value

I'm a bit more cautious these days than when one and twenty. This explains the reflecting singlet I've bought for night running. It's an ugly thing that I would never wear if not to keep the cars off. The singlet is of purely *instrumental value* to me. If I stopped running, or stopped running at night or if they (finally!) abolished cars from the road, I would no longer need it for anything at all. This is a feature of things that are merely *instrumentally valuable*: their value depends on context.

Instrumental values are important for no other reason than they help us to other, more important, ends. If there are no other ends, then there are no instrumental values. Those other ends, those things which should be the ultimate end of all our aiming, are the *intrinsically valuable*. Intrinsically valuable things are valuable independent of context; they are good in and of themselves.

This doesn't mean merely instrumental things aren't important. Think of the shoes runners buy, the socks, the energy products, the runners' magazines (maybe even this book), etc. . . . All instrumentally valuable. But you don't buy these tools because a life with gel-cushioned shoes or power bars (or gel-cushioned power bars) is necessarily a better life on its own, but because those tools will be useful – here in this life, in this context – to creating other things that are valuable on their own: good health, perhaps, a long life, maybe; happiness, pleasure, knowledge, success, possibly. We make a dangerous mistake, then, when we confuse the instrumental for the intrinsic. An energy bar is no good to you if it doesn't help you run longer (or if its taste gives you no pleasure) and running longer is no good to you unless running longer brings some intrinsic good into your life.

This, then, may be the most important question in life: *what is intrinsically valuable?* What is it for which we should "do all our doing"?

Hedonism

The simplest and perhaps most compelling theory of intrinsic value is called *hedonism*. Hedonists claim that only pleasure is intrinsically good, and only pain is intrinsically bad. The most influential modern progenitor of this idea was the philosopher Jeremy Bentham (1748–1832). "Nature," he told us, "has placed mankind under the governance of two sovereign masters, pain and pleasure."[1] This view is compelling because while most things some one person values are disputed by some *other* person (you like strawberry, I hate strawberry; you like Van Gogh, I hate Van Gogh), there is widespread agreement on the value of pleasure and pain. Almost no one hates pleasure; almost no one likes pain. This isn't something that can be said for most values.

The hedonist view of the good life is simple: pursue those things that give you the most pleasure or happiness; avoid those things that cause you pain or unhappiness. The traditional image of a hedonist is of someone pursuing the basest pleasures: eating sweet and fatty foods, looking for sex and drugs, and so on. A true hedonist, though, values all pleasure, whether it comes from classical music, or a great conversation, or a beautiful mountain, or solving a puzzle, or reading a philosophy book, or, yes, sex, or food. The wise hedonist will be sure to mention that if you want the very best life (and who doesn't?), you mustn't fool around with those things that give you only

---

[1] Jeremy Bentham, *An Introduction to the Principles of Morals and Legislation* (1780), ed. J. H. Burns and H. L. A. Hart (New York: Oxford University Press, 1996), p. 11.

Chris Kelly

moderate or temporary pleasures, not if there are things of extreme and constant pleasure nearby.

The hedonist in all of us has to wonder a bit about runners. Why do we choose such a hobby when pain is the one thing a wise human shouldn't want? There are, after all, so many pleasurable activities one can engage in with minimal chance of suffering; shuffleboard, going for a drive, eating out, listening to music, watching TV, having a conversation about molecular bonding: the list is endless. Isn't there something perverse about waking up earlier than you want to, going for a run in the bitter cold, running faster than your body tells you should, continuing to run despite increasing pain and all the other myriad sufferings we intentionally inflict upon ourselves?[2]

One Answer: Running as Instrumental

No pain no gain

There is an easy answer to the hedonist. Many of us became runners because the sport was a tool to some other goal; we became runners for instrumental reasons. Running, we knew, was good for the heart, the waistline, or the brain. We runners don't endure unpleasantness *for the sake of* unpleasantness (at least not most of us). That *would* be perverse. Rather, we think we are getting in shape, or getting faster, or winning something worth winning. Personally, running has allowed me to sleep better, feel stronger, have more energy, be more confident, think more clearly, make new friends . . .

One of the aptitudes of the wise is the ability to put off present pleasure or overcome present pain for greater reward down the road. It takes "the art of measurement," Socrates tells us, to make right choices. The art of measurement is the ability to see things for their real value independent of present appearances. By the evidence of appearance, the full moon in the sky is a much bigger object than any of the stars; but astronomers, experts in the art of astronomical measurement, tell us that the moon is smaller than each and every

---

[2] One doesn't have to be a hedonist to see the point here. Some of us want to deny the hedonist point that *only* pleasure is intrinsically valuable. Some of us think that knowledge, consciousness, beauty, life, freedom, to name a few, are also intrinsically valuable. Even so, surely we all agree that pain and suffering are still one of the *bads*, and, surely we all agree that we should do our best to avoid them.

star we can see with the naked eye. The art of measurement. What is a little pain now, if I live five years longer, and get five years more pleasure? What is a little pain now, if I avoid the big pain of a heart attack? What is a little pain now, if I get the big pleasure later of winning the race? The art of measurement.[3]

This is a wisdom most experienced runners possess. There are days we don't feel like running, yet we do. Rarely do I want to do the last interval of an interval workout, but I always do it. Our bodies tell us to stop or slow down at the end of a race, but we don't (if we can help it). Why do we do all of this? Because we've learned the art of measurement, and derive the concomitant benefits.

No pleasure no gain

That answer is too easy, though. We don't run just for glory or health benefits. To see this imagine a little blue pill with all the health benefits of running. Would you take the pill if *you had to give up running*? Most of us wouldn't. Why? Because we *enjoy* "the red pill" of running itself. When I was on the flat beneath *La Concha*, I experienced a *reduction* of my mental pain. I was satisfying the hedonist imperative. I felt better and better as I went upward. I was ecstatic at the mountain top, in a state of intense enjoyment. These are all good things, and even the hedonist would agree.

So, one reason we run through pain is because the pleasure of running outweighs the suffering. Aristotle made a point many centuries ago, "each type of person finds pleasure in whatever he is called a lover of, so that a horse pleases, e.g., the horse lover, a spectacle the lover of spectacles . . ."[4] If you truly love something you will derive some pleasure from the experience of it. Running lovers enjoy stellar cardiovascular systems *and* they enjoy running itself.

---

[3] "Socrates: Do not the same magnitudes appear larger to your sight when near, and smaller when at a distance? . . . Now suppose happiness to consist in doing or choosing the greater, and in not doing or in avoiding the less, what would be the saving principle of human life? Would not the art of measuring be the saving principle; or would the power of appearance? Is not the latter that deceiving art which makes us wander up and down and take the things at one time of which we repent at another, both in our actions and in our choice of things great and small? But the art of measurement would do away with the effect of appearances, and, showing the truth, would fain teach the soul at last to find rest in the truth, and would thus save our life" (Plato, *Protagoras*, 58b).
[4] Aristotle, *Nicomachean Ethics*, book 1, 1099a.

No pain no virtue

Even this last, though, overlooks something important about a runner's relationship to pain. Sometimes the pain *itself* is instrumentally valuable. Ask yourself this, if running were always *easy*, would it be as valuable to you? Sure, I would love to have limitless energy and sprint for an hour whenever I wanted. That would be a pretty good superpower. Nonetheless, something important would be lost. Running would no longer be a challenge. Running's difficulty is part of its value.

One reason for this is that experiencing pain and unpleasantness is necessary for developing some of the most desired virtues. You can't be courageous if there is nothing to fear. You can't be charitable if there is no one in need of charity. There is no value in temperance unless there is some pleasure one must forego (on the hedonist scale a lost pleasure might as well be a pain). Running builds character because it is difficult, and because many of the virtues can neither be exhibited nor developed in the absence of hardship.

In addition, we should not forget, there is pleasure in achieving these virtues. Paradoxically, no small part of the pleasure I felt at the top of the mountain was due to the amount of pain I went through on the way up. Part of the pleasure was due to the fact that I had accomplished something difficult. And that is what would be lost if running lost its pain: mountain peaks would be as attainable as doorsteps, and there are very few doorsteps I would brag about scaling.

No pain . . . no pleasure?

Even this doesn't fully explain my attitude toward all of the pain experiences of my run up *La Concha*. So far I've suggested that runners accept the inevitable pain and suffering of running because (1) the running is instrumentally valuable to more pleasure *down the road*, (2) running *is itself* more pleasing than painful, and (3) *pain* as well can be instrumental to later pleasure or other goods like the virtues. I have one more (possibly bizarre) suggestion, though: sometimes pain sensations themselves *can be pleasing*.

As I was nearing the top of the mountain, I was definitely in pain: my legs burned, my calves were cramping. My gums were tender. My throat was dry. All in all, though, I was *enjoying the experience*. I was happy I was doing it *as* I was doing it. Here's the weirdness: pain itself seemed to constitute an enjoyable experience.

Now, I don't enjoy *all* pain. I didn't enjoy the bruises; I didn't enjoy the knee pain. I'm not a masochist (at least not an indiscriminate one): I don't enjoy pain *because* it is pain. Nonetheless, I did enjoy my pain experiences as I topped the ridge. Is this possible? Is it really pain if I like it? If I did, am I being perverse? Do you have any idea what I'm talking about?

What is Pain Anyway?

Pain seems so unequivocally bad, sometimes, that you might be tempted to join many famous philosophers and define it that way. On such a view, pain equals bad sensation; that is, any pain is a bad sensation and any bad sensation is a pain.

For a definition to be adequate there should be no significant counterexamples. A counterexample is an example that disproves a rule. The orbit of Mercury was a counterexample to Newton's laws of motion. Because Mercury moved in ways that Newton's laws said they shouldn't, Mercury proved those laws couldn't govern all motion. If "pain" really meant "bad sensation," there would be (1) no examples of pain that weren't bad sensations and (2) no bad sensations that weren't pain. If there were, they would be counterexamples to the definition.

Let's start with counterexamples to the claim that there are no bad sensations that aren't pains. Not all unpleasant sensations are pains. Nausea, for instance, is an unpleasant sensation, but it would be a stretch to call it a "pain." I didn't have a "pain in my stomach" while jogging down the mountain. If I told you I did have a pain in my stomach, you'd think I had a cramp, or indigestion, or incipient appendicitis or had been punched or some such thing. When I became nauseated from dehydration, it was one more unpleasant sensation added to the others. It was not one more *pain*. The same can be said for the sensation of cottonmouth and my inability to swallow. This is a really (really) unpleasant feeling, but it is not pain. There was no pain in my throat, no pain in my tongue or on the roof of mouth, but it definitely seemed bad.

A similar unpleasant but not painful sensation – one that I do not remember experiencing on *La Concha* – is itching. One might think that itching is just a less intense pain. We can test that theory. Pinch your wrist until you feel the lightest pain. Was that an itch? No? Now recall the most intense itch you've ever felt and compare it to that pinch. Itching sensations can be as intensely unpleasant as and more intensely unpleasant than pains. That does not make them pains.[5]

Now for examples of pain sensations that aren't bad sensations. Those final meters up *La Concha* show, if I described the situation accurately, that pain doesn't always seem bad; it is not always unpleasant. But was I really feeling pain? Can a sensation really be a pain without being unpleasant?

Imagine you are working at your computer in your office, or eating at the kitchen table, or you are any other everyday place, not making any particular effort, minding your own business, when all the sensations of a final sprint overcome your body. The muscles between your ribs, your diaphragm, expand forcefully, then contract. Then again and again until you are panting vigorously. Your legs burn intensely in the thighs. There are tight little knots of muscle in your calves. Your breath narrows at the back of your throat; your gums fill with lactic acid. Every muscle is straining and stretching.

Imagine this happening in detail and you can recover what it feels like to be a novice runner on a hard run. Sometimes we forget how unpleasant running seems to some people. These are genuinely alarming sensations; they would seem bad in our office or most any other place; we would want them to stop. And the first time we feel them on a run, even if we know why they are there, they seem horrible. But they feel different to us now, don't they? Even if you don't positively enjoy some of them as I do, you've learned to accept them. They no longer alarm you; you no longer hate them. This shows that the seeming badness of pain is dependent on our *attitude* toward the pain sensations. If this is right, then unpleasantness is not a feature intrinsic to an experience, but a relation between us and our experience.

One might argue that I'm really not feeling pain anymore if I like it. The burning in my thighs has ceased to be a pain, if I'm enjoying the burning. Then it's a pleasure. This isn't right though, and one can look at medical studies on pain to see why. Pain medications can be

---

[5] It is interesting to note that the conceptual analysis I just did of pain, nausea, and itching has now been backed up by neurobiologists. Nausea is caused by a completely different biological mechanism than either pain or itching. And though itching and pain both enter the nervous system through similar neurons, they follow independent pathways to the brain. Not all bad sensations are pain.

classed into two different categories: there are those that make pain go away – anti-inflammatories, for instance – and those that make the *badness* go away – morphine, for instance. Say you rank your knee pain at an "eight." You take some ibuprofen and soon after you rank your pain at a "five." If instead you had taken morphine, you will still rank it at "eight" afterward. It just won't seem bad anymore.

The same thing happens to the runner as she goes from being a novice to a veteran. She reduces or removes the badness of the pain sensations. She still feels pain sensations, though. And, so, badness can be separated from the pain experience, and the proposed definition must be false.

This, on its own, doesn't mean that pain isn't bad, though. Perhaps, we runners are just confused. Endorphins work, biologically speaking, much like morphine after all. Why should we trust what someone on morphine says? Contemporary philosopher Irwin Goldstein makes this point:

> Not disliking those sensations we call "pains" may seem extraordinary, but this is not reason to say a sensation would not *be* a pain were it not disliked. The idea of hungering for pain, like that of craving castration, represents an empirical anomaly, a response psychologically queer; it is not self-contradictory, merely linguistically disordered.[6]

Are we runners psychologically queer? To answer this question, we still need to determine what pain is.

Start with the evidence. We know that pain is not nausea; neither is it itching. What is the difference between a pain sensation and nausea or itching? All three are unpleasant, but they *seem* different. This difference in seeming is apparently due to a difference in what they mean to us. Those meanings are probably fixed by the evolutionary purposes of those sensations. Physical pain implies a breaking, a puncture of the skin, a tearing of the muscle, a bursting of the capillaries, a burning or a freezing of the cell walls. It is evolutionarily appropriate that we react strongly to such events; and, so, pain seems bad. Itching seems to mean "something foreign moving over the skin." Nausea means, maybe, "poison inside."

---

[6] Irwin Goldstein, "Pleasure and Pain: Unconditional, Intrinsic Values," *Philosophy and Phenomenological Research* 50, 1989, p. 261.

Perhaps it is not the way pain feels that is bad, but what pain *represents* that is (generally) bad: broken bones and damaged organs and such. If that's right then it's no surprise that pain sensations seem bad to us. We don't like bad news, after all. It *would* be psychologically queer and perverse to generally like bad news or want to receive it. Bad news is intrinsically the type of thing that we would forego if we had the option. This is not because there is anything intrinsically wrong with *bad news itself* – with, for instance, the *words* in bad news. It is silly to hate the *sign* that tells us the road is closed; it is the *fact* that the road is closed that is distressing. We don't want to get bad news because of what bad news tells us is true about the world.

Imagine you are having tea with your mother. The waiter hands you a note, says he just received a phone call for you, and the caller left a message. The note says, "Your mother died yesterday at 5 a.m." As your mother is sitting right across from you eating a crumpet, you know this news is false. You might at first find this unpleasant – we are conditioned not to like bad news, after all – but after a few moments you'll know it is a mistake. In other words, there is a difference between *suffering* pain and merely *feeling* pain. We suffer an experience when that experience seems bad to us. I can suffer many non-painful experiences: a visit from my mother-in-law, or a stubbed toe, or making an embarrassing gaffe in conversation. I can also have these experiences without suffering.

All the same considerations apply to pain. If pain represents or indicates bodily damage, then pain is a form of bad news. People don't like pain because of what pain represents. Bad news should stop being unpleasant when we know it's false (remember the note about your mother). This explains why I, as a runner, no longer feel the burning in my legs as bad. I realize that the apparent bad news is false. Indeed, I know that sometimes this burning sensation is actually *good* news despite my body's protestations. I *intended* to do that to the tissues of my thigh. Such micro-tears will, I know, make my muscles stronger in a couple of days (longer, unfortunately, as I get older). On the other hand, the walnut cracking sensation in my knee felt appropriately horrible, and stopped me immediately. That was truly bad news and I, as an experienced runner, knew it.

It may be "psychologically queer" to like or not mind pain, but it is not (necessarily) perverse. As long as we know that the apparent bad news is not really bad, it is good and appropriate to not mind the sensations. The bruise on my calf and the scrape on my tailbone were not very bad news, not really, and so it was appropriate to ignore them. If, in addition, we know that the apparent bad news is good, as with some muscle pain, we should (and can) learn to like the sensation.

This doesn't mean, obviously, that runners like all pain, nor does it mean we manage to like all pain associated with healthy running. I still dread the ends of races, the nausea, the extreme fatigue. Millions of years of evolution are hard to overcome with rational arguments. Nonetheless, the average runner has the skill to counter much of that biological urgency. We still finish races, after all. We know how to turn pain's evolutionary meaning on its head.

The Good Life

And this is clearly one key to reaching the good life: the ability to see through the appearances of things – especially the appearances created by our biology because they can be so powerful – and see things as they are. This is the art of measurement made general. Unpleasantness is not intrinsic to things (if it isn't to pain, it's hard to imagine it being intrinsic to any other sensation). Therefore, if we spend our lives, as the hedonist suggests, avoiding things we find unpleasant, we may be wasting our time. And worse, we may also lose all opportunity to achieve those things that require us to go through experiences generally considered unpleasant: running races, human relationships, challenging classes, challenging jobs, pregnancy, international travel, and so on.

Much the same can be said for the other half of the hedonist equation, the injunction to seek out pleasant experiences. Heroin is widely reported to be pleasurable, but most of us know that it is something we should not seek out. The hedonist might agree; being an addict may not be that pleasurable actually. But now we have deeper wisdom than hedonism available. Not only should we be aware that this heroin sensation will lead to suffering later, we should also cease to find the sensation pleasant. We should see it for what it is; see it for the damage it causes us. Not to be funny, but heroin is bad news; it just doesn't seem like it at first. The same can be said, to a much lesser extent, for the pleasurable sensations of double fudge whole-cream ice cream and deep-fried chicken when taken in excess.

The End of the Story

In the end, I was sitting there in the dark wishing the moon were out or I had a flashlight. My knee was feeling a bit better, but I really couldn't see anything. Then a little miracle happened. The mountainside was awash in light, as if someone had flicked on the moon. The beach town had opened for business, and all at once, the neon lights, the street lamps, the carousel, the boardwalk lit up as if in response to my wishing. It was a wholly unlooked for revelation. And what did the light reveal, but that was I sitting on a path! One moment, I was lost on a mountainside, sitting among the bushes and brambles, civilization inaccessible. A moment later, with a little light and a new perspective, I was on my way home. And this is the key to happiness: turn the lights on and look around. Or rather wait for the lights to come on. With a little patience and then a little light, you will discover where you really are, what your status really is. Give your experience as much meaning as it can take, which is as much as it deserves, and savor it, even if that experience happens to be the one we call pain.

Chapter 10
Performance-Enhancement and the Pursuit of Excellence

William P. Kabasenche

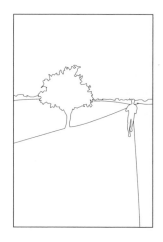

Have you ever wondered what it would feel like to run *really* fast? Would it be different from how your own best efforts have felt? Would it have a new quality to it? Apparently, my friend Franklin had been wondering about this.[1] While running once, he asked me if I would ever take EPO (erythropoietin, a red-blood-cell booster that acts as an illegal performance enhancer), if it were declared legal and medically safe.[2] I said I doubted I would. For his part, Franklin said he would "just to know what it would feel like to run a sub-eight minute two-mile." Daniel Komen currently holds the world record for two miles, at 7:58 and change, so Franklin had set his sights pretty high. I expressed some reservations about this line of thought. Does it really feel different, in a meaningful way, to break eight minutes as opposed to breaking nine, ten, or eleven minutes, depending on your ability? I appealed to philosopher Alasdair MacIntyre's idea of the goods internal to a practice to try to make my case. This chapter represents my attempt to offer a more complete answer to Franklin's question,

---

[1] 'Franklin' is a pseudonym, although the conversation that follows really took place.
[2] For those already feeling tempted, WADA (the World Anti-Doping Agency) has declared EPO illegal, and the drug's use is not without serious medical dangers. Some people appear to have died from using it, usually by making their blood so thick with red blood cells that their heart fails in its efforts to pump. WADA is an organization that conducts drug testing, primarily for performance-enhancing drugs. Most countries and most international athletics bodies accept its jurisdiction.

to explain why I would not take EPO to experience the feeling of running an eight-minute two-mile.

My line of reasoning might have broader application than just to Franklin's question. Appealing to the goods internal to running could also explain why we wouldn't, as runners, necessarily want or need to seek out fast downhill or wind-aided courses, use shoes with springs in them, or indulge in other means of "artificial" aid in an effort to achieve new levels of excellence in running.

MacIntyre on Practices and Internal Goods

To set up my response to Franklin, I'd like to use and expand on the ideas of Alasdair MacIntyre concerning internal and external goods and his notion of a practice. I'll start with practices. MacIntyre offers the following, somewhat convoluted, definition of a practice:

> By a "practice" I am going to mean any coherent and complex form of socially established cooperative human activity through which goods internal to that form of activity are realized in the course of trying to achieve those standards of excellence which are appropriate to, and partially definitive of, that form of activity, with the result that human powers to achieve excellence, and human conceptions of the ends and goods involved, are systematically extended.[3]

Let's unpack this definition. A practice is form of social activity. So, for instance, Americans are in the practice of driving on the right and running facing traffic. But MacIntyre uses the word to refer to more complex activities than just where we drive or run. He lists playing football and chess, designing architecture, farming, scientific and historical inquiries, painting, and music as examples of complex practices (p. 187). What distinguishes these activities as practices in MacIntyre's sense is that they have a complexity concerning the ways we might *excel* in engaging in them. Players of football or chess engage in an ongoing conversation about how best to play those games. Often the "conversation" just manifests itself in the way participants play. Although, excellent play usually leaves people talking for some time afterward too. Sometimes somebody comes up with

---

[3] Alasdair MacIntyre, *After Virtue*, 2nd edn. (Notre Dame, IN: University of Notre Dame Press, 1984), p. 187. From here on, I'll cite references to *After Virtue* by page numbers in the text.

an innovative way to achieve the aims of game; perhaps a new style of play revolutionizes "how the game is played." All of this differs, of course, from driving on the right-hand side of the road. Nobody looks for a new or innovative way to do this and nobody thinks there are any particular goals or excellences to achieve in this form of activity other than just driving safely where people (including runners) expect you to be driving.

But MacIntyre's notion of a practice contains another idea that makes it somewhat unique. He believes that for the kinds of practices he's talking about, there are goods internal to a given practice. To make sense of this, we should distinguish internal and external goods. External goods would be things like money, status, and prestige (p. 188). Obviously, people achieve these in many different ways. The money you earn in your job is no different, except perhaps in quantity, from the money Paul Tergat earns when he sets a world record. And you can achieve status and prestige within a society in a lot of different ways. So, these external goods are *external*, in part, because they can be gotten in a variety of ways; they are not fundamentally internal, or intrinsic, to particular practices. But internal goods differ in this regard. MacIntyre says that whatever qualifies as a practice in his sense will have internal goods. And internal goods are particular to practices. The "good" of achieving excellence in playing football or in painting is unique to that practice. Revolutionizing the way people play football (or do the high jump, as Dick Fosbury apparently did with his "Fosbury flop") might earn you money, status, and prestige. But even if you didn't earn those external goods, MacIntyre argues you would still have the internal good of having achieved a new height of excellence within a practice. You could know the experience of having done the activity well. And whereas nobody, except maybe novice drivers, feels especially proud of how well they keep that car on the right, many have experienced the sense of achievement inherent in playing an organized sport or an instrument well. Thus, many have experienced goods internal to a practice.

Although he never says it explicitly, I believe MacIntyre commits himself to the idea that people can achieve the goods internal to a practice regardless of their skill level, so long as they excel relative to their own innate, or God-given, abilities.[4] That's a relief to those

[4]   Or, relative to how well they have used these abilities so far in their development as a practitioner.

of us who don't imagine ourselves revolutionizing any of the practices we engage in. In response to an objection, MacIntyre points out that someone could be immensely skilled in a practice but only care about external goods (p. 274). By contrast, he says, another person could be relatively less skilled but be able to enjoy something from the same practice that the hypothetically more skilled practitioner cannot (namely, internal goods).[5] The difference between those who run simply for the money as opposed to those who run for the enjoyment of achieving a PR (personal record) illustrates the difference MacIntyre mentions.

I'd like to point out two other aspects of MacIntyre's account of practices and internal goods before moving back to focusing on running. First, MacIntyre discusses two kinds of internal goods (p. 189–90). One type of internal good would be the "product" of one's pursuit of excellence in a practice. If painting is a practice, as MacIntyre says, then excelling in painting will result in an excellent product and that product is an internal good of the practice of painting. However, the product does not have to be a literal object. For playing an instrument, the "product" could be an excellent performance. But a second kind of internal good exists as well. This would be the discovery, in the pursuit of excellence in the product, of "the good of a certain kind of life" (p. 190). While trying to achieve excellence, whatever that is for our ability level, we can be changed as people. The honest pursuit of excellence forms and transforms us as persons. Sometimes people like to identify themselves by their participation in particular practices – "I'm a football player," or a ballerina, or an artist, or a runner, etc. – because of what they believe this says about the kinds of people they are. This amounts to an acknowledgement that we are shaped as persons by our practices.

The final aspect of MacIntyre's account that I call attention to here is his claim that while external goods are scarce and thus competitive, internal goods are not competitive in this way (p. 190). Typically, because they are often scarce, external goods become the objects of competition. But the same need not be said of internal goods. These can be shared by many, and they can be shared in at least two ways. First, a revolutionary achievement of excellence within a given

---

[5] As MacIntyre says in a different but related context, "Excellence and winning, it is scarcely necessary to repeat, are not the same" (Alasdair MacIntyre, *Whose Justice? Which Rationality?* Notre Dame, IN: University of Notre Dame Press, 1988, 31–2).

practice "is a good for the whole community who participates in the practice" (p. 190). Everyone can share in the joy of the achievement.[6] Frequently, world-class runners rush to congratulate one amongst their numbers who sets a world record. In doing so, they celebrate the achievement of a new height of excellence. Internal goods can also be shared in the sense that many can enjoy these goods simultaneously. Although only one runner will be declared the winner, or the new record-holder, a number of runners might set PRs and so have achieved a new height of personal excellence in the course of the race. Achieving personal excellence within the parameters of a practice, as I've already argued, constitutes gaining goods internal to the practice, even if one is not the most skilled or able practitioner.

Running as a Practice with Internal Goods

I have been suggesting that running might be a practice in MacIntyre's sense of the word. But MacIntyre never mentions running on his list. He includes a sport and a game (football and chess), but he also *excludes* certain athletic activities (throwing a football with skill), saying they do not constitute practices in his sense (p. 187). And running is a pretty basic athletic activity. It is probably the simplest "sport." Almost everyone can do the basic movements involved in running, certainly more than can master the skill of throwing a football. So maybe running compares better with driving your car on the right side than it does with other activities MacIntyre identifies as practices. Is running a practice?

I will only defend the claim that a certain kind of running activity constitutes a practice. But I'm open to discussion aimed at convincing me that other running activities could also be considered practices as well. What I have in mind is competitive running. This need not be *professional* running. Nor need a "competitive runner" (in my sense of that term) be "competitive" in the sense of always finishing near the front in international, national, or even local races. Competitive running, as I envision it, involves the training and preparation one

---

[6] Unless, of course, someone had hoped to receive the external goods which sometimes accompany excellence in a practice, external goods which will likely only go to a relative few.

does to prepare to maximize one's efforts for one's ability level and the actual performance that all this preparation culminates in.

Kenenisa Bekele trains to run under 26:20 for 10k (6.2 miles or 25 laps on a track), and you may train to break 50 minutes for the same distance. Paula Radcliffe trains to see how far below 2:20 she can go for the marathon – pretty far under as it turns out – while you may be hoping to break three or four hours. If you set up a training schedule (however informal) and strive to prepare yourself to see just how well you can run at a given distance, then you are a competitive runner in the sense I am talking about here. You likely know the kinds of setbacks that might hamper your training, and maybe a few tricks to overcome stiff muscles or sluggish running. Perhaps you've discovered a few key workouts to which your body responds especially well and some other workouts you avoid for fear of overtraining. You have probably thought about the kinds of mental tricks you could use to distract yourself from pain in the course of trying to run faster than you ever have before. All of this differs from putting one foot in front of the other. This is a more complex activity, and it definitely aims at the achievement of excellence in the course of engaging in the practice. For those reasons, I believe competitive running deserves to be considered a practice in MacIntyre's sense.

Competitive running is also a social practice.[7] Even if you do most of your training alone, you likely compare notes with other runners. Perhaps you also consult books or magazine articles to learn how better to maximize your own performance. At races you seek to key off of other runners you know will set a good pace for you. I once ran the last 10 miles of a marathon with a total stranger. We probably said less than 15 words during the entire distance, but each of us spurred the other on to achieve a time goal we had set as individuals. Since we only barely met our goal, and since the last 10 miles *really* hurt, I was very grateful to share his company. I'm pretty sure I would not have met my goal had I been running alone at that point. So running (in my sense, as well as others) is a social practice.

As a social practice, competitive running includes internal goods that can be shared within the community of those who are practitioners. In the story I just told, my running companion beat me at

---

[7] This is another part of MacIntyre's definition of a practice, quoted above. I haven't said much about it thus far, but I do think it is an important aspect of the definition.

the end (winning would seem to be a kind of external good),[8] but more important to both of us was that we'd achieved our time goal and that we knew we'd wrung just about every last drop of effort out of ourselves to do it. Those are two important goods internal to the practice of running. Those who don't run or who don't attempt to see just how fast they can go cannot know the "good" of achieving some success in this endeavor, of maximizing their efforts by training and racing to the best of their ability.

Back to Franklin's Question

I've tried to set myself up to be able to answer Franklin's question. He wants to know why I would not take EPO to know what it feels like to run an eight-minute two-mile. My answer: I believe I can achieve any goods internal to the practice of competitive running while aiming and striving towards goals appropriate to my own ability level, which is not eight minutes for two miles. Regarding *internal goods*, I don't believe there are any additional ones to be had running at eight-minute pace as opposed to a minute (or more) slower. I suspect the main reasons to use EPO concern gaining external goods like prestige, status, and money. If I set a goal to break nine minutes, plan, train, and otherwise prepare to do it and then achieve that goal on race day, then I don't believe there are additional goods to be gained by doing all the same things while injecting EPO and upping my goal correspondingly. Franklin wants to know how it feels to run eight minutes, but I don't think it feels different provided that you are striving to maximize your abilities the way Daniel Komen was when he broke eight minutes. And interestingly, if Daniel Komen didn't care at all for the goods internal to competitive running, if he was just as happy to cheat his way to success in order to acquire

---

[8] Although I think winning – which usually brings some level of status, even if it's just "That's the guy/girl who won the race" – is an external good, I also believe that winning a race or beating a competitor might bring with it some internal goods. If you've always been outkicked by a particular rival, you might achieve some goods internal to competitive running by figuring out and executing a race plan that enables you to turn the tables. Maybe you begin to kick earlier, or set a faster pace through the second half of the race, or whatever. This case represents a form of excelling by maximizing your own abilities, and MacIntyre says that even internal goods can be "the outcome of competition to excel" (p. 190).

external goods such as fame and prestige (the first person ever under eight minutes!) and a lot of money, then I have enjoyed aspects of running that Komen never has (or didn't then anyway).[9] By contrast, if Komen loves running the way I do, if he savors the joy of setting a PR the way I do, then – also interestingly – he and I have shared in the *same* kind of internal goods of running.

Franklin might have an objection at this point though. He might say, what if I just set my running goals a little higher, knowing that the EPO will give me a boost? I have argued that where the internal goods are concerned, Franklin has no reason to seek to boost his abilities. If Franklin cares mainly about *external goods*, he might have reason to use EPO. (In reality, Franklin does *not* care mainly about external goods when it comes to running.) But this raises a question: What activities would be consistent with achieving the goods internal to the practice of competitive running? In other words, setting aside external goods, what activities could I appropriately engage in to achieve internal goods? EPO "unnaturally" boosts the number of red blood cells in the body, but what counts as "unnatural?" Is using an altitude tent?[10] What about living at a higher altitude if you previously haven't? These are tough questions. They could be used to "deconstruct" arguments against using performance-enhancing drugs by breaking down distinctions between what we think we know is wrong and activities we commonly accept. For instance, I don't know of anyone who thinks living and training at altitude in order to enhance performance is a form of cheating, but many people – including WADA (World Anti-Doping Agency) – think using EPO is cheating. Some might ask what the difference is. Which activities constitute cheating your way to excellence and which are legitimate?

Recall that MacIntyre claims that internal goods come in two kinds. The "product" (not necessarily a physical object) would be one internal good. In the case of competitive running as a practice, the "product" would be the particular occasion on which you put it all together. You have a race worth recalling for a long time and you savor the experience of running well and the memory of having done

---

[9] I do not want to suggest that I believe Komen cheated to break eight minutes. I am only making a point similar to the one MacIntyre makes which I have discussed above.
[10] An altitude tent simulates the thinner air at high altitude. Endurance athletes sometimes sleep in them to gain the benefits of the body's adaptive response to the thin air, and the results are somewhat similar to what EPO does – an increase in red blood cells which carry oxygen.

so. But the other kind of internal good MacIntyre discusses is the formation of your person, of your character – at least with respect to the practice in question (p. 190). Discussing portrait painting as a practice, MacIntyre says, "what the artist discovers within the pursuit of excellence in portrait painting – and what is true of portrait painting is true of the practice of the fine arts in general – is the good of a certain kind of life" (p. 190). A part of the goods internal to a practice is becoming the sort of person who can live "a certain kind of life." This idea might help us to answer some of those tough questions concerning which activities would be legitimate to use in pursuit of the "product" of a practice. MacIntyre doesn't privilege one kind of internal good over the other, and I'm inclined to think we should not either. If so, then we should only engage in those activities which are consistent with both achieving the "product" *and* forming our person with respect to the practice of running.

How should we form our person with respect to running? The old saying is "sports build character," but, of course, not everyone plays sports in such a way as to build good character. Some people cheat on the golf course or the baseball diamond and form their character correspondingly. In competitive running, we set goals and do a lot of hard work to achieve them. That, in part, is what makes our successes so sweet – all the hard work we put in, the knowledge that it could have gone wrong through injury, bad race tactics, or whatever. So runners understand that the kinds of goods they can achieve at the end of a training cycle (the "products") are a result, in part, of the hard work they put in now. They know that learning to deal with pain and adversity in training will set them up to deal with it on a grander scale when they try to go faster than they ever have before. This seems to be an appropriate part of the runner's formation as a person.

Running also tends to teach people that they are embodied and that their bodies have limits. To engage in competitive running is to enter a course in discovering your bodily limits. How much work at a certain pace can I do before I risk overtraining? How fast can I start a race and still maintain the pace I began with? So another part of the runner's formation is to appreciate bodily limits. This, it seems, might be what the EPO user is trying to deny or evade. Activities that teach us about the hard work necessary to achieve our goals and about the limits we have as embodied persons strike me as part of the appropriate formation of runners. These activities would be consistent with the goods internal to running, particularly the "formation" good. Training at altitude will do this. When I run at altitude I experience the effects of the thinner air and perceive the effort my body will need to make to overcome this. By contrast, if I injected EPO, I wouldn't experience any of these things. So as a rough judgment, I'm inclined to believe that altitude training can be part of achieving the good of a certain "product" – an excellent performance – and part of the formation of my character as a runner.[11] But EPO use can't.

Running Downhill and Going Professional

I have argued that I need not use EPO to achieve the goods internal to the practice of competitive running and that, assuming external goods which can be gotten elsewhere don't enter into our consideration, no other goods exist which I might achieve by using EPO. Despite Franklin's assumption to the contrary, it does not feel different in any meaningful way to run an eight-minute two-mile as compared with some slower pace, provided you are striving to maximize your own abilities. The shape of the argument I have offered here might also explain why competitive runners would not necessarily seek out downhill or wind-aided race courses or use shoes with springs in them to try to set PRs. Would such activities enhance the goods internal to the practice of running? Arguably, they would not.

My argument might not apply as well to the case of professional runners. We might need a different kind of argument to show why cheating is wrong for these runners. For them, running is both a source of income and prestige *and* a means for achieving the pleasures of the goods internal to running. Since they can be motivated by external goods alone, they might be happy to cheat in order to gain more external goods. But if they could be reminded of what motivated them to begin running – assuming they didn't start solely with the hope of getting good and therefore rich – or of the internal goods

[11] MacIntyre would probably say that the kinds of judgments I am making here are the kinds that ought to be deliberated over by the community of those engaged in a particular practice. Those of us who are competitive runners are best suited to make the kinds of practical judgments in question.

William P. Kabasenche

they came to enjoy along the way, perhaps they could be persuaded not to cheat. If so, it will be because someone was able to show them that the goods internal to running make the efforts involved worthwhile.[12]

[12] Thanks to John Hardwig and Colin Young for discussion of the ideas in this chapter.

Chapter 11
The Freedom of the Long-Distance Runner

Heather L. Reid

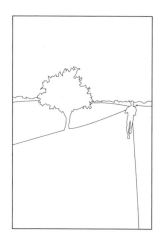

Runners often say that running makes them "feel free." To non-runners this can be puzzling; they associate running not with freedom, but with compulsion. They remember being forced to run the junior high cross-country course or being punished by their coaches with running laps around goal posts. Even regular runners may be hard-pressed to feel free as they push themselves to run for fitness, weight-loss, or competitive advantage. Few of us last long enough or are lucky enough to discover the sense of freedom achievable in activities like running, which is to say that few of us experience running as play, rather than work or necessity. But those who do discover freedom and playfulness in their running experience may learn to preserve and savor that feeling even when it seems all but absent from the rest of their lives. A sense of freedom is one of the most valuable gifts that running can give to us. An appreciation of that gift, and how it is connected to choice and attitude, is one of the great lessons of Alan Sillitoe's famed novella, *The Loneliness of the Long-Distance Runner*.[1]

Interpreted in light of existentialist philosophy, the story might better be titled "The Freedom of the Long-Distance Runner." Its main character, Smith, can be seen as a kind of existentialist hero who uses running to escape his worldly situation (he's a prisoner in

---

[1] Alan Sillitoe, *The Loneliness of the Long-Distance Runner* (New York: Signet, 1959).

a youth detention facility), to develop an authentic sense of self, and finally to actualize his freedom through an outrageous choice. Smith says during one of his runs:

> ...I knew what the loneliness of the long-distance runner running across country felt like, realizing that as far as I was concerned this feeling was the only honesty and realness there was in the world and knowing it would be no different ever, no matter what I felt at odd times, and no matter what anybody else tried to tell me. (Sillitoe, p. 37)

The "honesty and realness" that Smith finds in running reflects the experience of many runners who cherish their time on the road as if it were the most genuine part of their lives. The time we spend running is somehow the time when we feel most ourselves. What most people see as a pointless waste of time or a form of fitness-slavery, we see as an oasis of freedom. By combining Sillitoe's story with concepts from the philosophical movement known as existentialism, we may better understand why.

Escaping the Herd

Existentialist philosophy seeks meaning within individual existence, rather than externally imposed social or religious values. It emerged partly as a response to some of the dehumanizing aspects of modern Western life. Rising industrialization, for example, shifted people from artisan occupations which emphasize individual skills and personality, to cookie-cutter jobs in factories and office buildings which view human beings as replaceable cogs on a wheel. As a result, existentialist philosophy emphasizes individuality and disdains the social pressure to conform. Friedrich Nietzsche (1844–1900) brilliantly called society "the herd," thereby capturing the domesticating effects of our lives as social animals.[2] Like animals in a herd we tend to go wherever the group takes us, never looking up or thinking for ourselves. Society, Nietzsche observes, rewards us for conformity thereby suppressing individuality: "When the herd animal is irradiated by the glory of the purest virtue, the exceptional man must have been

---

[2] Friedrich Nietzsche, *On the Genealogy of Morals and Ecce Homo*, trans. Walter Kaufmann and R. J. Hollingdale (New York: Random House, 1967).

devalued into evil" (Nietzsche, p. 330). The problem with all this is that the pressures of the herd work against our need to discover and express our true selves, to achieve what existentialism calls "authenticity."

The journey toward existentialist authenticity, therefore, usually begins with a separation from day-to-day reality – some kind of escape from the herd. Jean-Paul Sartre (1905–1980) associates this escape with a change in attitude from seriousness to playfulness.[3] The world makes serious demands on all of us; we must work, we must follow social customs, we must be concerned about our social position. It is normal that we feel tied down, maybe even imprisoned or enslaved by these serious demands of the world. But these feelings often reflect an ignorance – or at least a forgetting – of the real freedom that we have. Like cattle we overlook the freedom we have to go our own way, preferring the comfort of the herd. "It is obvious," says Sartre, "that the serious man at bottom is hiding from himself the consciousness of his freedom" (Sartre, p. 580). To experience our freedom, we must first acknowledge that we have it, and then distance ourselves from the seriousness – we must play. "As soon as a man apprehends himself as free and wishes to use his freedom . . ." says Sartre, "then his activity is play" (Sartre, p. 580).

The way in which running can provide this kind of escape could hardly be more explicit than it is for Smith, who is a prisoner. Unlike many literary prisoners, however, Smith is hardly innocent. He blithely recounts his burglary and the bit of bad luck that led to his being caught, as if life itself were a game in which the opponents are bourgeois businessmen, authority figures, and cops. Smith has obviously spent his life resisting the social pressure to conform. Having landed in the Borstal (youth detention center), the game continues, only now his chief opponent is the Borstal governor, who sees in Smith the potential for a victory. As Smith puts it:

> The pop-eyed potbellied governor said to the pop-eyed potbellied Member of Parliament who sat next to his pop-eyed potbellied whore of a wife that I was his only hope for getting the Borstal Blue Ribbon Prize Cup For Long-Distance Cross-Country Running (all-England), which I was, and it set me to laughing to myself inside, and I didn't say a word to any potbellied pop-eyed bastard that might give them

---

[3] Jean-Paul Sartre, *Being and Nothingness*, trans. Hazel E. Barnes (New York: Philosophical Library, 1956).

real hope, though I knew the governor anyway took my quietness to mean he'd got that cup already stuck on the bookshelf in his office among the few other mildewed trophies." (Sillitoe, pp. 33–4)

Even though he's a prisoner, Smith's running potential earns him special permission to go on early morning training runs outside the prison grounds. At first the guards drive close behind him, but eventually they trust him enough to let him get out of sight – it would seem like the perfect opportunity for escape.

And escape Smith does, but not the kind of escape you might be expecting. "... I'm not so daft as I would look if I tried to make a break for it on my long-distance running," he explains, "because to abscond and then get caught is nothing but a mug's game, and I'm not falling for it. Cunning is what counts in this life, and even that you've got to use in the slyest way you can . . ." (Sillitoe, p. 7). Smith's runs take him outside the socially constructed environment of the Borstal and into a natural environment, one that liberates him from the herd. Getting up before sunrise, slinking past his snoozing comrades, and running out into a frosty morning makes him feel, "like the first and last man on the world" (Sillitoe, p. 8). Smith somehow senses that true freedom comes not from running away, but from running itself. His brief escape from the confines of the prison is most importantly a mental escape *to* the place where he is free to explore his own psyche:

> Sometimes I think that I've never been so free as during that couple of hours when I'm trotting up the path out of the gates and turning by that bare-faced, big-bellied oak tree at the lane end. Everything's dead, but good, because it's dead before coming alive, not dead after being alive. (Sillitoe, p. 10)

There is a sense in which we are all prisoners. Like Smith, we need some form of escape, and running can provide it both by physically removing us from that serious world and more importantly by mentally removing us from it. Pulling on our shorts and tying up our shoes, we don a uniform not accepted at work. Leaving behind the briefcase, cell phone, and car keys, we detach ourselves from the "real world" and enter a special space and time. When we play, says Sartre, we transform the environment and appropriate it for ourselves (Sartre, p. 581). Often we seek pathways that lead away from our workplaces, our cities, or our homes. But even the most familiar place looks different when we run. To use Sartre's words, running "strips the real of its reality" (Sartre, p. 580). Like the police car shadowing Smith on his runs, life's demands never completely disappear. But the act of running can make them slip out of sight – just long enough to get a glimpse of our selves.

Exploring Authenticity

The existentialists' concept of "authenticity" – being who you really are – is central to their idea of the good life. Running can provide an escape from the "real world" of "the herd," which sets the stage for discovery of our authentic selves. But play activities do not allow us to authentically be whoever we want to be. The runners' escape from what Martin Heidegger (1889–1976) calls the "tranquilizing"[4] effect of society should actually force us to face up to certain unavoidable facts about ourselves – such as our freedom to choose, and our responsibility for our choices (Heidegger, p. 298). As Sartre puts it, human beings are "condemned to be free" (Sartre, p. 439), and the function of play activities like running is "to make manifest and present . . . the absolute freedom which is the very being of the person" (Sartre, p. 581). Our choice to run away from the herd demonstrates our authentic freedom to us, but this discovery is not all sweetness and bliss. Freedom is an essential part of our human condition that we must consciously acknowledge, actualize through choice, and ultimately take responsibility for.

It was Heidegger who explored most richly the concept of authenticity. Although he never associates it with running, he makes it clear that authenticity results from doing and not merely being. Authenticity requires us to "become what we are" not just through passive reflection but through actively raising consciousness of our own significance as individuals and of the world's relative insignificance (Heidegger, p. 186). By actively choosing to run, we experience our own freedom. By reaching the boundaries of our strength and endurance, we also experience our human limitations. To be authentic according to Heidegger, we must acknowledge not just our free choice but also our mortality. And this dual awareness of freedom and death produces

---

[4] Martin Heidegger, *Being and Time*, trans. John Macquarrie and Edward Robinson (New York: Harper & Row, 1962).

anxiety or *angst* because it reminds us simultaneously that our time is limited and that we are responsible for how we spend it. Here the concept of anxious, mindful authenticity is contrasted with the mindless drifting typical of the herd. Says Heidegger, "Anxiety brings [us] face to face with [our] *Being free for (propensio in . . .)* the authenticity of [our] Being, and for this authenticity as a possibility which it always is" (Heidegger, p. 232). We realize the urgency, to put it simply, to *do* something with our lives.

Smith's descriptions of his lonely runs suggest that they provide for him just the kind of consciousness-raising that existentialism prescribes for those who would achieve authenticity. As he runs, he's not merely thinking about his current predicament, he's thinking about life as a whole with its inherent absurdity and inevitable end.

> And it's daft to think deep, you know, because it gets you nowhere, though deep is what I am when I've passed this half-way mark because the long-distance run of an early morning makes me think that every run like this is a life – a little life, I know – but a life as full of misery and happiness and things happening as you ever get really around yourself – and I remember that after a lot of these runs I thought that it didn't need much know-how to tell how a life was going to end once it had got well started." (Sillitoe, p. 17)

The reality of death seems as though it's never far from Smith's thoughts. He describes with approval his father's suicide, thinly veiling the horror he experienced at finding the body. When the governor offers to make him the best runner in the world, Smith imagines himself being shot just as he charges away from the pack: ". . . CRACK! CRACK! – bullets that can go faster than any man running, coming from a copper's rifle planted in a tree, winged me and split my gizzard in spite of my perfect running, and down I fell" (Sillitoe, p. 34). Smith knows that death is unavoidable and what counts is making the most of life while you can.

For all his consciousness of absurdity and death, however, Smith is anything but a morose character. He's full of life and in love with his life – with all its misfortunes and ugly realities. Smith's authentic existence gives him a fullness that is starkly contrasted with the conventional authority figure:

> Our doddering bastard of a governor, our half-dead gangrened gaffer is hollow like an empty petrol drum, and he wants me and my running

Heather L. Reid

life to give him glory, to put in him blood and throbbing veins he never had. (Sillitoe, p. 42)

The great potential of the running experience is that it can fill us, ultimately, with awareness: awareness of the *un*importance of social conventions and traditional authority, awareness of the true importance of acknowledging our freedom, responsibility, and inevitable death. Yes, this awareness creates a kind of anxiety, but it also discloses the power of choice. It creates the opportunity to stand up to life's absurdity and express our inner freedom through consciously exercised choice.

Choosing Freedom

Ideally, running should be voluntary. It should not be something required by anyone for any reason; it should be something we choose for ourselves. A runner is something we should choose to be; something we make ourselves into. The awareness that who we are is a matter of what we choose is central to the existentialist world view. Sartre says, "As we have seen, for human reality, to be is to *choose oneself*" (Sartre, p. 440). We must actively make ourselves who we are. Authenticity cannot be imposed on a person from without, we must choose it as a way of being in the world. Likewise our freedom comes from nothing external, we must actualize it through the exercise of choice. The athlete who says her coach forces her to run is not free because she doesn't acknowledge her freedom. The athlete who unquestioningly follows his coach's commands is not free because he doesn't exercise his freedom to choose. Neither athlete is taking responsibility for what he or she does. Before we can be free, we must first choose to choose. Choice does not follow automatically from freedom, freedom is actualized though exercised choice – even if it's just a choice of attitude.

This connection between freedom and choice is perhaps best illustrated by Camus's essay "The Myth of Sisyphus."[5] Albert Camus (1913–60) recalls the fate of Sisyphus who, in Hellenic mythology, was condemned by the gods to the eternal torture of rolling a boulder

[5] Albert Camus, *The Myth of Sisyphus and Other Essays*, trans. Justin O'Brien (New York: Random House, 1955).

up a hill, only to see it roll back down again. Camus sees a connection between the absurdity of Sisyphus's task and the meaningless tasks to which so many modern workers devote their lives. The gods expect Sisyphus to be punished because they assume that he will lament and despair in the hopelessness of his task. They never realize that he might *choose* to roll the boulder. A choice of attitude is the only freedom Sisyphus has left. By refusing to view his fated task as drudgery, Sisyphus avoids being punished. Camus explains, "The lucidity that was to constitute his torture at the same time crowns his victory. There is no fate that cannot be overcome by scorn" (Camus, p. 90). By choosing to roll his rock, Camus's Sisyphus finds freedom within the inevitability of his fate. Existentialism asks us to acknowledge freedom within our own fate of death by choosing, quite simply, to live. Camus concludes that "one must imagine Sisyphus happy" (Camus, p. 91). We too, through the conscious exercise of choice, might achieve such happiness.

The actualization of freedom through exercised choice is brilliantly illustrated in Sillitoe's novella. The awareness of freedom that Smith has cultivated in his training begins to sour him on the idea of racing. He contrasts the richness of his training runs through the countryside, where he chews on bark and takes in the silence, with the starkness of the racecourse populated by noisy fans and assistance personnel trying to hand him water. The fans seem to be more interested in Smith winning than he is himself. "You should think about nobody and go your own way," he concludes (Sillitoe, p. 38). Eventually Smith realizes that he must take back his running from those who would have him win for *their* own glory. To do this he will have to overcome both the temptation of reward and the threat of punishment. To express his independence, to actualize his freedom, to achieve authenticity he must exercise an outrageous choice.

In the race for the "Borstal Blue Ribbon Prize Cup for Long-Distance Cross-Country Running (all-England)," Smith enters the stadium for the last lap of the track well ahead of the other runners. The "pop-eyed potbellied governor," various other VIPs, and many of Smith's comrades are there cheering wildly for his victory. But just short of the finish-line, Smith stops in his tracks.

> And I could hear the lords and ladies now in the grandstand, and could see them standing up to wave me in: "Run!" they were shouting in their posh voices. "Run!" But I was deaf, daft and blind, and stood

where I was, still tasting the bark in my mouth and still blubbing like a baby, blubbing now out of gladness that I'd got them beat at last. (Sillitoe, p. 45)

Meanwhile the second-placed runner comes onto the track and crosses the line for victory. But Smith has won his battle for independence from authority. Like Sisyphus, he actualizes his freedom by choosing what no one ever thought he would. Like Sisyphus, he will gladly bear the governor's punishment of six months hard labor because that too was part of his defiant choice.

Even for those of us who never enter a race, even if we never have the opportunity to make as outrageous a choice as Smith does, running can give us many of the existential benefits that it gave to him. First of all, running can provide a needed escape from the pressures of our day-to-day lives and the distorted values of the "herd." Second, running can provide a play space which diminishes the reality of that other world and gives us the chance to become aware of our freedom, our limitations, and the need to take responsibility for our actions. Third, running can teach us about the power of choice. It is only by actively choosing to be who we really are that we can achieve authenticity. Ideally this choice will be expressed in our lives beyond running, but the first choice must be simply to run.

Smith concludes:

. . . when you've had enough of feeling good like the first man on earth of a frosty morning and you've known how it is to be taken bad like the last man on earth on a summer's afternoon, then you get at last to being like the only man on earth and you don't give a bogger about either good or bad, but just trot on with your slippers slapping the good dry soil that at least would never do you a bad turn. (Sillitoe, p. 40)

Chapter 12
Existential Running

Ross C. Reed

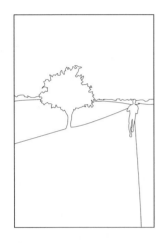

You are obviously a runner and a thinker. If you weren't, you probably wouldn't be reading this. So, my question at this point is: why *are* you reading this? Do you expect me, a running philosopher, to tell you why *you* run? Or why running is inherently philosophical, more philosophical than, say, bowling or football or golf? Barring contact injuries, it seems clear that running is more *painful* than bowling or golf, or, dare I say football? In fact running *seems* to be all about the pain, running seems to be the *sine qua non* of sports pain, the Mecca of tripartite suffering. If you're a non-runner and you have no clue what I'm talking about, put down this volume, go outside, and run full out for five minutes. Okay, so running is painful. Even really slow running is painful if you go far enough. Even world famous ultramarathon runner Dean Karnazes (who has run well over 200 miles at a clip) has this to say: "There's really no mystery to what I do . . . It hurts me just as bad as anyone else" (we won't stop to ponder how he "knows" this).[1] This being the case and ruling out the hypothesis that runners are of necessity sado-masochistic, why do you – I – we – run? It's certainly *not* for the glamour. (Unless, of course, snot, drool, and occasional vomit in the midst of an ostensible death struggle constitute glamour.) I once saw three cheerleaders at a high school cross-country meet. I assumed they were lost. They

[1] Dean Karnazes, *Ultramarathon Man* (New York: Penguin, 2005), p. 231.

weren't. Apparently, the school had no football team. Possibly, I'm the wrong one to tackle this question, it being the case that I really haven't ever *not* run. This, I suppose, would be a good time to get to that: my life as a runner.

My Life as a Runner

Growing up in a one-traffic-light town in southeastern Pennsylvania, there wasn't a plethora of activities for the (relatively) bright-eyed adolescent, so at $13^{1}/_{2}$ years of age I began to run cross-country for the local high school. That was 30 years ago this past June and I'm still out there slogging the miles (albeit not for the local high school), only now even slower than back in my "glory" days. I heard about cross-country in eighth-grade health class. It seemed like the perfect sport for people with no talent who preferred invisibility to shame. And there was a direct relationship between what you put into it and what you got out of it, or at least that's what it seemed like at the time. I don't think I yet realized that life is fundamentally unfair, but that's a whole other issue. Anyway, I won't bore you with too many details except to say that I've run nearly 100,000 miles since June of 1975 and competed in races at distances of 800 meters through the marathon. This is not including road biking, mountain biking, exercise bicycling, backpacking, hiking, race walking, and swimming. I've done plenty of these foolhardy activities too (but at least not bungee jumping). In fact, at this point I'd like to recommend Bill Bryson's *A Walk in the Woods*[2] if you're an eco-aerobic adventurer. Even if you're not, it can provide a vestigial sense of vicarious vertigo.

A few times I ran even farther than a marathon, even managing to cover 45 miles in a day once, the whole time philosophizing about why I "had" to do it. What would Nietzsche do? Would Schopenhauer run even with runner's knee? Would the Buddha run Boston? Aristotle with shin splints? The reflective barrage was almost as ghastly as my incipient physiological demise.

During the early years, I dreamt of Olympic Marathon fame, and, due to extraordinary powers of self-deception, continued to fan this obvious delusion even after my abysmal NCAA (National Collegiate Athletic Association) division two "career" in track and cross-country.

[2] Bill Bryson, *A Walk in the Woods* (New York: Broadway, 1999).

These last 10 years or so I've barely raced at all, and let me tell you, I couldn't care less. Because it's the running that I love. Without the running, there might not even be an "I" at all.

When I started to run as a boy, I began reading all the running magazines I could find (Anyone for a copy of *New Jersey Ultra Runner*? If it doesn't exist, it will have to be invented) and I bought all the books on running I could afford. I read George Sheehan's first book (if you don't count the medical encyclopedia, but then, of course, I read that too) *Dr. Sheehan on Running*[3] about the time it appeared, and I did the same with his second.[4] In the context of writing about running, Sheehan always referred to the poets and philosophers. In fact, every time I read Sheehan, I got a dose of one or more of the greats: Plato, Nikolai Berdyaev, Nikos Kazantzakis, William James, José Ortega y Gasset, Gandhi, Kierkegaard, Bertrand Russell, Pindar, Kant, Nietzsche, Gabriel Marcel, Keats, George Santayana, Ralph Waldo Emerson, William Blake, Eric Hoffer, Aristotle, G. K. Chesterton, Viktor Frankl, Pythagoras, Aquinas. Is it any wonder that from an early age I connected running and philosophy? Sheehan claims that he can't write without running, and assuming as he does that philosophizing is necessary for writing, then it's clear that for him, running and philosophizing are inextricably intertwined. I'd philosophize even if I couldn't run (maybe I'd philosophize about *not* running), but running without philosophizing would be *unthinkable*.

I came to realize that an awful lot of runners thought a great deal, but when you think about it, what else can you do during all those hours of . . . running? Almost inevitably, runners end up reflecting on just why it is that they are out there to begin with – especially when it is 102 degrees Fahrenheit or there are 14 inches of snow on the ground or you manage to glimpse the dog out of the corner of your eye *just before* it lunges into your left calf. I mean, could tennis ever be *this* bad? My guess is, if you're like most other runners, young, old, female, male, you'll be out there again in short order, wondering all over again just what the heck you're doing out there and why a bad day running is better than a lot of things and on some days

---

[3] George Sheehan, *Dr. Sheehan on Running* (Mountain View, CA: World Publication, 1975).

[4] George Sheehan, *Running and Being: The Total Experience* (New York: Simon and Schuster, 1978).

everything. But when you run, the endorphin-fueled stream of consciousness runs on even longer than that last sentence. And nobody seems to mind at all. Okay, okay: to philosophers and running.

What can the Philosophers Tell us about Running?

What can the philosophers tell us about running? Can philosophy help us understand why we run, especially when there are so many other human endeavors with much more obvious extrinsic benefit? What kind of being are we that we find it worthwhile to engage in an activity such as running? (Have we no shame? A grown man in spandex tights? In public? Even the gods avert their eyes). What is the meaning of the running being? What human questions and concerns does running address? To this end, let's consider the writings of a couple of existential philosophers: Søren Kierkegaard (1813–55) and Jean-Paul Sartre (1905–80). Although neither mentions running (and their names appear conspicuously absent from any race results), both philosophize at length about what it means to be human.[5] But before we discuss running and existential philosophy, it seems appropriate – even downright smart – to talk a little about existentialism. We've all heard about it, but just what the heck is it?

Existentialism as a philosophical "movement" or "school" is traced back (by those who say they know, that is, university professors) to the aforementioned Søren Kierkegaard. Other important existential philosophers include (but are certainly not limited to) Friedrich Nietzsche, José Ortega y Gasset, Karl Jaspers, Martin Heidegger, Albert Camus, Simone de Beauvoir, and Jean-Paul Sartre. There is also much in the field of literature that is deemed "existential," including writings by people like Fyodor Dostoevsky, Franz Kafka, and Walker Percy. What ties these thinkers and writers together are the common themes of existentialism. Here is a brief outline of some of the concerns of existential thinkers.

1 *Freedom.* Existential writers stress the fact that we are free beings and that we are effectively forced to choose each day, each moment, among various competing alternatives. Awareness of this fundamental inescapable reality – our freedom – is the source of dread, anxiety

---

[5] And this seems good enough for our purposes. We're assuming here that all runners are human. A bold assumption? As is already obvious, the argument herein presented is by no means airtight. We're philosophizing, that's all.

(Kierkegaard) and anguish (Sartre). Runners seem to know all too well that each step *is* a choice, and that without ongoing choice, collapse would be imminent (it could be imminent anyway).

2   *Selfhood*. Existentialists either claim that we co-create ourselves – as partners with the Divinity (Kierkegaard) or that we are wholly free to create ourselves (Sartre: his famous line is "existence comes before essence," or "existence precedes essence").[6] As Dean Karnazes says in *Ultramarathon Man* after the Western States 100-mile run: You're just not the same person after running (a totally heinous) 100 miles. No, because if you had to *actually remember* what you *voluntarily assented* to, you'd go mad with suffering, which brings us to (3).

3   *Self-deception/duplicity*. Because of the elasticity of our nature as humans, as described in (2), we have a monumental capacity for self-deception, with a corroborating talent of deceiving others when we are lucky enough to know the truth. Consequently, existentialists are often concerned with the question of becoming aware of that of which we are not aware, and the morality of self-deception (as well as the morality of lying in general). Running, as a visceral art, can provide momentum to allow one to surmount sedimented patterns of self-deception through the processes of deconceptualization/reconceptualization (to be discussed later in this chapter).

4   *Truth*. This aspect of existential thought will be further developed throughout the rest of this chapter, but suffice it to say here that for the existentialist, truth is not simply a matter of cognition. Existential truth is a function of all aspects of human experience, including cognitive, affective, volitional, kinetic, olfactory, tactile, and visual components. Running, by this measure, may be the ultimate primal existential event.

Truth

Trust no thought arrived at sitting down. The seated spectator is not a thinker; he is a knower.[7]

Sheehan, *Running and Being*

---

[6]   Jean-Paul Sartre, "Existentialism is a Humanism," in *Existentialism from Dostoevsky to Sartre*, ed. Walter Kaufmann (New York: Meridian, 1975), p. 348.

[7]   Having said this, there is no guarantee that the thought of those standing up or, God forbid, those running, has an ounce of veracity either. Maybe truth *is* elusive for the reflective biped.

Knowledge (of concepts) is static, frozen in time, whereas thinking is a process, a flux, an activity, and, in this sense, running promotes thinking through deconceptualization. Just as the runner must do her own work of running, the thinker must do her own work of reflecting – the thinker, as such, cannot simply borrow concepts and consider the "thought" her own. Philosophers have a name for that branch of their discipline that deals with truth: epistemology, or theory of knowledge. Epistemological questions philosophers ask include "What is truth?", "How do I know if something is true?", "Can I know if I can't know something?", "What does it mean to know something?" and "What does it even mean for something to be true?" Another perennial favorite of running philosophers: "Is it true that I look *that* bad in running shorts?"

> There on a country road, moving at eight miles an hour, I discover the total universe, the natural and supernatural that wise men speculate about. It is a life, a world, a universe that begins on the other side of sweat and exhaustion. (Sheehan, *Running and Being*, pp. 246–7)

Out on the road, we burn glycogen and accumulate lactic acid, but our passion drives us into existential truth. This truth, we realize, goes far beyond cognition, far beyond the static nature of concepts, far beyond the borrowed experiences of others. It even seems that some individuals perceive running as their first *real* experience, their first non-borrowed experience, or, quite possibly, their *only* real experience. For it is *our* experience, born of passion and suffering, *our* truth, however ephemeral. A truth that is inexplicably beyond the eye of cognition, although dimly acknowledged and respected by such. We run to glimpse the perennial, universal (but revealed only in the particular), mystical yet personal truth (see Sheehan, *Running and Being*, p. 230), to escape from the prison of the intellect.

The "founder" of modern existential philosophy, the Danish thinker Søren Kierkegaard, talked about truth in his pseudonymous *Concluding Unscientific Postscript*:

> Here is such a definition of truth: An objective uncertainty held fast in an appropriation-process of the most passionate inwardness is the truth, the highest truth attainable for an existing individual.[8]

---

[8] Søren Kierkegaard [Johannes Climacus, pseud.], *Concluding Unscientific Postscript to the Philosophical Fragments*, trans. David F. Swenson and Walter Lowrie (Princeton, NJ: Princeton University Press, 1968), p. 182.

This "highest truth" is beyond cognition for Kierkegaard, but the passionate inwardness and resolve required of the runner produce the possibility of such experiential, personal truth. This "revelation" is often a part of the experience of running and cannot be separated from it: to run is to participate in altering one's vision of the world. This truth the philosophers call "existential" truth because it is "realized" through existing (rather than merely through thinking by itself), in this case existing *as a runner*.

"Before I run, I am a Cartesian" says George Sheehan in *Running and Being* (p. 252). What does this mean? Sheehan is referring to the French philosopher René Descartes (1596–1650), for whom truth was a function of the intellect alone (what Descartes smartly and philosophically called "non-extended substance"). The thinker, for Descartes, was effectively a disembodied "knower," the inverse of the existential knower fully embodied in the runner. Existential philosophers and runners know better: truth is a function of embodiment, the result of desire, passion, and volition as well as cognition. Every facet of the runner's being is present and integrated with each step, and the runner "knows" this. This kind of existential knowledge is what Sartre calls "phenomenological" because our knowledge is a result of our direct "presence" to being or reality. We don't know the "thing" in some abstract way – we bump into the thing. Bumping into the thing *is* phenomenological knowledge. Bumping into the thing is what the runner does with every breath, with every step. And with this knowledge, the runner transcends ordinary logical categories of knowledge. With this integration the runner is prepared for the mystical adventure that awaits.

Sartre speaks at length about truth in a way directly relevant to running:

> The foundation of truth is freedom. Thus man can choose non-truth. This non-truth is ignorance or lie . . . The unveiling behavior is *activity*: to allow Being to appear as it is, we have to *go back* and *look* for it . . . truth reveals itself to *action* . . . not passive contemplation [emphasis added].[9]

This is an expression of truth that the runner can recognize as she participates in the revelatory changes brought about through the

---

[9] Jean-Paul Sartre, *Truth and Existence*, trans. Adrian van den Hoven (Chicago: The University of Chicago Press, 1992), pp. 13–15.

sport of running. Up ahead on the road, we await our own truth, a truth that must be realized existentially. Up ahead on the road, we await the truth of ourselves. Our own truth. As we come into contact with being on the road, we pursue that self that is to be, or the self that may be. (Aristotle as well as many of the existential philosophers make a great deal of this distinction between actuality and potentiality, or between that which is and that which could be. The latter is dependent, at least in part, on human volition). Because potentiality is just that. In the words of Kierkegaard (through the pseudonym Anti-Climacus): "The self does not actually exist, [it] is simply that which ought to come into existence."[10] Running is an ongoing choice to live into oneself.

"Being is knowable. And this does not mean at all that Being is rational" (Sartre, *Truth and Existence*, p. 16). As runners, we interface our bodies with the exigencies of the world, and, in so doing, open ourselves in a deeper way to existence itself. Make no mistake, the runner is on a journey, no matter how slow or fast. And this journey takes her to places she could not otherwise go. The physical transcends itself into the metaphysical.

Freedom and Self-Knowledge

> Then I discovered running and the long road back. Running made me free.
>
> Sheehan, *Running and Being*

In order to become a self, we need to make choices, for choice defines the self. Choosing the lifestyle of the runner requires an ongoing commitment not only to the activity of running but to the self. It involves the choosing of a certain kind of self. Kierkegaard through Anti-Climacus says this regarding selfhood:

> The self is freedom. But freedom is the dialectical aspect of the categories of possibility and necessity. The more consciousness, the more self; the more consciousness, the more will; the more will the more self. A person who has no will at all is not a self; but the more will he has, the more self-consciousness he has also. (Kierkegaard, *The Sickness Unto Death*, p. 29)

---

[10] Søren Kierkegaard [Anti-Climacus, pseud.], *The Sickness Unto Death*, trans. Howard V. Hong and Edna H. Hong (Princeton, NJ: Princeton University Press, 1983), p. 30.

If Kierkegaard is right, it looks like running is almost insurance against non-selfness and possibly a condemnation to hypertrophied self-consciousness. For is it possible to be running, in pain, and not *will* each step as you continue? Could one possibly experience a *will-less* death shuffle? Or is the relation to the self only that much more pronounced with each incremental increase in pain?

> A person cannot rid himself of the relation to himself anymore than he can rid himself of his self, which, after all, is one and the same thing, since the self is the relation to oneself. (Kierkegaard, *The Sickness Unto Death*, p. 17)

Kierkegaard must have been a runner.

> Suffering . . . directs a man's attention inward.[11]

Furthermore, Kierkegaard must have been a marathon runner.

Out on the road, we seek freedom, truth, and selfhood. All are elusive, and none can be forced. Even the pilgrimage itself must be altered according to the body's demands. Intellect is a necessary but insufficient condition to complete any run, long or short, slow or even slower. In choosing to run, we are (at least implicitly) bowing to the fundamental forces of being. We are choosing to accept without knowing. But as we choose to accept, we transcend our acceptance and seek freedom, truth, and selfhood. We seek that which escaped us on the sedentary plane. It may yet again escape us on the plane of sweat and suffering. Exertion brings the possibility, but cannot force the reality.

> But if the self does not become itself, it is in despair, whether it knows that or not. (Kierkegaard, *The Sickness Unto Death*, p. 30)

The self, in seeking itself through running, seeks to escape the despair of an empty life, a life of squandered potentiality. Dr. Sheehan puts it this way: "For when I run, I am a hunter and the prey is my own self, my own truth" (Sheehan, *Running and Being*, p. 13). Paradoxically, introspection has limitations when it comes to self-discovery. Running, for Sheehan, goes beyond the limits of reflection and allows

---

[11] Søren Kierkegaard, *The Gospel of Suffering*, trans. David F. Swenson and Lillian Marvin Swenson (Minneapolis, MN: Augsburg Publishing House, 1948), p. 55.

for the possibility of a deeper level of self-revelation. In the end, Sheehan proclaims "I run, therefore I am" (Sheehan, *Running and Being*, p. 92).

As we construct our "running epistemology," it is clear that Kierkegaard, Sartre, and Sheehan are in agreement. For the three of them, truth is a confrontation with being, a clear example being that which takes place between the runner and the rest of the universe. Running is an approach to being that allows truth to be revealed.

> We forget that the opposite of the present is not past or future; it is absence. (Sheehan, *Running and Being*, p. 128)

> The runner lives in an eternal present. (Sheehan, *Dr. Sheehan on Running*, p. 165)

> What is the criterion of truth? There is no doubt on this point: it is Being as presence. (Sartre, *Truth and Existence*, p. 61)

In making an active approach to being through running, the runner at times experiences the feeling of "really living," of an adventure, of a timeless memory. (This can be true even for one's all-time worst race or the proverbial run from hell!)

Running is a great opportunity for spontaneous imagination, and in imagining we transcend who we are to realize other possibilities for our freedom, for our selves. Without imagination, we have no personal future, no real hope, no transcendent self. Imagination is essential for the realization of our own freedom. Sartre puts it this way: "We may therefore conclude that imagination is not an empirical and superadded power of consciousness, it is the whole of consciousness as it realizes its freedom."[12] As she oxygenates every cell in her body, the runner opens herself to a world of endless imaginative possibilities, possibilities of her own, possibilities imagined through the simple process of running. Because we are free, we always of necessity transcend ourselves. The runner seeks not to squander her transcendence, but to meet it on the road ahead, a meeting beyond cognition alone. This is the experience of being fully present to being, being fully present in one's life. This *is* the experience of running.

[12] Jean-Paul Sartre, *The Psychology of Imagination* (Secaucus, NJ: Citadel Press, n.d.), p. 270.

Play

Let's go back to the beginning of our inquiry. "Why run?" we asked. What is the meaning of people out in public in tights? (I also suggested that possibly you should look elsewhere for answers, but at this point I continue to forge ahead with my own, since, for whatever reason, you are still reading). At this point I am going to assert that running is a form of play and that humans *need* to play in order to become authentic, in order to strive towards their potentiality. Play is not optional for the human being striving towards her potential: play is necessary. (Obviously, we cannot here develop a complete theory of human authenticity, but are relying on arguments derived from the writings of Sheehan, Kierkegaard, and Sartre on the issue. I recommend to the reader the writings of all three for illuminating discussions of authenticity and much more). Without play, humans fall prey to fanaticism in its nearly infinite guises, whether political, religious, cultural, or other.

Why is play so important? To address this question, let's look a little more closely at Sartre's philosophy. Almost all commentators on Sartre end up accusing him of holding an intensely and unnecessarily bleak perspective, a perspective pervaded by meaninglessness and useless struggle. What seems to escape them is Sartre's final call for play as the singular solution. (Maybe the critics aren't runners? Possibly they sit too much? Possibly they . . .). To demonstrate this solution, here's a brief overview of Sartre's philosophy, an overview so brief that it will be 87 minutes less than 90 minutes, produced after 25 years of rumination.

For Sartre, there are only two kinds of "being" (even here it's tricky, because one *is* being and one *is not* being but the "negation" of being) – free being (human being) and everything else. Sartre refers to the human being as "nothingness" because free being "has no essence" or, put simply, is not a thing. So we have two kinds of "being": (1) freedom and (2) thingness (essence). But for Sartre the conscious human being can't stand the fact that she is nothing(ness) because she wants to be something (she wants to have an essence). People are afraid of and therefore flee their freedom. (The literature driving home this point is so voluminous that the reading of it alone would take a lifetime: Dostoevsky, Nietzsche, Freud, Erich Fromm, R. D. Laing, Alice Miller, and certainly Kierkegaard and Sartre). If a free being (nothingness) could become something this would mean that the human being could be a thing (essence) and nothingness (freedom) at the same time. For Sartre, this is impossible. (For Sartre, this is impossible not only in fact but in theory. The way *he* defines being and nothingness, it only makes sense). Unfortunately, the fact that it's impossible doesn't stop us as human beings. We just keep going with our hopeless project to use our freedom to get away from our freedom in order to become something, to have a being, an essence. Sartre tells us that we are "condemned to be free,"[13] but we want to be anything but free, we want to be something. The human being, for Sartre is the "useless" project to use our freedom to try to escape from our freedom (into thingness) and guess what? We are never successful. But of course we still don't desire to give up. We keep trying. Is there a way out, a glimmer of hope? There is only *one* way, says Sartre, for human beings to escape the "seriousness" that plagues them and seemingly condemns them to an endless struggle. This way is the way of play.

Sartre says this about play:

> The first principle of play is man himself; through it he escapes his natural nature. (Sartre, *Being and Nothingness*, p. 581)

This "natural" nature tries to escape from its own freedom, from that which makes it human. This "natural" nature is that which tries to inject "thingness" into the human being, instead of acknowledging its infinite freedom. For Sartre, if humans could succeed in being both free and determined (thingness once again), they would be God:

> Thus the best way to conceive of the fundamental project of human reality is to say that man is the being whose project is to be God . . . man fundamentally is the desire to be God. (Sartre, *Being and Nothingness*, p. 566)

For Sartre, authenticity is possible if and only if one is able to abandon this "God-project." Abandonment of the God-project is possible only after a "radical conversion" (Sartre, *Being and Nothingness*, p. 412). And the radical conversion is possible only through play (Sartre, *Being and Nothingness*, pp. 581, 626). Therefore, without play, humans are condemned to a futile quest to become

---

[13] Jean Paul Sartre, *Being and Nothingness*, trans. Hazel E. Barnes (New York: Philosophical Library, 1956), p. 439.

unfree and free at the same time ("God"). Running, as a form of play, allows for Sartre's "radical conversion" to play, which means that authenticity is possible.

What is "authenticity"? As with many philosophical concepts, authenticity is a thorny and possibly ineffable topic. Having said that, let me proceed to "eff" the "ineffable" with the reckless abandon characteristic of a Pennsylvanian cross-country runner. An individual is authentic when she no longer seeks to hide from her own freedom, when she is able to confront the reality of her own history and existence, when she no longer actively seeks to deflect her consciousness away from her freedom by means of subterfuge. Authenticity is a way of relating to one's own freedom, it is a way of embracing the fragile, ephemeral, essenceless being that we are, instead of rejecting it in favor of some unrealizable ideal (be it the God-project or some other inhuman standard of moral purity) that we for some reason deem more palatable. The key to authenticity, however, must be found in play. After the effort and pain (and snot) have been acknowledged, in the final analysis, running fundamentally is a form of play.

Let's go back to Dr. Sheehan as he weighs in on running and play:

Play ... is the answer to the puzzle of our existence. (*Dr. Sheehan on Running*, p. 183)

Shakespeare was wrong. To play or not to play: that is the real question. (*Running and Being*, p. 71)

Playfulness becomes a pervasive attitude in that the runner develops a playful approach toward the absurdities of everyday existence. (*Dr. Sheehan on Running*, p. 31)

In Alan Zweibel's novel *The Other Shulman*, Shulman's outlook on life is radically altered after he begins running: "And though he had no answers to just about anything, he becomes more optimistic about everything because the questions didn't seem as hard."[14] Shulman cemented his optimism with a blazing 8:22:17 New York City Marathon. Finally, we are able to transcend the narrow confines of Rene Descartes's rationalism. Dr. Sheehan tells us that

"I think, therefore I am" is the philosophy of the incomplete man ... I play therefore I am. (*Dr. Sheehan on Running*, p. 186)

---

[14] Alan Zweibel, *The Other Shulman* (New York: Random House, 2005), p. 87.

To be an authentic human being, play is as necessary as eating, drinking, and sleeping. Running is both an ancient and a timeless form of play, play that can be solitary or with others, play that requires almost no equipment or special conditions. It requires neither wealth, nor intellect, nor education, and, as I found out long ago in my one-traffic-light town, just about no talent whatsoever. It is the universal form of play, acknowledged by children as such the world over.

The next time you're out there, running at who-knows-what pace, philosophizing about truth, selfhood, and existence, maybe you'd like to think about our final philosophical musing, compliments of Shulman, our 8:22 marathoner:

> If a thigh pulsated during a marathon but no one felt it, would it still hurt? (Zweibel, *The Other Shulman*, p. 165)

And if it did, would we have to stop playing?

Chapter 13
Can We Experience Significance on a Treadmill?

Douglas R. Hochstetler

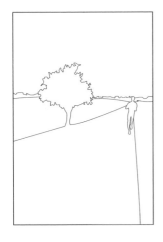

The Warm-Up

In recent years, all sorts of cardiovascular equipment – treadmills, elliptical machines, rowing machines, stair climbers, stationary bikes and so forth – have become extremely popular forms of exercise for millions of people. These pieces of equipment have, at times, replaced other more traditional forms of movement, such as running or walking outside and playing team sports.[1] Many use cardiovascular equipment for reasons of convenience, safety, economics, and perhaps comfort. Former Boston Marathon champion Amby Burfoot notes that treadmills are "unparalleled for hard, scientific training, since you can vary your speed precisely and monitor your heart rate at once."[2] Indeed there are some individuals who, if exercise equipment were not readily available, would not move at all – at least in an aerobic sense.

Despite its popularity, however, treadmill running does not produce the same experience as running in natural surroundings. On one level, treadmill running appears to be innocuous – what is problematic about running on a treadmill once in a while or even regularly? As a modern culture of increasingly sedentary individuals, perhaps we

---

[1] Robert D. Putnam, *Bowling Alone: The Collapse and Revival of American Community* (New York: Simon and Schuster, 2000).

[2] Amby Burfoot, "Run anytime with a home treadmill." *Runner's World*, Available at: http://www.runnersworld.com/article/0,7120,s6-240-322–1053-0,00.html.

should rejoice that people are moving at all. This point I concede, in that treadmills can be effective places to achieve physiological and health-related goals. For individuals who run solely to lose weight or burn calories, the treadmill may suffice. Treadmills are, however, the sort of places that discourage people from encountering movement in a richer sense.

Movement holds the potential for shaping our lives in ways that go beyond the physiological. Our actions, even seemingly small ones, the things we do repeatedly, bring about significant changes in the way we operate and how we perceive the world. The kinds of activities we take up in part define us. One who runs repeatedly and with commitment begins to define him or herself as a runner. What happens then if we begin to define ourselves as "treadmill runners?" Is it possible to encounter treadmill running as significant?

By significance or meaning I refer to the way our lives cohere and make sense. We live in this way when our daily activities matter. There is a purpose to our existence, a hope that our present and future coalesce in a valuable way. Our doing coincides with who we want to be, and we find ways to make sense of the traumatic or difficult. American philosopher John Dewey (1859–1952) described an experience happening "when the material experienced runs its course to fulfillment."[3] In other words we seek to incorporate the breadth of life opportunities (including running) – the dramatic and the mundane, the joys and the sorrows. In this way our experience encourages curiosity, promotes growth, and strengthens individual and collective initiative.

We experience our lives from a particular location in time. *Where* we choose to live shapes our experience in a certain sense, precluding us from being in other locations at the same time with the same experience. People running on treadmills live their bodies, time, and space very differently than those who run on mountain trails or around tracks. Later in this chapter we will look in greater detail at how the phenomenon of running outdoors differs from running on treadmills. My point is not that the treadmill necessarily prevents experiencing significance, but rather that treadmills are places where such possibilities are more difficult to actualize, and the experience is importantly different.

---

[3] John Dewey, *Art as Experience* (New York: Capricorn Books, 1934), p. 35.

Douglas R. Hochstetler

I do want to allow for individual preferences, however, and recognize that some people actually prefer tedious repetition when they run. For these individuals treadmill running (or even running around a track) provides significance. Other runners prefer an out-and-back or loop run but enjoy running the same path day after day. In some way the place and type of run fits into their life story and personal goals. For many others, I argue, a richer experience is to be found while running outside with changes in terrain, weather and the like.

Thinking about a Significant Life

As a way to examine significance through movement, I turn to the writings of Henry David Thoreau (1817–62) and William James (1842–1910). These philosophers were intent on finding and describing meaningful ways to live. Moreover, both Thoreau and James argued that place does matter in terms of this quest. Thoreau magnified this importance by intentionally living beside Walden Pond (a secluded place of outstanding natural beauty) for a two-year period. James wrote about this topic in his manuscript "What Makes a Life Significant?"

Thoreau recognized that *where* he *lived* made a difference. He realized that residing with family in Concord often hindered his goals as a writer and poet. The house, abuzz with family and friends, allowed few opportunities for the solitude and reflection that Thoreau desired and considered important. At the urging of mentor Ralph Waldo Emerson, Thoreau built a 10′ × 15′ cabin beside Walden Pond. Even though his cabin was quite small, Thoreau remarked that he "did not feel crowded or confined in the least. There was pasture enough for my imagination."[4]

Thoreau realized the importance of *where* he *moved* as well. He advocated walking to locations that held promise. For him, this direction was generally to the south and west of Walden where "the earth seems more unexhausted and richer" (Thoreau, p. 603). The direction he chose held woods and farmlands – ground not yet tamed by Massachusetts expansions. He described his walking at length, detailing everything he experienced – the sights, sounds, and smells. In sum,

[4] Henry David Thoreau, *The Portable Thoreau*, ed. Carl Bode (New York: Penguin, 1982), p. 340.

Thoreau realized that finding the right place to live – somewhere with rich possibilities – was a central part of a meaningful life.

James wrote at length about the importance of place as well, in particular his time at Chautauqua Institute, an educational and retreat center in New York. While at Chautauqua, James and other attendees had the opportunity to take a wide range of educational courses and listen to engaging speakers and enthralling orchestral concerts. At this pristine location, James wrote, "you have culture, you have kindness, you have cheapness, you have equality, you have the best fruits of what mankind has fought and bled and striven for."[5]

After some time, however, he found himself ready to leave this version of utopia, and this bothered him. James thought what he missed at Chautauqua was the element of precipitousness or "living on the edge," of "strength and strenuousness, intensity and danger" (James, p. 289). This locale of tranquility called upon very little need for struggle, except, James noted, in the occasional ballgame.

> Sweat and effort, human nature strained to its uttermost and on the rack, yet getting through alive, and then turning its back on its success to pursue another more arduous still – this is the sort of thing the presence of which inspires us, and reality of which seems to be the function of all higher forms of literature and fine art to bring home to us. (James, p. 290)

For James, the significant life involved finding places that were, in some respects, untamed and savage. Striving towards a significant life requires deliberate choices, as both Thoreau and James suggest. This applies to movement and most certainly to the locations where we run.

Treadmill as Short of Significant Life

When we think about the phenomena of treadmill running as compared with running outside on roads or trails, it becomes clear that while some things are similar – we sweat, exert effort, feel the impact in our feet and knees – many things are different. Running on a treadmill is a distinct, and somewhat impoverished, running

---

[5] William James, *Essays on Faith and Morals* (Cleveland: World Publishing, 1962), p. 288.

experience. I now want to suggest several ways in which running regularly on a treadmill can impact our experience and overall life significance as well.

First, we might run on a treadmill at the expense of our own muse, *our* thought process and consciousness. Douglas Anderson defined musement as "a phenomenological act; it involves an element of perception. It then, with continuity, proceeds to an interrogation of what is found phenomenologically or perceptually."[6] This process happens as we take in our surroundings, leading us to ponder, reflect, imagine, and so on. Too often we are bombarded by the noise of daily life, from televisions to cell phones to stereos and computers. It can be quite challenging to find open space to think for *ourselves*. Thoreau realized that nature and solitude provided a vehicle for his thinking and writing.

Repetitive activities in general are conducive to musement. Thoreau spent hours hoeing beans in the summer sun, and found that "labor of the hands, even when pursued to the verge of drudgery, is perhaps never the worst form of idleness" (Thoreau, p. 406). Treadmills, like forms of manual, repetitive labor, would appear to hold the same potential for reflection and musement. Prison reformers introduced treadmills in nineteenth-century British penitentiaries hoping that prisoners would have plenty of time on the wheel to dwell on their transgressions and possibly repent.[7]

Part of the difficulty with treadmills, however, is that individuals tend to approach them with an attitude of distraction rather than seeking musement. They carry Walkmans and iPods, watch television or read magazines. Most individuals are merely hoping to cope with the boredom, and then move on to other more significant activities. Rather than movement as reflection or an enterprise of its own accord, the treadmill becomes a place to put in one's time, a monotonous means to health and fitness ends.

The very notion of distancing oneself from experience is at the heart of Thoreau's critique of early American culture, and holds true today as well. Why would we purposefully engage in activities, especially leisure ones, where our prime motivation is to distract ourselves from the very experience? Perhaps we have not thought enough about

---

[6] Douglas R. Anderson, *Strands of System: The Philosophy of Charles Peirce* (West Lafayette, IN: Purdue University Press, 1995), p. 146.
[7] See James Hardie, *The History of the Tread-Mill* (New York: Samuel Marks, 1824).

the purpose of our movement, or at least have not fully considered its potential.

It is possible to experience insights while engaged in monotonous activities like treadmill running. In fact, because of the mind-numbing repetition and boredom, treadmill running might even enhance the reflective and/or meditative qualities. With the reduced stimuli present, the runner may become more focused on her breathing pattern, foot strike, or arm position, almost in a Zen-like fashion. Or the runner may intentionally think about anything except the task at hand in order to cope with the boredom. But this inwardly focused process is vastly different from that of the outdoor experience.

I also acknowledge, along with James, that even people engaged in repetitive, dreary, manual labor pursuits (including those who run on treadmills) can still find significance in the doing – if they are linked with some great vision or ideal. These individuals, in spite of their location and circumstances, are able to display the traits of heroism, courage, and strenuousness which James held so dear. In this way the treadmill runner may put up with the boredom and drudgery in order to realize a particular goal, such as running inside in inclement weather in order to train for an upcoming race. If we have a choice, however, running outdoors provides the inroads for a richer running experience.

Diminished Aesthetic Complexity

Treadmill running also differs in terms of the overall aesthetic complexity. Aesthetics, which relates to how we perceive experience, involves the way we approach the world via our senses. Our encounters with stimulating environments could be described as complex, with changes in smell, contour, texture, and so on. Much of the spontaneity or playfulness of running is sucked out of treadmill running, however, leaving a sterile, unchanging environment. One example is the exercise environment itself. Many treadmills are in fitness centers with a fixed environmental temperature day after day. Some treadmill runners even turn on a fan or adjust the thermostat if the temperature is not to their liking, especially if the treadmill is in the confines of their home. Running outside provides no such control. The runner may deliberate between a long or short sleeve t-shirt, wearing a hat, gloves, or not. Temperatures may range between hot and sticky summer runs to those with cold and severe wind.

The terrain on treadmills remains unchanged as well – the belt continues to move beneath the runner's feet, whirring along mile after mile. The friction, resiliency, and absorption all remain constant. The path continues to point straight ahead without any variance, gradual shift, or fork in the road. The treadmill surface is much different than sidewalk, grass, trail, or macadam. These elements have a different sound and feel, compared with the treadmill belt. They take us somewhere – to places with wildlife and perhaps even traffic, offering the possibility to explore and wander. They prompt us to make decisions about direction, to consider forging ahead or turning back.

Running on a treadmill certainly provides very objective feedback – miles run, calories burned, current heart rate, and so forth. In fact, the treadmill has become a benchmark for research equipment because of its ability to standardize the experience. With their subjects on a treadmill, researchers control the location, speed, incline, workout length, temperature, and other assorted variables. It is much more difficult to standardize the running experience outdoors. Even the same five-mile path, while consistent for distance, may vary according to weather conditions, temperature, lighting, and, of course, speed.

On treadmills we may also lose a certain amount of experience that arrives via spontaneity. Running on a treadmill allows very few chance encounters. No dogs will chase us. No neighbors will greet us. We will not step in a pothole or come upon new terrain or unexplored territory. We select our program – hills, cardio, fat burning, or manual – enter our time, level, and then begin to run. Depending on the day, the exercise routine may range from mildly interesting to bearable to numbingly boring.

When running outside we are, at times, forced to make changes concerning the route. Recently I experimented with a new one-hour run loop. Unbeknownst to me a portion of the road was closed due to construction. My options were to turn back or complete the loop as best I could. I chose the latter. This meant running several hundred yards through mud, past a flock of not-so-friendly geese, and through a bean field.

Treadmills also present fewer opportunities for spontaneous interaction with others. Some people enjoy exercising beside a friend while on a treadmill. These social aspects of running are valuable but limited in that running outdoors with others provides much greater flexibility and degrees of freedom. Unlike the fixed relationship of treadmills, lined up side-by-side, running with people outdoors allows for gradual shifts in position and encounters to occur. This might include the gradual movement to the front or back of the pack, the side or middle of the group, as well as moving closer to one runner or away from another.

Diminished Experience and Discovery

The treadmill also limits us by restricting our sensory experiences – the things we see, hear, smell, and feel. For example, treadmill running requires a focused gaze in order to maintain balance. When a running partner and I choose to run indoors on days of inclement weather, I am not able to casually look at him as we chat like we do when on our runs outdoors. I'm fearful that, while turning to look for more than a brief period, I will lose my balance. The field of vision is limited and often changeless as well. The runner looks at the treadmill much of the time – the readouts with time spent, distance covered, and calories burned. The lighting, shapes, and sizes of objects nearby remain constant throughout the run, at a fixed point with respect to the runner. Those running in fitness centers may see some variety but only in a limited sense.

My gaze while running outside is typically 10–15 feet ahead. I may become locked into the pavement or path, picking a spot ahead and continuing to gaze at that portion of the road or trail. But at other times I may look from side to side, admire fields of corn or soybeans, and extend my step to avoid a puddle, or make eye contact with an approaching car or bicyclist. The horizons that running in natural settings provide are replete with possibility. Even a five-mile loop run every day throughout the year changes in terms of scenery – with variations throughout the seasons – providing an encouragement to observe. Quite often these variations are subtle and slow, requiring a great deal of perceptive skills to notice.

With recent advances in virtual reality one could run in front of a screen showing a bucolic countryside or breathtaking ocean view. In this way it would be possible to "experience" the outdoors, in a virtual sense, without the necessary risks of weather, insects, or traffic. As the technology improves, this option may be even more appealing to some runners, but these virtual runs appear impoverished on two counts. First, to a certain degree risk is part of the attraction to running outside. Running through adverse conditions – rain and snow, over potholes and through ravines – promotes the kind of precipitousness of which James wrote and upon which significance, at least in part, hinges. Second, the appeal of virtual reality only further underscores our human desire for variety of experience and our resistance to boredom and meaningless repetition. We, like Sisyphus, try to avoid activities that involve pushing rocks up inclines without any express purpose.[8]

Movement activities such as running provide a powerful vehicle for discovery, of both self and environment. This discovery process is diminished, however, when running on treadmills. When I think of places I've run, favorites come to mind – the golf course in State College, around the section near our farm in Iowa, on the trail in the Little Lehigh Parkway, and many more. I often think of memorable runs, conversations, sights, and experiences in conjunction with these particular places. On the other hand, it is difficult to think of any memorable run on the treadmill, apart from any significant physiological measures. There is no change in scenery, temperature, or wind speed. These runs are largely about finishing and getting on to something else, hardly the stuff of stories and memories.

Movement also holds the potential for self-transformation. Those who encounter movement in a significant fashion develop into different human beings by virtue of the activity. To illustrate, two consecutive summers spent bicycling across the United States changed me in both subtle and dramatic ways. I became adept at bike maintenance (especially changing flat tires), found I was a bit less patient than I previously thought, and came away from the trips with a desire to try bike racing. In short, I emerged from these five-week, 3,000-plus mile trips a different person. Of course it would be possible to spend five weeks and 3,000 miles on a stationary bike, but the transformation would be much different and much less picturesque. Movement that is significant has a way of promoting change, particularly in terms of the spontaneity and risk involved.

---

[8] Sisyphus was a Greek mythological figure, condemned to spend eternity performing meaningless labor. His task was to roll a large stone up a hill, only to have the stone roll back down once it reached the top.

Decreased Risk

Finally, treadmill runners may encounter fewer risks than their outdoor counterparts. Because of the nature of running outside, there are more things that could and do go wrong. We develop safety measures to run in natural surroundings – we carry Mace, wear identity bracelets with medical information, tell family members or friends our route, choose safe places and times to run, vary our routes, and run in well-lit areas.

Treadmills do include a certain amount of risk consistent with running outside. In both places the runner may experience fatigue, disappointment, muscle strain, or even serious physical injury. On the treadmill, however, a great deal of risk is reduced. Manufacturers attempt to reduce the chances of risk (and therein reduce their own chance of lawsuits) by providing warning labels and safety features. Treadmills also provide respite from inclement weather and other unwanted intrusions.

Running on a treadmill is certainly safer than running outdoors. In fact that is why many people choose to run indoors. Either in the gym or in their home these individuals are able to exercise a great deal of control over their personal safety. They need not worry about someone hiding in the woods or about getting lost. Medical professionals, or at least a telephone, are close by, should they pull a muscle while running. The terrain is level the entire time, without potholes, tree roots, or sidewalk ridges. Finally, if they fall the machine will automatically shut off, (provided the runner is attached to a safety strap by the wrist) thereby preventing further injury.

The downside of reducing the majority of risk, however, is an impact on the overall experience. As James noted, there is also less chance of doing something heroic or of developing a meaningful story, for good or bad. It is hard to imagine a life-changing event taking place on the treadmill. This is not to say that a significant life necessitates an overabundance of risky behavior. We should certainly note the importance of seeking balance between reckless abandon and sterile safety.

Running outside involves a certain degree of precipitousness not found on the treadmill. *Runner's World* writer, John "The Penguin" Bingham, confirms this aspect of risk and the importance it plays in our lives:

Running lets us rediscover what we knew as children: That being safe all the time isn't very interesting. There are no air bags in our running shorts. We are vulnerable to the whim of fate and the blindness of serendipity. But we are not held hostage to fear. We boldly go where we know we belong. The fun is at the edge of the unknown.[9]

The Cool-Down

In conclusion, running (and movement in general) need not be only a means to another end. The doing itself may also be valuable. We risk limiting this experience when confined to a treadmill. We risk experiencing movement primarily as an instrumental endeavor, rather than an avenue toward the significant life championed by Thoreau and James.

Is it possible to experience significance on the treadmill? It is possible to find meaning, or perhaps create a significant life, out of the direst circumstances. But when we have the freedom to choose where we move, it would be prudent to choose a place that provides the most opportunity to experience life in its richest sense. Running outside puts me in a position to be the kind of person I want to be – unconstrained, free to roam and make decisions about direction and path (not just about speed or incline) – and that is a good place to be.

[9] John Bingham, "No Need for Speed – The Edge of Running," *Runner's World*, 39/6, June 2004, p. 62.

Chapter 14
Running in Place or Running in Its Proper Place

J. P. Moreland

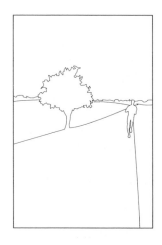

I've jogged for 35 years. I have sore ankles and a strong heart. I've gained some weight in the last 10 years but not as much as some of my non-jogging friends. I've had many tennis shoes and lots of memories. Depending on the year, I've averaged three to five times per week and three miles each time I go for a run (that's been pretty steady). And I am a philosopher who jogs, though I would never admit to being a jogger who philosophizes.

Is jogging (which I'll use synonymously with "running") worth it? In a large and pretty obvious sense, yes; in a super-sized sense, maybe. All things being equal, jogging is a good thing to do and is immensely rewarding. It enhances health, releases stress and anxiety, and helps elevate one's mood, it gives a person time to be alone and meditate. All this is pretty obvious.

But when you try to assess the value of jogging in a more comprehensive way, in a manner that goes beyond these obvious benefits, things aren't so clear. Therein lies a big story, one too big for us to chase down here. So I'm going to give some good and bad news about jogging. I'll start with the bad news and end with the good. As it turns out, the good news is better than you might expect, and for reasons you might not expect. But I get ahead of myself. Let's start with the bad news about jogging.

Jogging, the Exercise Craze, and the Empty Self

Currently, a three-way worldview struggle rages in our culture among ethical monotheism (especially Christianity), scientific naturalism, and postmodernism. I want to say a brief word about the latter two relevant to our topic.

First, *scientific naturalism* is the view that the physical cosmos science studies is all that exists. Scientific naturalism has two central components, one metaphysical and one epistemological. Metaphysically (having to do with reality), scientific naturalism implies that everything that exists is composed of matter or emerges out of matter when it achieves a suitable complexity. Epistemologically (having to do with how we know things), it implies that physical science is the only, or at least, a vastly superior way of gaining knowledge.

The second worldview is *postmodernism*. Postmodernism is a loose coalition of diverse thinkers from several different academic disciplines, so it is difficult to characterize postmodernism in a way that would be fair to this diversity. Still, it is possible to provide a fairly accurate characterization of postmodernism in general, since its friends and foes understand it well enough to debate its strengths and weaknesses.[1] As a philosophical standpoint, postmodernism is primarily a reinterpretation of what knowledge is and what counts as knowledge. More broadly, it represents a form of cultural relativism about such things as reality, truth, reason, value, linguistic meaning, the self and other notions. On a postmodernist view, there is no such thing as objective reality, truth, value, reason and so forth. All these are social constructions, creations of linguistic practices and, as such, are relative not to individuals, but to social groups that share a narrative. Roughly, a narrative is a perspective, such as Marxism, atheism or Christianity, that is embedded in the group's social and linguistic practices.

The pervasive denial by naturalists and postmodernists of truth and rationality outside the hard sciences has left many people without hope that true, rationally defensible forms of wisdom can be discovered as guides to a flourishing life. As a result, people have turned to emotion and the satisfaction of desire as the decisive factors in adopting a worldview and an approach to life. This approach to life

---

[1] For a helpful introduction to postmodernism, see Joseph Natoli, *A Primer to Postmodernity* (Oxford: Blackwell, 1997).

has created the conditions for the emergence of a new personality type that psychologists claim is present in epidemic proportions in American society. This personality type is called *the empty self.*

Since the 1960s, for the first time in history a culture – ours – is filled with what are called empty selves. According to Philip Cushman, "The empty self is filled up with consumer goods, calories, experiences, politicians, romantic partners, and empathetic therapists. . . . [The empty self] experiences a significant absence of community, tradition, and shared meaning, . . . a lack of personal conviction and worth, and it embodies the absences as a chronic, undifferentiated emotional hunger."[2]

There are two essential traits of the empty self. First, the empty self is *inordinately individualistic and narcissistic* in orientation. A healthy form of individualism is a good thing. But the empty self that populates American culture is a self-contained individual who seeks meaning by defining his own life goals, values, and interests as though he were a human atom, isolated from others with little need or responsibility to live for the concerns of his broader community. But as psychologist Martin Seligman warns, ". . . the self is a very poor site for finding meaning."[3]

The values of the empty self also reflect a radical change in our culture's understanding of happiness. Americans are terribly confused about what happiness is and, as a result, seldom find it. Since the time of Moses, Solomon, the Greek philosophers Plato and Aristotle, the church Fathers like Augustine, through the Reformation and until around the 1700s in Britain, almost everyone agreed about what happiness was – a life of wisdom and virtue. Unfortunately, to make progress in happiness so understood, one needs to gain non-empirical knowledge of values, virtues, teleological goals and the nature of objective meaning.

In the last hundred years or so, happiness has come to mean something quite different. A recent dictionary definition of happiness is "a sense of pleasurable satisfaction." Note very carefully that happiness is identified with a feeling, and more specifically, a feeling very close to pleasure. Thus, we say "I got an A on the exam and I am so happy!" "I set a new 10k PR and I am psyched and happy!" Today,

---

[2] Philip Cushman, "Why the Self is Empty," *American Psychologist* 45, May 1990, p. 600.

[3] Martin E. P. Seligman, "Boomer Blues," *Psychology Today*, October 1988, p. 55.

the good life is a life of happiness, and it is the goal of most people for themselves and their children.

So what, you may be asking, is so wrong with happiness understood as a sense of pleasurable satisfaction or fun? In one sense, nothing. All things being equal, I would rather have fun than not have fun. But in another sense, everything. There are two main problems with this understanding. First, it represents a serious departure from a more ageless and richer definition. Second, the contemporary sense of happiness cannot be obtained by seeking it. If you have ever tried to be happy, you know this is true. Pleasurable satisfaction makes a very poor lifetime goal; it is, however, a wonderful by-product of striving after happiness in the classical sense. Think about it. If happiness is having an internal feeling of fun or pleasurable satisfaction, and if it is our main goal, where will people place their focus each day? It will be on them, and the result will be a culture of people who can't live for something bigger than they are.

What does all this have to do with jogging, you may be asking? Simply this. Far too often today, the exercise craze in general, and the emphasis on jogging in particular, is an expression of empty selves trying to be happy by indulging a narcissistic, self-absorbed emphasis on body-image and sexual attraction as the holy grail of life's most important quest – the satisfaction of immediate bodily desire. It is no accident that the emergence of the empty self and the inordinate preoccupation with exercise and jogging coincide. This, I take it, is the bad news about jogging. Does it follow that there is no good news? Certainly not. I have already acknowledged that in its proper place in a life well lived, jogging can be of immense benefit. I also believe that jogging can be a strategic part of an overall employment of spiritual disciplines that, taken together, can help to produce virtuous, flourishing people of wisdom and character. To support this claim I will sketch out a framework of spiritual disciplines as they are found in classic virtue theory stemming from Aristotle and Thomas Aquinas and from New Testament teaching.

Jogging, Spiritual Disciplines, and a Life of Character

We all know what it means to learn some particular activity, for example, to play golf or the piano. Consider golf. We start by becoming motivated to learn and by reading about how to play or by watching, say, a golf video. But no one in his or her right mind would stop with daily reading and with listening to inspiring golf-music designed to make us feel deeply about learning golf! Yet this is exactly our view of making disciples. We think that if we preach to people once a week (twice if they are really committed!), if they read a bit of the Bible or other inspirational literature each day, and if they listen to inspiring music, they'll really grow in character and virtue.

Returning to golf, what is missing in this strategy? Practice, practice, practice. The great players are those who practice over the course of their careers. To learn golf, we go to a driving range, and, focusing on specific movements under the instructor's direction, we repeat those movements over and over again until a habit is formed. The same thing is done in learning how to play the piano, speak French, make pottery, or learn math.

The sad thing is that we know what to do to learn golf or some other specific activity, but we don't know the relevance of repeated bodily practice and discipline for learning to be good at life taken as a whole. Long ago, Plato (428–348 BC) wisely noted: "There is no question which a man of any sense could take more seriously than . . . what kind of life one should live" (*Gorgias*, 500c). Elsewhere Plato observed that it would be a tragedy if a person could be content with life by having good health, wealth, great looks, and a lot of ease and pleasure while, at the same time, not giving a moment's thought to the cultivation of skill at living life as a whole with virtue and character (*Laws*, 661a–c).

So what does learning to play golf, make pottery, or even jogging have to do with the good life? As a first step toward an answer, let's look at a number of New Testament texts that seem a bit odd at first glance. It's hard to know how to take them if we do the right thing and interpret them literally.

I urge you therefore, brothers and sisters, by the mercies of God, to present your *bodies* a living and holy sacrifice, acceptable to God, which is your rational service of worship. (Rom. 12:1)[4]

This verse is unpacked earlier in Paul's letter:

[4] All quotations are from the New American Standard Bible. In this quotation I have replaced "spiritual" with "rational," the literal rendering of the term.

Even so, consider yourselves to be dead to sin, but alive to God in Christ Jesus. Therefore do not let sin reign in your mortal body that you should obey its lusts, and do not go on presenting *the members of your body* to sin as instruments of unrighteousness, but present yourselves to God as those alive from the dead, and *your members* as instruments of righteousness to God . . . I am speaking in human terms because of *the weakness of your flesh*. For just as you *presented your members* as slaves to impurity and to lawlessness, resulting in further lawlessness, so now *present your members* as slaves to righteousness, resulting in sanctification. (Rom. 6:11–13, 19)

Do you not know that those who run in a race all run, but only one receives the prize? Run in such a way that you may win. And everyone who competes in the games *exercises self-control* in all things. They then do it to receive a perishable wreath, but we an imperishable. Therefore I run in such a way, as not without aim; I box in such a way, as not beating the air; but I *bruise my body and make it my slave*, lest possibly, after I have preached to others, I myself should be disqualified. (1 Cor. 9:24–7)

Discipline yourself for the purpose of godliness; for *bodily discipline* is only of little profit, but godliness is profitable for all things, for the present life and also for the life to come. (1 Tim. 4:7–8)

As mentioned above, at first glance these texts – especially the words that I have italicized – may seem a bit puzzling, but as we will now discover, they express insights about human nature and flourishing so very deep that, once again, the insights of this biblical teaching and, more generally, classic virtue theory expose the shallowness of our own culture in breathtaking fashion. To understand this biblical teaching, we must first clarify four concepts: *habit, character, flesh,* and *body*.

A *habit* is an ingrained tendency to act, think, or feel a certain way without needing to choose to do so. The way a person writes the letters of the alphabet is not something he or she needs to think about. It is a habit, and one concentrates on what one is writing, not on the habitual style of handwriting used. *Character* is the sum total of one's habits, good and bad. Penmanship character is the sum total of one's good and bad writing habits; it is one's handwriting style.

Biblical terms such as "flesh" (*sarx*), or "body" (*soma*) have a wide field of meaning. Sometimes "flesh" and "body" mean the same thing, but in the passages above, there is a unique and important meaning for each. "Body" is pretty obvious. In contrast to the soul, it refers to one's living, animated physical aspect. The body can be seen and touched, and it is composed of tissue, skin, and bone. The "flesh" in these texts refers to the sinful tendencies or habits that reside in the body and whose nature is opposite that of the Kingdom of God.[5] To understand these more fully and to appreciate their importance more deeply, let's look at jogging. What I am about to say may sound a bit forced, but I mean for it to be taken quite literally.

When a person jogs, he or she has a "jogging character," that is, the sum of good and bad habits relevant for jogging. One's "jogging flesh" is the sum of one's bad jogging habits. Where do these bad habits reside? They dwell as ingrained tendencies in specific body parts, particular members of the body. One's jogging abilities may be weakened by bad habits in the legs, the shoulders, or somewhere else. One may have good habits in one's shoulders but bad habits, jogging flesh, residing in one's legs. For example, many joggers are guilty of overstriding, and this has a tendency to produce injuries. Others run with tense shoulders, which can limit the distance and speed that they are able to jog. Joggers also have notoriously tight hamstrings, and the experts of the sport encourage a regular discipline of stretching to counteract this condition. Jogging flesh, then, resides in the specific members of one's body.

How does one develop a good jogging character? Not simply by daily jogging readings coupled with regular exposure to motivational jogging music! No, one must present one's members to a jogging instructor either in person or through the guidance of a running book as instruments of jogging "righteousness" instead of following one's jogging flesh as an instrument of jogging "unrighteousness." These are not figures of speech. They are literal indeed. By so presenting one's members, one gradually gets rid of bad jogging habits and replaces them with good ones.

How does one present one's members to a jogging instructor? Two things are involved. First, one must dedicate oneself to the pursuit of jogging righteousness – to getting good at jogging – and choose to submit as an apprentice to a master-teacher. (Many people think of jogging as a simple activity. You just put on a t-shirt and shorts, lace

---

[5] For a useful discussion of "body" and "flesh," see G. E. Ladd, *A Theology of the New Testament* (Grand Rapids, MI: Eerdmans, 1974), pp. 464–75. "Flesh" may actually refer on occasion to a fleshly community, one that walks according to a legalistic adherence to the old covenant. But even in these cases of the corporate use of "flesh," the term *sarx* is derivative of the ethical usage in reference to individuals. See Walter Russell, *The Flesh/Spirit Controversy in Galatians* (Lanham, MD: University Press of America, 1997).

up your shoes, and go. However, joggers with any experience know that there is much wisdom to be gained from others. The perennial popularity of *Runner's World* magazine and how-to running books testifies to this fact.) Second, when presenting one's members to a jogging instructor, one does not simply engage in a one-time act of dedication to the master-teacher. To "present one's body" to a jogging instructor requires repeatedly engaging specific body parts in regular activities done over and over again, with the instructor in charge, and practicing different activities. For example, one may present the members of one's body, say, the shoulders, to the instructor by practicing over and over again a specific relaxation technique or stretching exercise. The result of such habitual bodily movement will be the replacement of bad habits that dwell in the shoulders with good habits. The jogging flesh that resides in the shoulders will give way to jogging righteousness.

A jogging discipline is a repeated jogging exercise, a bodily movement involving specific body parts, repeated over and over again, that is done for the purpose of getting rid of jogging flesh and gaining jogging righteousness in one's body. A jogging discipline is done repeatedly not to get good at the discipline, but to become a better runner. Consider the fact that joggers who only jog are prone to injury, and that because of this many coaches encourage even the casual jogger to incorporate biking, swimming, or weight-training into their fitness programs. A jogger may engage in cross-training, such as bicycling or weight-lifting, not to become better at biking or lifting weights, but to become a better jogger.

The parallels with becoming good at life should be clear. When one presents one's body to God as a living sacrifice (Rom. 12:1), it involves not only a one-time act of dedication, but a habitual, repeated bodily exercise (1 Tim. 4:7–8; 1 Cor. 9:24–7) involving specific body parts (Rom. 6:12–13, 19), resulting in putting to death one's bad habits (Col. 3:5), i.e., removing the flesh that resides in those body parts, and replacing them with righteousness that comes to reside in the members of one's body. *A Christian spiritual discipline is a repeated bodily practice, done over and over again, in dependence on the Holy Spirit and under the direction of Jesus and other wise teachers in His way, to enable one to get good at certain things in life that one cannot learn to do by direct effort.* A related definition could be given to a spiritual or simply virtuous discipline without the specifically Christian elements.

Just as jogging flesh resides in specific body parts, for example, the shoulders, so sinful habits often reside in specific body parts, for example, anger in the stomach area, anxiety in the chest or shoulders, gossip in the tongue and mouth region, and lust in the eyes and other areas. A spiritual discipline is a repetitive practice that targets one of these areas in order to replace bad habits with good ones in dependence on the Spirit of the living God.

Some spiritual disciplines, for example, the practice of journaling (the habit of writing down one's prayers to God, one's daily experiences of answered prayer, good and bad events, and so forth), are mere means to an end (learning to remember answers to prayer, learning to concentrate on incidental daily events as occasions that have spiritual significance, learning to talk deliberately and with emotion to God). Other disciplines are both a means to an end when done as a discipline and intrinsically valuable in their own right when done during the actual "game" of life. The habit of expressing kindness is an example.

The philosopher Dallas Willard points out that there are two categories of spiritual disciplines: those of abstinence/detachment and those of engagement.[6] This list is not exhaustive, but it does contain most of the classical disciplines:

Disciplines of Abstinence: solitude, silence, fasting, frugality, chastity, secrecy, sacrifice;
Disciplines of Engagement: study, worship, celebration, service, prayer, fellowship, confession, submission.

In disciplines of abstinence, we unhook, detach, abstain for a period of time and to varying degrees from the satisfaction of normal, appropriate desires – food, sleep, companionship, sex, music, comfort, financial security, recognition, and so forth. These disciplines help us address sins of *commission*. In general, it is not a good idea to detach from something without filling the resulting void with attachment to something positive. Thus, disciplines of engagement go hand in hand with those of detachment, and the former help us address *sins of omission*.

---

[6] Dallas Willard, *The Spirit of the Disciplines* (San Francisco: Harper & Row, 1988), pp. 154–92.

It is crucial to understand that on the biblical and, more generally, the classical understanding of virtue theory, the formation of a good character essentially requires repeated employment of bodily practices relevant to the development of character. Within this framework, jogging can play an essential role as a spiritual discipline in the broader task of becoming a virtuous, flourishing person. First, repeated bodily exercise is, itself, a sort of spiritual discipline in that it forms the habit of saying no to the body's resistance to change and discipline, it is a form of control over and discipline of the body, subjecting it to the will. In this way, jogging is itself a discipline of abstinence. 1 Cor. 9:24–7 is directly relevant to this aspect of jogging. Second, progress in bodily discipline in one area spills over into other areas and makes other bodily disciplines easier. Thus, growth in solitude and silence can facilitate growth in fasting and conversely. Similarly, my own practice of jogging has made it easier to practice other spiritual disciplines and, in this way, jogging can help one develop other habits relevant to character.

In sum, there are some obvious benefits to jogging such as health and stress relief. But beyond that, there is good news and bad news about jogging. As an expression of the empty self, it will enslave people in a failed approach to life. This is tantamount to spending one's life running in place. It doesn't take one anywhere important. But as part of a life seeking virtue, it can be a wonderful means to a much larger end. This, I believe, is running in its proper place.

Chapter 15
The Running Life
Getting in Touch with Your Inner Hunter-Gatherer

Sharon Kaye

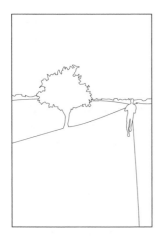

What is the good life for human beings? Philosophers have been asking this question ever since Socrates (469–399 BC). In fact, it would be hard to deny that this question has driven the development of philosophy and therefore the development of Western civilization itself. Although the answers philosophers have proposed over the past 2.5 millennia vary in interesting ways, they by and large fall into two main categories: the religious and the cultural.

By "religious," I have in mind someone like Thomas Aquinas (1225–74) who maintains in the *Summa Theologica* that the purpose of human life is to worship God. While casting Aquinas as a paradigm, I define the "religious" category as any life philosophy devoted to a supernatural creator of the universe.

By "cultural," in contrast, I have in mind someone like Aristotle (384–322 BC) who asserts in the *Nicomachean Ethics* that human beings should strive for moral and intellectual excellence. In line with Aristotle's intention, I define the cultural category as any life philosophy devoted to politics, science, or art.

Although religion and culture have clearly dominated discussions of the good life, in what follows, I reject both categories, proposing instead a third: the biological. I define the "biological" as any life philosophy devoted to physical fitness, though I will focus on runners in particular. The running life holds the long elusive secret to human happiness.

Biology

There is just one premise of weight in my argument for this thesis and it is a premise that every reasonable person accepts, namely, EVOLUTION IS TRUE. Charles Darwin's theory of natural selection, as enhanced by more recent discoveries in genetics, geology, and other fields, is the only correct account of the history of the planet earth. Although every reasonable person accepts this premise, many fail to recognize its far-reaching ramifications.

The members of our genus, *Homo*, first appear in the fossil record about 2.5 million years ago, along with the oldest-known stone tools. We lived as hunter-gatherers until the rise of agriculture, which began a mere 10,000 years ago. The difference between a hunter-gatherer and a farmer is as profound as the difference between an ant and a spider. Ants are always on the move; spiders spin their webs and wait. In the same way, life in an agricultural society is sedentary as compared with life as a hunter-gatherer, especially when slavery or industrialization makes it unnecessary for many members of the farming society to actually work in the fields. What this means is that the modern lifestyle we think of as "human" is not human at all in the grand scheme of things.

This point is widely neglected because it is so difficult to grasp the timescale. If we compare our biological history to a single 24-hour day, we are hunter-gatherers from the wee hours, past dawn, through morning, all afternoon, and into the night, until about five minutes to midnight. Farming changed our entrenched lifestyle suddenly, radically, and recently – so much so that there has not been enough time for it to have any significant effect on our physiology. Only roughly 500 generations of humans have lived and died as farmers. Natural selection by random mutation takes much longer than that. So, despite our civilized carrying on, we are all still hunter-gatherers deep down.

Not only are we hunter-gatherers, we are runners. Have you ever noticed that the human being is the only member of the animal kingdom that is known to run voluntarily for 26 miles at a strenuous pace without stopping? Sure, other animals are on their feet a lot and many can sprint faster than we can, but do they marathon? No they do not. And there is good reason: they have no buttocks. True, most animals have hindquarters of some kind but only human beings enjoy a true gluteus maximus. Recent studies show that evolution designed this glorious anatomical adaptation specifically for the particular stability and strength required by endurance running.[1] This is to say that, through the sheer accident of a random mutation, one of our ancestors was born with an overdeveloped butt. Because the resulting increase in mobility enabled him to escape predators and hunt more effectively on the African plains, he survived and reproduced while his flat-reared peers either died or cowered in the jungle. Consider our nearest relatives, the great apes. They lack buns (and other crucial equipment, such as the Achilles' tendon). They walk, they shuffle, they lurch along; they do not run. Hence, they have always stuck to the trees. Meanwhile, our running forerunners spread far and wide, developed advanced brains, and before long took over the world.

The Biological Life

What does all of this imply? Achieving the good life requires escaping the way of the spider and rediscovering the way of the ant. To find happiness we must get in touch with our inner hunter-gatherers.

The reason why "the mass of men lead lives of quiet desperation," as Henry David Thoreau (1817–62) so poignantly put it, is that we are no longer doing what we are built to do. Let's face it, almost all of us have to work for a living, and, unfortunately, there is no modern job that effectively approximates hunting and gathering. Loren Cordain writes:

> Hunter-gatherer males typically spend between 19.6–24.7 kcal/kg/day in physical activity whereas the sedentary office worker would expend only 4.4 kcal/kg/day. Even if a 3.0-mile walk . . . were added to the office worker's activities, the resulting value of 8.7 kcal/kg/day would be significantly lower than that which would be normal for our pre-agricultural ancestors. Only when higher level activities are engaged in (say running 12.1 km/h for 60 min) do modern sedentary workers simulate the energy expenditures of our stone age ancestors. . . . Although human lifestyles have changed almost inconceivably since the advent of the agricultural revolution and the more recent industrial revolution, our exercise capacities, limitations and requirements remain the same as those selected by natural selection for our stone age ancestors.[2]

---

[1] Dennis M. Bramble and Daniel E. Lieberman, "Endurance Running and the Evolution of Homo," *Nature* 432, 2004, pp. 345–52.

[2] Loren Cordain, R. W. Gotshall, and S. B. Eaton, "Evolutionary Aspects of Exercise," *World Review of Nutrition and Diet* 81, 1997, pp. 55–8. See also, Loren Cordain, R. W. Gotshall, S. B. Eaton, et al., "Physical Activity, Energy Expenditure and Fitness: An Evolutionary Perspective," *International Journal of Sports Medicine* 19 (1998), pp. 328–35.

A day in the life of our stone age ancestors was extremely physically active. Today we feel as though we spend a great deal of time "running around," but back then, this was literally true. Moreover, when we weren't on the move, we were digging, pounding, lifting, hurling, climbing, carrying, fighting, and – don't forget the constant prospect of having sex.

The modern-day job that most closely approximates this lifestyle is that of Senate Pages, who are reported to scuttle around Capitol grounds to an average distance of seven miles per day. Unfortunately, only high school students are eligible for that particular job. Nor is there enough wilderness left in the United States to support true hunting and gathering, even on a small scale.

What it boils down to is that, thanks to the agricultural revolution, we can no longer hope to live the life our bodies secretly crave. So, in order to avoid self-destruction, we must do the next best thing: we must cram our hunting and gathering into the fraction of the day we call our "free time."

How much free time does the average person have in a day? Sit down sometime and record how you are spending your time. Next (after the shock and disgust die down) make a chart showing how you *should* be spending your time. It might look something like the following:

Sleep	8 hours
Work	8 hours
Meals	2 hours
Transportation	1 hour
Chores, personal hygiene, etc.	1 hour
Unexpected and miscellaneous	1 hour
Total	21 hours

It's rough being a modern human – dull necessities take almost all day! If this chart is correct, however, it suggests that you have three hours left per day for pursuing the good life. Three precious hours. What are you going to do with them?

According to the biological account I have been developing, you should do some hunting and gathering. In fact, depending on just how sedentary your job is, you may need to condense a full day of hunting and gathering into those three hours. This means strenuous exercise every day. Every day? Yes, every day – well, with an occasional day off, never more than once per week. Your inner hunter-gatherer is screaming to get out. Once it does, it will not want to go back in. The endorphins alone will keep you coming back for more.[3]

Although I just used the generic term "exercise," and although cross-training is always a good idea, I want to stress that running is still the ideal primary focus for the modern hunter-gatherer. Biking the equivalent takes twice as long. Walking, much longer. Water aerobics? Elliptical trainer? Pilates? Forget about it. To get in touch with your inner hunter-gatherer you simply must accept that you have to sweat buckets and it has to be hard and it has to hurt. Think of it this way: your workout needs to generate the adrenaline induced by a pack of hungry wolves on your tail. You can do this safely and easily in a two-hour period: run a brisk 10k with warm-up and cool-down, then lift weights or do abs on alternating days along with extensive stretching. (No skipping stretching! Skipping stretching causes the injuries that give people the excuse not to run.) Running is your primal need whether you are aware of it or not. If you satisfy it in an efficient manner, then your third hour is free for that other more obvious primal need, which, by the way, benefits from physical fitness in countless ways.

It should be clear by now that this "biological" account of the good life is really just a new, enlightened form of hedonism. The ancient philosopher Epicurus (341–270 BC), who is known as the father of hedonism, maintains that the good life for human beings is to be found in the pursuit of pleasure. Unfortunately, he did not know that the ultimate pleasure lies in maximal health, that maximal health is achieved through physical fitness, and that physical fitness requires a daily commitment to strenuous exercise, as is best exemplified in running.

Of course, compared to religion and culture, running looks like a passing fad. Is there nothing to be said for these more time-honored traditions?

---

[3] "Endorphins (ĕndôr′fĭnz): neurotransmitters found in the brain that have pain-relieving properties similar to morphine. . . . Besides behaving as a pain regulator, endorphins are also thought to be connected to physiological processes including euphoric feelings, appetite modulation, and the release of sex hormones. Prolonged, continuous exercise contributes to an increased production and release of endorphins, resulting in a sense of euphoria that has been popularly labeled 'runner's high'" (*The Columbia Encyclopedia*, 6th edn., © 2001–5 Columbia University Press).

The Religious Life

According to a very large number of people around the world, the secret of the good life lies in devotion to a supernatural creator of the universe. It is difficult to estimate how many subscribe to what I am calling "the religious life" because calling oneself a believer is not the same as cultivating this belief as one's life philosophy. True believers make sense of everything that happens to them in terms of divine providence. Their self image, their conception of reality, and their hope for the future all hinge on the existence of God. To them, our time on earth is best spent serving him through our daily activities and worshipping him in our free time.

The problem with the religious life is that its only plausible interpretation collapses squarely into the running life. If God exists (and that is a big "if"), then he created the world as we know it today through the epically slow and gradual process of natural selection. Because, as premised at the beginning of this chapter, and as every reasonable person knows, EVOLUTION IS TRUE.

I say the existence of God is a big "if" because the theory of natural selection is completely sufficient to account for the history of the natural world without the need of any supernatural intervention. Nor do we need a God to set off the Big Bang since matter may have pre-existed this apparent beginning in another form. (If God can be eternal then so can the universe.) Nevertheless, the God hypothesis is consistent with evolution and evolution does not prove that he does not exist.

So, suppose God exists. On the supernatural version of evolution, sometimes known as "intelligent design theory," the mutations that lead to new species and that appear to us to be random are actually instances of divine guidance. Hence, God designed us to be hunter-gatherers. He need not have arranged for us to grow buttocks and the Achilles tendon. He need not have subjected us to 2.5 million years of violently intensive physical training. In fact, he could have designed us for kneeling on the floor, sitting in pews, or standing around chatting while downing cheap doughnuts and coffee. He manifestly did not. People who spend their free time doing these things die of heart disease, cancer, and diabetes – all modern ailments completely unknown to our athletic ancestors.[4] If God exists, then

---

[4] See Michael D. Lemonick and David Bjerklie, "How We Grew So Big: Diet and Lack of Exercise Are the Immediate Causes – But Our Problem Began in the Paleolithic Era," *Time*, 163/23, June 7, 2004, p. 23.

it seems we ought to do what he built us to do, namely, live the running life.

The Cultural Life

The life of culture, on the other hand, does not collapse into the running life. In fact, its devotees often openly disdain physical activity, preferring instead to sit and study something, be it people, books, pictures, music, or even television. For the purpose of this discussion, there is no need to make a distinction between "high" and "low" culture. Moreover, I am happy to include sport spectators in this category as well, since, for the spectator, sport is equivalent to an artistic performance. Culture devotees regard politics, science, and/or art (all very broadly construed) as the greatest good for human beings.

It would be absurd for anyone to deny the value of politics, science, or art. We all enjoy the fruits of these endeavors every day. But these endeavors constitute a life philosophy only if they are regarded as ends in themselves. Consider our other two categories. In the case of religion, the worship of God is the end to which all other activities are subordinated. If one eats, if one sleeps, if one goes somewhere or does anything at all, it is ultimately for the greater glory of the creator. Likewise for the biological way of life: one's every thought and deed is supposed to support and enhance physical fitness; anything inconsistent with this goal is pernicious and to be avoided. Proponents of religion and biology can both agree that politics, science, and art are all worthy enough insofar as they serve religion and biology respectively. Proponents of the cultural life philosophy, however, recognize no greater good than culture, and so regard culture as an end itself. This is problematic in each of the three areas of culture I have identified.

First, politics, which divides into two distinct camps. On the one hand, there are those who seek politics for its own sake, in other words, those who seek power. But power corrupts and the corrupt life is not the good life. On the other hand, there are those who seek politics for the sake of some vision of the good life. In so doing, they themselves prove that politics is not itself a life philosophy, but only a means to it.

Second, science. When attacking this area, I do not mean to attack practical knowledge or any kind of career training. The target is knowledge for knowledge's sake. As John Stuart Mill (1806–73) argues, grasping a wide range of background facts and thinking critically makes one better at any career, better at voting, and, most importantly, better at trivia games. Likewise, the value of scientific research lies in its applications, from the most frivolous high-tech toy to the most urgent medical cure. The only compelling challenge to this thesis concerns research done originally for its own sake that only later, perhaps by accident, resulted in an important application. But this challenge actually just proves my point: the application is what makes the knowledge valuable, even if retrospectively.

Third, art. Sensible people *use* art, for example, paintings to decorate the walls, film as a destination for a date, music as an accompaniment for driving, reading as a way to fall asleep, theater as a threat against sullen teenagers, etc. It is not sensible, however, to view art as an end in itself. To say that something is an end in itself is to say that it is the greatest good, the most important thing of all. This means you should sacrifice your life for it. Would you put a bullet in your head to save the Mona Lisa? Not me. We all know stories about crazy artists who sacrificed their lives for the sake of their art. That's why we call them crazy.

Objections

It becomes easy to see why fitness is the greatest good for human beings. Fitness is life, and life is the only legitimate end in itself. There is just one thing worth sacrificing one's own life for, namely, that of someone else. But this does not threaten my thesis.

Any conception of the good life for human beings is going to have to, not just be consistent with, but promote and nourish authentic interpersonal relationships. Most versions of the religious life mandate either family or other communal commitments while the cultural life conspicuously celebrates romance and citizenship. I contend that the biological life is equally if not more apt to accommodate our social needs and the possibility of true love. The reason is that strenuous exercise is the natural companion of sport. Serious runners, for example, typically race now and then – for fun and for inspiration. There is no better vehicle for human bonding than the teamwork and competition involved in sport. The triumph of victory, the agony of defeat, and even the steady ups and downs of daily striving create a compelling human drama. Sport is an excuse to spend time together. It facilitates our desire to know each other, to rely on each other, and to root for each other. An athlete is no less likely than a priest or a poet to be a true friend.

I suppose few would disagree with this last point. The salient objection I tend to encounter when discussing the running life concerns the idea of progress. Many reason that the modern sedentary lifestyle is a welcome improvement upon cave dwelling. Our ancestors fought their way out of this hardship. It took eons to separate the human species from the other animals. Surely intelligence is the crowning achievement of nature! If we are to follow the direction of evolution, it seems we should live by brain not by brawn. Accordingly, reverting to the primitive values involved in the running life seems backward and counterproductive.

My response to this objection is twofold. First and foremost, it is a mistake to see evolution as having a direction. Dinosaurs died out, not because they were inferior to lions, tigers, and bears but because environmental conditions happened to change. It is true that the human brain is a highly effective adaptation, enabling survival under a very broad range of environmental conditions. But this does not change the fact that our bodies are still calibrated for the active life. Fortunately, we don't need to go back to the caves. We can instead use our intelligence to design highly sophisticated sports equipment, such as tennis shoes with air bubbles in the soles, to make our exercise more enjoyable.

The second point I would like to make against the objection is that intelligence need not be equated with the domestication of modern life. It may be necessary to re-evaluate the alleged achievements of our mental machinations thus far. The philosopher John Zerzan, an outspoken critic of contemporary society, writes:

> Domestication involved the initiation of production, vastly increased divisions of labor, and completed the foundations of social stratification. This amounted to an epochal mutation both in the character of human existence and its development, clouding the latter with ever more violence and work. . . . Indeed, [primal] peoples had no conception of private property, and Rousseau's figurative judgment, that divided society was founded by the man who first sowed a piece of ground, saying "This land is mine," and found others to believe him, is essentially valid. . . . Work, as a distinct category of life, likewise did not exist until agriculture. The human capacity of being shackled to

crops and herds devolved rather quickly. Food production overcame the common absence or paucity of ritual and hierarchy in society and introduced civilized activities like the forced labor of temple-building.[5]

My concerns about both religion and culture crystallize in the notoriously inhumane and historically recent activity of temple building. Oppressed peasants built the pyramids, and how many of them were maimed or killed in the process? This tragedy is symbolic of civilization itself. It is worth asking, what is progress, and should we pursue it at the price of our collective health?

Conclusion

I conclude that the good life for human beings lies, not in religious or cultural pursuits, and especially not in philosophy, but rather in biology, and in running in particular. I should, however, give credit where credit is due. Philosophy is responsible for unlocking the secret in an indirect way. Philosophy gave birth to science, which made it possible for Darwin to discover evolution, which enables us, today, to know just exactly how we should be spending our time.[6]

[5] John Zerzan, *Elements of Refusal* (Seattle: Left Bank Books, 1988), p. 67.
[6] I would like to thank Earl Spurgin for critical comments on an earlier draft of this chapter.

Chapter 16
John Dewey and The Beautiful Stride
Running as Aesthetic Experience

Christopher Martin

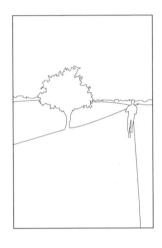

I have friends who seem unable (or unwilling) to grasp the value of running. When I debate with them about the value of road racing, jogging, or any other type of running as a worthwhile athletic endeavor, they often argue that while running may perhaps be a "healthy" practice, its place remains rather low on the podium of athletic activities. Why, they ask, would you spend hours on desolate trails or on the side of traffic-clogged roadways as you struggle through the tedious repetition of running, when you could better spend that time playing team sports like hockey or basketball that are both more social and more entertaining? For the dedicated runner, of course, these protests carry no great weight. We all know that running need not be repetitive or solitary.

Many of us runners are used to countering the concerns of the non-runner with detailed accounts of how we do things like change our route to keep things fresh or join up with running partners to aid in our training. Of course, at the end of our spirited defense, the non-runner will often politely (if not patronizingly) concede our points. Yet, we cannot help but notice that although they might acknowledge our passion and dedication to our chosen way of life, the non-runner is not completely convinced. Despite our best efforts to persuade them otherwise, running can appear to the outsider to be nothing more than obsessive nonsense, a cult whose deity is one of masochism. For them, running stands as the silly preoccupation of a group of people who would be much better off if they saw the light and joined the rest of humankind on the soccer pitch, football field, or (most lamentably in my opinion), the golf course.

Is there a more compelling justification for running, one that might enlighten the non-runner as to running's true value? Yes, running has a strong *aesthetic* value. Running fashions a powerful and unique *aesthetic*, that is, an artistic or beautiful experience for the runner. The idea that running could be aesthetic or beautiful is strange at first blush. When we think of aesthetic beauty, we usually think of the kind of artistic beauty seen in fine arts such as painting or sculpture. How is running supposed to be like fine art? Clearly, sweaty running clothes, skin chafe, and foot blisters are not aesthetically pleasing. The difficulty in recognizing the aesthetic in running is actually a problem of how we understand the nature of aesthetic experience itself. The philosopher and educator John Dewey (1859–1952) can help us here. In his classic book, *Art as Experience*, Dewey expands our idea of what commonly stands as the aesthetic. Dewey was part of a larger school of thought called pragmatism. Pragmatism, broadly conceived, argues that meaning and truth are determined by the success of our actions. If we act on a belief and the resulting action is satisfactory, then we say that our belief was warranted. Dewey applied his particular pragmatic theory to such areas as ethics, education, and aesthetics.

Running as Experience

Aesthetics is mainly about the study of the beautiful. When we sense something in our surroundings that appeals to us, we usually say that we are responding to its aesthetic nature. Philosophers curious about the nature of the aesthetic often try to find those standards by which we judge something to be aesthetically pleasing. What is it about a great work of art, for example, that allows us to respond to it so deeply? According to Dewey, traditional philosophy gives the aesthetic a status that sets it apart from the day-to-day experiences of human beings. Most theories of the aesthetic, in Dewey's view, have mistakenly taken the intensity of our experience of beauty to mean that it is somehow completely disconnected from our usual experience of the world. Because of this, many understandings of the aesthetic take fine arts as the ideal example of the beautiful. Consequently, the experience of the beauty of fine art is thought to be separate and distinct from daily experience. The "ideal" of the aesthetic is supposed to be a matter of escape from those things that are worldly and common such as the body and its sensations.

According to Dewey, the separation of the aesthetic from daily life is caused by modern society's valuing of the work of the mind over physical labor. This destroys a complete view of experience which recognizes that the body and mind work together. The body is then undervalued. As Dewey tells us, "prestige goes to those who use their minds without participation of the body and who act vicariously through control of the bodies and labor of others . . . under such conditions, sense and flesh get a bad name."[1] Consider, for example, the lower status unfairly afforded to manual labor. The devaluing of the body requires that the aesthetic be placed in a realm free from the material world of the body and rescued, so to speak, from the environment we live in. In this context, understanding the beautiful becomes more a case of grasping ideal forms that exist somewhere beyond our worldly existence. Fine art is believed to be beautiful because it is thought to come closest to embodying these forms.

This popular idea of the aesthetic as being divorced from the body and the everyday world makes the case for running as an aesthetic experience a difficult one to make. At best, we could perhaps argue that running is aesthetic when it is embodied in the near perfect form and motion of the professional runner, someone whose training and discipline have brought them to a state akin to a living work of art. Here, our understanding of the aesthetic in running might be more about the muscular form of the runner, the living sculpture wrapped in spandex and Ray-Ban sunglasses. In this case, the runner represents an ideal *object*. However, the runner is not himself or herself having an aesthetic *experience* as such (other than, perhaps, a vain appreciation of his or her own appearance).

Thankfully, according to Dewey, popular notions of the aesthetic are woefully inadequate. A more complete theory of the aesthetic, one he offers to us in *Art as Experience*, seeks to "restore continuity between the refined and intensified forms of experience that are works of art and everyday events, doings, and sufferings that are universally recognized to constitute experience" (p. 2). In other

[1] John Dewey, *Art as Experience* (London: Perigree, 1980), p. 22. All further page references in the text are to this work.

words, Dewey wants to stress the connection between the aesthetic and everyday experience. The aesthetic lies within this connection. But how?

Dewey begins by reminding us that people are always in contact with their surrounding environment. As we live our lives, we are always adjusting and adapting to the demands of our surroundings. For example, we all need food and shelter, and we all thrive on fresh air and in a pleasant living space. When these needs are met we enter into equilibrium, or balance, with our environment. However, our relationship with the environment is not always smooth. Our needs are not always met. As living creatures, our lives "[consist] of phases in which the organism falls out of step with the march of surrounding things and then recovers unison with it – either through effort or by some happy chance" (p. 12). In other words, being alive means experiencing moments in which the environment leaves us unable to meet our needs and wants, followed by moments where we experience the satisfaction of having these needs and wants fulfilled.

For Dewey, this struggle to gain equilibrium between ourselves and the environment reaches to the core of aesthetic experience. We become *conscious* or aware of being out of step with our environment, a consciousness that is experienced in the form of emotion. Needs, for example, can be satisfied, leading to an emotional state of fulfillment. Attempts to have needs met can also be defeated, leading to an emotional state of frustration. Consider the wide range of emotional states we pass through as we deal with situations in our daily lives, both good and bad. Lived experience becomes the source of those expressive and emotional moments that enable us to both recognize and create art.

In this way, connection with our environment is the *foundation* of aesthetic experience: "instead of signifying being shut up within one's own private feelings and sensations, [experience] signifies active and alert commerce with the world; at its height it signifies complete interpenetration of self and the world of objects and events" (p. 18). The rhythm of falling in and out of equilibrium that is experienced by all living things as they struggle to adapt to their environment, combined with a human, conscious awareness of this struggle, serves as the source of aesthetic experience. When we consider the nature of the aesthetic from this point of view, it makes no sense to see the aesthetic as something beyond the worldly. Rather, it is because experience is indeed "the fulfillment of an organism in its struggles and achievements in the world of things, it is the germ of art. Even in its rudimentary forms, it contains the promise of that delightful perception which is esthetic[2] experience" (p. 19). The link between our everyday lived experience and the aesthetic is undeniable.

The argument for an aesthetic experience specific to running, though not entirely clear at this point, at least becomes a possibility. Running is an experience because running involves an absolute "interpenetration" of the self and the world. The activity of running is defined by the terrain that we travel through: while running the world is never far from our feet. Be it through a forest trail or through a suburban neighborhood, running is indeed an experience that is continuous with the world we interact with. Hills and slopes, twists and turns all contribute to the completeness of such an experience. The importance of the environment to running becomes clear when we try to separate the bodily activity of running from our surroundings by trying, through the use of technology, to minimize and control the challenges presented by the environment. Most would agree that the treadmill, though allowing the runner to mimic the activity of running indoors (so that we are sheltered from the bad weather and difficult terrain) somehow takes away from the satisfaction and fulfillment of running. By contrast, authentic running is an activity that is completely open to the challenges and "disruptions" created by our surroundings. The runner focused on the *experience* of running remains open to the difficulties offered by a steep hill or high humidity. Runners do not try to control the environment, they become part of it. In fact, environmental change and disruption are conditions required for the *possibility* of running as an experience. Consider the enthusiasm that most runners have for trying out new routes in different places. Runners commonly use the Internet to find favored running routes at their vacation destination. The more different from our usual surroundings the better. Differing conditions, in presenting new challenges, combine with our running activity to produce radically different running experiences.

The runner's openness to his changing surroundings is due, in part, to the that fact that the relationship between environment and organism in running is more deeply connected than in many other activities. As we have seen, intimacy with our surroundings is required of running because the challenge offered by the terrain creates the

[2] Dewey uses the spelling "esthetic" for "aesthetic."

running experience. This intimacy contributes to the intense vitality of running experience. Recall that for Dewey, the emotional quality and vitality of experience is caused by the shifting between disorder and equilibrium that occurs as we struggle with our environment. While this kind of vitality can potentially occur in almost any kind of activity we undertake, the *aesthetic* character of experience is derived from the *intensity* of this vitality: "Experience in the degree that it *is* experience is heightened vitality" (p. 18).

Running as an activity is at the peak of vitality because of its deep relationship with its surroundings. The runner and environment come together to create a complete experience. In other words, the power of the experience of running lies partly in the fact that running *is* disorder and equilibrium. When we run, we are in constant communion with our terrain. We have segments of a run where we feel we are at equilibrium with the environment, as well as segments where our struggle with our environment becomes intense. When we begin our route, the body has to adapt to the new conditions of stress and movement that it has been subjected to as it "warms up." Muscles ache; we begin to perspire as a way of cooling down as body temperature rises; our breathing becomes more focused and regimented. Eventually the body adapts (hopefully!) and we achieve a fairly fluid and comfortable pace. We may begin to drift into our own thoughts, almost forgetting that we are running because our harmony with our surroundings becomes so complete. Yet, Dewey reminds us that were we to remain in this harmonious state indefinitely, we would not be having an experience: "without resistance from surroundings would the self become aware of itself; it would have neither feeling nor interest, neither fear nor hope, neither disappointment nor elation" (p. 62). Runners can become lost in the comforts of equilibrium: entire stretches of their run can be lost to memory. For the runner, this means that disequilibrium, or disorder, is crucial for running experience. Our comfortable pace, for example, can be stressed when we begin the upward climb of a steep hill. Consequently we become more aware of what we are doing. Experienced runners intuitively know that they need to do this. They actively move out of equilibrium by using the environment as a source of stress. Many of us include sprints in our route in order to increase the stress that the terrain causes the body. An otherwise mindless stretch of running route can become an engaging challenge. One reason for moving out of equilibrium is to condition the body. Another is to heighten our awareness of what we are doing, helping us to shape our activity into an authentic, complete experience.

Running as Aesthetic Experience

How exactly does this running experience become *aesthetic*? What is exceptional or distinctive about running? According to Dewey, though the potential for an aesthetic experience lies in many activities, such experience is often left unfocused. In our effort to get things done in our day-to-day activities, we tend to have a narrowed and incomplete experience. We fall into routines, for example, that are designed to make our tasks as easy and as smooth as possible. Ergonomics and efficiency are the dominant values of the day, preventing the fullness of an experience that would otherwise become aesthetic:

> the enemies of the esthetic are neither the practical nor the intellectual. They are the humdrum; slackness of loose ends; submission to convention in practice and intellectual procedure. Rigid abstinence, coerced submission, tightness on the one side and dissipation, incoherence and aimless indulgence on the other, are deviations in opposite directions from the unity of experience. (p. 42)

In other words, what separates us from the aesthetic is not its supposedly "ideal" or otherworldly nature. Rather, it is our modern way of life that undermines the kind of experiences required for aesthetic experience to happen.

Consider by contrast to this the focus of an experience intimately tied to the environment like running. Here we have an activity that can challenge Dewey's "enemies of the esthetic." Authentic experience has that "esthetic quality that rounds our experience into completeness and into unity" (p. 43). Running clearly qualifies, having a distinct beginning and a distinct end. By comparison, our usual activities blur together in a collection of small tasks, "dispersed and miscellaneous" (p. 46) as we are increasingly called upon to multi-task at the office or complete an endless list of errands at home. Running, on the other hand, has a clear and overriding focus. When we run, we have a certain beginning and end to our route. More importantly, we make sure that the task at hand is running and nothing else. The runner who wants a unified and integrated running experience does not run in order to complete errands. This does not mean that we cannot choose to literally run to the corner store instead of taking the car. It just means that this experience would be unlikely to become aesthetic. For the runner who wants an *aesthetic* running experience, the focus of his activity should remain on running and nothing else.

The Runner as Artist

This brings us to the final aspect of aesthetic experience. When we think of aesthetic experience as a matter of appreciating an art object like a painting or a sculpture, we tend to make a distinction between *making* the art object and *appreciating* it. Due to this distinction, we often make the further assumption that aesthetic experience is passive, as in listening to a beautiful piece of music. Of course, our emphasis thus far has been on the aesthetic as a particular *activity*, namely running. Indeed, the aesthetic does involve passive aspects of experience such as appreciation, perception, and enjoyment (p. 49). Furthermore, these more "passive" aspects are not necessarily foreign to the perspective of a runner in the midst of his running activity. Rather, aesthetic experience involves the combination of both active and passive elements. For Dewey, this combination of active and passive in aesthetic experience involves a balanced relationship between what, in his words, is "done" and what is "undergone" (p. 49). For any activity that we *do* also has the consequence that we *undergo* something. The action of running, for example, involves undergoing muscle strain and the sensation of the surface that we run on.

It is here that our analysis of running experience arrives at a more complete concept of the aesthetic. Aesthetic running is the deliberate creation of an experience that requires an intense, *vital* interaction between self and world that is valued as both an act that we do *and* as something that we undergo. Aesthetic running activity has the same qualities that Dewey says are characteristic of the activity of the artist:

> perception of [the] relationship between what is done and what is undergone constitutes the work of intelligence, and because the artist is controlled by the process of his work by his grasp of the connection between what he has done and what he is to do next . . . a painter must consciously undergo the effect of his every brush stroke or he will not be aware of what he is doing or where his work is going. (p. 47)

We runners do not have to strain too far to see the similarities between Dewey's description of the activity of the artist and the activity of the runner. As we run, we are controlled, to a degree, by what we undergo. We must attend to the movement of our legs, consciously monitor our speed, and make all sorts of intelligent assessments of our bodily state and surroundings, using the information at hand to guide our actions. Like the artist, our experience of the world can proceed at a level that is truly poetic. The relationship between body and world changes as the division between our self and surroundings is overcome. On the one hand, we do more than race to our final destination; we experience what we *undergo* while running *as* running. On the other hand, we do more than indulge in the movements of our body; when we run we *do* something that has direction and purpose as we approach the end of our route. *If* we allow ourselves to undergo disruption and equilibrium, *if* we allow ourselves to be open to the surroundings through which we run, *if* we undertake the action of running as an activity in itself, *if* we have an endpoint at which we can say that we have finished running, if we have all these things, we can look back and say that we've had an aesthetic running experience. Compared, for example, to the soccer player who sprints with single-minded purpose to the soccer ball in an effort to attain his goal, the runner's entire being is involved in the composition of an aesthetic running experience.

Chapter 17
"Where the Dark Feelings Hold Sway"
Running to Music

Martha C. Nussbaum

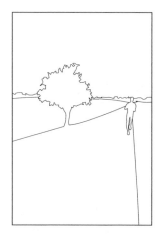

Like many runners, I run to music. But, like many serious distance runners, I don't approve of earphones. The usual points about danger and distraction have some weight with me, but my deeper reason is that I like to play music in my head. That way I can be my own programmer and conductor, shifting the tempo to harmonize with my speed, choosing the work, or section within the work, to suit my rhythm, fatigue level, and emotional state. Because I am a great lover of opera, it is primarily opera to which I listen in my head, although other pieces of classical music, Cole Porter songs, and Gilbert and Sullivan sometimes enter in. (What I say here about opera could, however, easily apply to other types of music that the reader may prefer.) When I am really tired at the end of a long run, I find myself atavistically returning to early childhood and the Episcopal hymns I used to sing in the junior choir in Bryn Mawr Pennsylvania, most of which have plodding, march-like beats, and some of which have lyrics indicative of suffering and endurance. I have gotten through the final mile of a training run pretty often to the tune of "Those dear tokens of His passion / Still His dazzling body bears / Cause of endless exultation / To His ransomed worshippers. / With what rapture with what rapture / Gaze we on those glorious scars." (I converted to Judaism in my twenties, so there's no longer a theological meaning in this for me.) In jauntier moments, I might end a training run to the hymn-tune version of Blake's "Jerusalem."

On the Road to Another World

Hearing music in your head takes preparation, because you have to know the music very well if you are going to play it to yourself in your head. That is part of the fun. For each half-marathon or marathon for which I'm training, I choose an opera, and I play a good CD of it over and over, often while I am dressing and stretching before a run, looking at the libretto and trying to memorize it. I then listen to bits of the work in my head during training runs, especially long runs (along the Chicago lakeshore), working up to a more sequential "playing" during the race itself. So in effect I focus intensely on that one opera for around three to four months.

Some operas that I love don't work well for running. Wagner operas, for example, are hopeless, because of their lush late-night quality. (For related reasons, I never play in my head, while running, the works of Mahler, a composer who is very important to me.) Verdi and Puccini seem on the whole not to work very well, or only isolated bits of them. I have run happily to *Fidelio*, and I recently ran a race during the holiday season to Humperdinck's *Hansel and Gretel*. But Mozart operas are my particular favorites because of their endless variety of emotion and mood, and because of a deeply affirmative and humane serenity that appears to underlie all their shifts of tone and rhythm. I have run races to *Figaro*, *Così Fan Tutte*, *Don Giovanni*, even *Die Entführung aus dem Serail*, but on balance *Figaro* is particularly superb, and I am just now planning to run a second long race to it, thus favoring it over all others.

I usually have a general plan, such as: I'll run the first hour to act 1, the second hour to act 2, and so on. That means that I play to myself the salient parts of that act, more or less in order – leaving out recitatives and sometimes ensembles. As a former singer, I find it a lot easier to learn the arias than the rest. (So *Così Fan Tutte* has been unusually difficult for me to learn, with its larger proportion of ensemble to solo.) But usually I don't stick to the plan, because I like to repeat things, or I jump ahead to find something that is more in keeping with my mental state. Often in the middle of a long run I want something very serene, and I jump ahead to the Countess's "Porgi amor" ("Give, o love") or, in a recent *Don Giovanni* period, to Ottavio's "Dalla sua pace" ("My peace depends on hers"). During the later parts of a long run, I often need to be revved up a little, so I jump ahead to a part about anger or vengeance, such as the Count's aria "Vedrò mentre io sospiro" ("Shall I, while I live, see my servant happy?"), or Osmin's, "Ha, wie will ich triumphieren" ("Ha, how I shall triumph when they take you to the place of judgment and slit your necks right through"), both of which are *great* at mile 15 along the lakeshore, especially the part that goes "und die Hälse schüren zu," "and they slit your necks right through," which is sung to such a jaunty cheerful melody that it cannot be resisted, even by tired feet. (Some readers may have this experience in connection with angry hip-hop, or heavy metal.) A more mercifully angry song, on the note of which I ended one lovely half-marathon in northern Wisconsin, is Elvira's "Mi tradi quell'alma ingrata" ("The ungrateful one betrayed me") from the end of *Don Giovanni*, in which she denounces the villainous betrayer, but promises to forgive him if he comes back to her. For speed drills on the track, still other parts are appropriate: I particularly like "Giovanette che fate all'amore" from *Don Giovanni* (the opening of Zerlina's wedding scene, where all the young girls are dancing around).

My habits produce cultural anomalies that I find amusing, and also significant, because they are examples of the fact that in today's world all cultures are heterogeneous and new minglings of allegedly separate cultures are always occurring. When I find myself listening to Humperdinck's "Tra la la, Hunger ist der beste Koch" ("Hunger is the best cook") as I run around Lodhi Garden in New Delhi, India – well, that's in one way very funny, and a triumph of cosmopolitan sympathy over racist exclusionism, because Humperdinck was a protégé of Wagner who probably would have been absolutely appalled to think of his music being conjured up by a Jewish woman in a stronghold of the allegedly lower races of the East. In another way, though, Humperdinck's insight into the struggles of the poor and the extreme importance of even one meal to a person living on the margins of society – the father is singing about the fact that poor people get by with almost nothing and are hungry all the time – chimes in very fittingly with the development work that I'm in India to do. I think that Humperdinck would actually have taken a keen interest in these development issues, if he could have managed to put his racism to one side. There are common human abilities and opportunities that link us all, despite profound cultural differences.

When I run, then, I do have some side-thoughts connected to my work in political philosophy, which focuses on issues of human need and capability and defends a set of cross-cultural norms.[1] For the most part, though, I enter a world of the imagination, a dreamlike invisible world where, as Mahler wrote, "the *dark* feelings hold sway, at the door which leads into the 'other world' – the world in which things are no longer separated by space and time."[2] The ability to enter this world is connected, I believe, to the way in which running opens up the body and makes it possible to think beneath the surface of articulate language – which, for Mahler, also meant to think fluently and creatively, beneath the surface of habit.

Music and the Expression of Emotion: A Philosophical Problem

Here we arrive at a difficult issue, which has frustrated philosophers over the years.[3] I don't believe I make progress on the issue while I am running, but it does seem to me that my musical experiences during running have helped me see where the solution to the problem might lie. The issue is how we should think of the fact, which seems evident enough, that music expresses emotions. We say of some music that it is joyful, of other music that it is sad. Some music seems to express tender longing; other music expresses the agony of unfulfilled desire. We make these judgments all the time, not only about opera and programmatic music, but about music with no storyline and no verbal accompaniment. We seem to assume, when we do so, that we are talking sense. But it has been very difficult to say exactly how these ascriptions of emotional properties to music work.

Three claims, all of them plausible, define our problem:

1 Music contains (expresses) emotions;
2 Emotions contain linguistically formulable propositions;
3 Music does not contain linguistically formulable propositions.

[1] See Martha C. Nussbaum, *Women and Human Development* (New York and Cambridge: Cambridge University Press, 2000) and *Frontiers of Justice: Disability, Nationality, Species Membership* (Cambridge, MA: Harvard University Press, 2005).
[2] Letter to Max Marschalk of March 26, 1896. Quoted in Deryck Cooke, *Gustav Mahler: An Introduction to his Music* (New York: Cambridge University Press, 1980), p. 54.
[3] I discuss the issues presented here more fully in Martha C. Nussbaum, *Upheavals of Thought: The Intelligence of Emotions* (New York and Cambridge: Cambridge University Press, 2001), especially chapters 5 and 14.

It is impossible to endorse, consistently, all three of these claims. So we must modify something, or give something up. Most people find (1) and (3) obvious. (2) becomes plausible on a little reflection. When we think of complex emotional experiences, experiences, let's say, of grief, or anger, we see that they are not simply powerful feelings or bodily states. They involve thought about an object, and these thoughts appear to be necessary constituent parts of the emotion itself. When I grieve, I don't just have a stomach ache: I am focused on the person I have lost, and my grief contains not only a representation of that person, but also a variety of thoughts about the person, prominently including the thought that this person is lost, or gone, or dead, and also the thought of the importance of the person in my life. Pain without those thoughts would simply not be grief. Again, I might be in a state of irritation, but I can rightly be said to be angry only if I have certain thoughts about what has happened: usually, the thought that someone has damaged willingly and inappropriately something or someone that is important to me, and that the damage is reasonably serious. We may, of course, argue about the precise family of thoughts that we want to include in an account of what makes an emotion anger, but some such thoughts seem to be crucial in making the emotion anger, rather than some other painful state, such as grief or fear.

How Might Music Contain Genuine Emotions?

Many philosophers have thought that (2) is correct, in the form in which I stated it. They therefore have problems seeing how music, which is not linguistic, can contain genuine emotions. Eduard Hanslick, the great nineteenth-century musicologist whose book *On the Musically Beautiful* is still one of the greatest works in musical aesthetics, decided that (2) had to be right, and that therefore all our ascriptions of emotional properties to music were merely metaphorical, ways of talking about musical structure that really should be eliminated in favor of a more precise musical language.[4] Arthur Schopenhauer, the highly influential nineteenth-century philosopher whose writing about music, in *The World as Will and Representation*

---

[4] Eduard Hanslick, *On the Musically Beautiful*, trans. G. Payzant (Indianapolis, IN: Hackett Publishing, 1986). (Hanslick's work was originally written in 1854.)

exercised enormous influence over his contemporaries, decided that (1) must be correct, music really does embody genuine emotions.[5] To solve the problem, he dropped (2): he held that emotions involve dynamic and rhythmic features, but not linguistically formulable thoughts, and not, indeed, thought of any sort at all. He thought that music was the representation of what he called the Will, by which he meant not willpower, but a force of erotic striving that he conceived of as fundamentally unintelligent, and present in all of nature, and he thought that all human emotions were forms of this unintelligent force. I believe that Schopenhauer's position cannot be adequate, for the reasons I just crudely sketched, though much more obviously needs to be said.

Modern philosophers of art have usually followed either Schopenhauer or Hanslick. (The very distinguished twentieth-century aesthetician Suzanne Langer produced a quite powerful account of a Schopenhauerian position in her important book *Feeling and Form*.)[6] Few have been willing to abandon (3), but the fine musicologist Deryck Cooke did so, producing an account of music as a genuine language, in a book suitably entitled *The Language of Music*.[7] I believe that his attempt, bold and interesting though it was, did not succeed, in part because he focused on semantics only and did not attend at all to morphology or syntax, crucial features of any language. But readers must judge for themselves.

In my view the entire debate goes astray very early, when it assumes that thoughts are intrinsically linguistic. So, if emotions contain thoughts, these must be verbal in nature, or straightforwardly formulable in words. But think about the fact that we begin to experience emotions as small infants, long before we can speak a language. After we learn to speak, language may often shape our emotions, but it seems implausible that we cannot have emotions without words. (Such emotions are often a part of the runner's experience.) Think, too, of the fact that very many non-human animals would appear to have emotions such as fear, anger, and even, in some cases, compassion. We should not dismiss that idea as a crude anthropomorphism:

[5] Arthur Schopenhauer, *The World as Will and Representation*, 2 vols., trans. E. F. J. Payne (New York: Dover Publications, 1969). (The work was originally published in 1818.)

[6] Suzanne K. Langer, *Feeling and Form: A Theory of Art* (New York: Charles Scribner's Sons, 1953).

[7] Deryck Cooke, *The Language of Music* (New York: Oxford University Press, 1959).

by now most cognitive psychologists who study animals would insist that they do indeed have emotions, and that emotions play a necessary role in their ability to function well in their environment, marking certain goals as salient, others as greatly to be avoided. A young creature without fear would not live very long.

Now the Schopenhauer position rears its head again. For people may be very tempted to say, yes, small children and non-human animals have emotions, but these emotions do not contain thought. They are just bodily states, or objectless feelings. They do not have the complex directedness and the thought-content that characterizes the emotions of a human adult. But can this be correct? What is it to have fear, if not to have a thought of bad things impending, things that are pretty important for one's well-being. Without that thought, directed outwards toward some object or objects in the world, a trembling is just trembling, not full-fledged fear. When a small child wakes up terrified in the night, is she just having a bunch of very unpleasant feelings? That is not what parents typically think, when they soothe the child by addressing its thoughts about the world: everything is all right, there is no monster under the bed, etc. Even if the child cannot yet speak, the parent adopts gestures and tones of voice aimed at convincing the child that the world is benign and not hostile.

The real problem here is what I might call language-imperialism, the tendency to think that all intelligence is essentially linguistic. (The philosopher Nelson Goodman argued well against language-imperialism in his important book, *Languages of Art*.)[8] We don't really believe that all intelligence is linguistic, since we recognize the existence of other intelligent media of expression: visual art, gesture, dance, and, of course, music. But the minute we admit them to the class of intelligent forms of symbolic activity, we tend immediately to think that we need to reduce them to language in order to show how they could possibly be intelligent.

The commonsense position, it seems to me, is that our minds register what is happening to our important goals and ends in many ways, some of them linguistic, some of them pictorial, some of them simply involving complex forms of perception, in which a creature sees some object in the world *as* good or bad for its well-being. What emotions require is that sort of complex object-directed thought,

[8]   Nelson Goodman, *Languages of Art* (Indianapolis, IN: Bobbs-Merrill, 1968).

which need not be linguistic. We see X as Y, where X is an object, and Y is something in the realm of good and bad, in reference to our own goals and projects. Often we may be able to make a rough and ready translation of these non-linguistic perceptions into words, describing the inner life of a baby in words that the baby could not possibly comprehend. (Psychologist Daniel Stern's *Diary of a Baby* is a very successful attempt to do just that.)[9] But we must always remember that the project is one of translation, not faithful replication.

En Route to a Solution: The Experiences of the Musical Runner

Here I believe that runners' experiences are quite helpful. For runners know that not all emotions are verbal, or easily verbalizable. The body has its own ways of perceiving the world, which often take over from language when one is settled into a rhythm. Joy is a way of seeing the world in which the whole body seems to leap forward toward the things that the eyes see as good. Longing is exemplified in the straining of muscles and tendons toward a perceived goal. In such moments we gain a better understanding of what the emotions of non-human animals may be like, and why it would be foolish to deny that such emotions exist, involve thought of a kind, and move creatures toward their objects of desire.

Music, like visual art, is a highly elaborate set of symbolic structures. But that gives us no reason at all to think of it as inherently linguistic. Music also exemplifies forms of striving, longing, and so on that involve us (insofar as we identify with the point of view of the music) in a set of thoughts that is genuinely emotional, such as the thought of the irrevocable loss of love, the thought of our agonizing distance from all that is good and fine, the thought of the wondrous beauty of life, and so forth. To put these thoughts into words is to translate and, usually, to distort them. The words are only a way of pointing us toward an experience that is intrinsically musical. On this point Hanslick was correct: we need to follow the symbolic activity of the music itself, not always to be treating it as a storyline that can be represented by a verbal outline. But we should not take

---

[9] Daniel Stern, *Diary of a Baby* (New York: Basic Books, 1990).

the absence of the word to be equivalent to the absence of thought. That is where both Hanslick and Schopenhauer go astray.

Indeed, Gustav Mahler insisted (in the many letters he wrote on these matters) that the thoughts embodied in music are frequently fresher, deeper, and more accurate than the thoughts that we express using words.[10] This is so because words are the shopworn medium of daily social exchange. They have become blunted by familiarity (a reason why great poets strive to recall us to the freshness of words, by using them in unconventional ways). Music can cut beneath habit and enter a part of the personality that is less defended, more receptive, than the parts we show one another in our daily conversations. (Readers will not have missed the fact that in my musical running I have access to a very powerful anger, and an unadulterated guilt-free pleasure in anger, which I do not permit myself in daily life. I mean, if Mozart can express it, it must be all right, at least for a short time!) We should not expect musical emotion-thoughts to involve clear logical progress, or even the recognition of distinct objects, he adds, because the world of music, unlike the visible world, is a dreamlike world, where things are often indistinct and dark. (In this way the world of music resembles the world of our early childhood emotions, a further source of music's tremendous power.)

Not all music embodies emotions, but a lot of music does. When we listen to that sort of music, it invites us to occupy a position from which, if we listen well and knowledgeably (with enough familiarity with the traditions in which the work was produced), we will have a series of emotions, sometimes highly specific, sometimes vague and amorphous. These emotions succeed each other with kaleidoscopic and tumultuous rapidity, and we often cannot trace the logical connections among them; there is rarely an orderly "plot line" of the sort that gives coherence to our experience of reading a novel. Our experience unfolds rather as it does in a dream, and often with the unusual intensity of dreaming. (As Mahler says, describing his own music, "A burning pain crystallizes.")

Even though the emotions embodied in music are often dreamlike and obscure, they may be in their own way extremely precise. It

[10] Gustav Mahler, *Selected Letters of Gustav Mahler,* ed. Alma Mahler and Knud Martner, trans. Eithne Wilkins and Ernst Kaiser (London and Boston: Faber and Faber, 1979); Alma Mahler and Gustav Mahler, *Memories and Letters,* ed. Knud Martner and D. Mitchell, trans. D. Creighton, 3rd edn. (Seattle: University of Washington Press, 1985).

would be difficult to differentiate the many varieties of love and longing in words with the same precision with which music often accomplishes that differentiation. The music of Wagner's *Tristan* embodies a love that is aching unassuagable longing, love that takes the lover straight out of life into death, because nothing in the world can satisfy it. The love-duet at the end of Monteverdi's *L'Incoronazione di Poppaea* also depicts an erotic fascination that blots out the world, but in a very different way, showing that sexual passion provides lovers with its own very powerful, and renewable, source of satisfaction, if only the lovers can kill off anyone who stands in their way. In both works we hear the quality of obsession, but in one case the obsession leads to death; in the other it celebrates the triumph of sex over morality, empire, and good sense.

Even when words go with music, as in opera and in parts of Mahler's symphonies, it is important to insist that the music is not just a vehicle for an emotional meaning that is primarily conveyed through the words. Words may give us a general orientation: for example, we're dealing with revenge, or with death and mourning, or even, with the death of a child. But the words usually don't tell us the precise shadings of such ideas. Often, indeed, the text of a song or a symphonic movement may be quite general, underdetermining the specific emotions that the music more precisely evokes – the reason why settings of the same poem by two different composers (and the interpretations of a standard by different jazz musicians) can be so revealingly different in their emotional trajectory. To take one of my running examples, we could imagine a composer who would set the words of Osmin's triumph aria to a very menacing and ugly melody, depicting in that way the hideousness of revenge, and suggesting that revenge is obviously hateful. Mozart's setting is very different – because it is so sunny, happy in a totally non-vicious way, even lovable. I would say that it expresses the revenge-thoughts of a childlike person who has no real conception of the damage that his plans will do to real people, and who is in that way unusually seductive because not ugly. (A good Osmin will caper about in a very endearing way, and will be loved by the audience.) Mozart shows us how tempting such revenge is, because it is so jolly. In that way (as usual), he provokes thought.

Similarly, when, at the end of *The Marriage of Figaro*, the Countess counters her husband's refusal of mercy with the wonderful line, "I am more gentle, and I say yes" ("più docile io sono, e dico di sì"),

Mozart might have set Da Ponte's words to music suggesting that she is being sly, or manipulative, or grudging – or perhaps that she is simply exhausted. Instead he chooses a phrase that expresses most sublimely the responsive and yielding quality of genuine love, a quality that accepts the vulnerability in the self that love, unlike revenge, entails, and that yields to that vulnerability. All that is not in the Da Ponte text, it is in the music. (And in the performance of the music, another important topic. The score is itself an indeterminate set of indications, to be brought alive only by the performer, and in this sense Kiri Te Kanawa's rendition of that line expresses the ideas that I have just mentioned more perfectly than many other renditions.)

My argument could only be carried further by turning, at this point, to the detailed analysis of musical works. Any good such analysis would not talk only about symphonic and operatic music in the Western tradition. It would also talk about jazz, blues, rock, hip-hop, and much more. (So it will have to be written by many people, since it can only be done well in each case by someone who knows the tradition in question and its musical idiom, including highly specific things, such as, in my own case, when I write on Mahler, how Mahler uses the clarinet, or the harp. Analogous details are crucial to the analysis of rock, jazz, and most other types of music.) It should also take up various types of non-Western music. Indian philosophy, for example, contains a rich tradition of analysis on this topic, which can only be adequately understood and conveyed to others by someone who knows Indian classical music and its subtleties.

In the background, however, I think that all work on that topic might bear in mind the experiences of the musical runner, especially such a runner's experience of thoughts that are embodied, surging, striving, yet not verbal, and of powerful emotions connected to those thoughts or, rather, partially embodied in them.

Chapter 18
The Power of Passion on Heartbreak Hill

Michelle Maiese

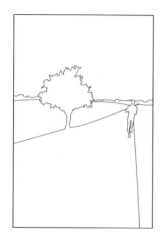

Living Through a Marathon

"What is it like to run a marathon?" I've been asked this question numerous times and never found it easy to provide a quick and informative answer. Running an endurance race is a unique experience that involves a myriad array of feelings and sensations. At some moments it feels like a journey through hell, while at other times it seems like one of the most thrilling days of one's life. Over the course of several hours, a marathoner is bound to undergo all sorts of bodily and emotional experiences. For better or for worse, what it's like to be running a marathon can change radically over the course of a mile.

As I struggled up "Heartbreak Hill" in the Boston Marathon several years ago, I felt a cramp forming in my side and pain in my quads. Suddenly I felt panicky and afraid: was I going to vomit? I knew that if the hill did not end soon, my legs were sure to give out on me. After several months of physical and psychological training and a few hours of running, the finish-line seemed out of my reach. I feared that my feelings of discomfort and delirium had settled in for good and that I was about to "hit the wall." Visions of me riding a medical vehicle to the finish-line danced in my head, and I was not sure if I dreaded this scenario or longed for it.

Dragging my weary body around a corner, I saw the throng of people in the crowd grow larger. Suddenly the cheering and clapping grew louder and I saw college students holding balloons and waving banners. Music blaring from boom boxes aroused feelings of pride, excitement, and hope. In a matter of seconds my cramps diminished, my strides lengthened, and my fears of "the wall" vanished. I tried to picture myself sprinting across the finish-line, and all of a sudden I felt energized and determined. Completing the race seemed possible again.

Could my zombie twin have accomplished this feat? Could she have overcome the pain and discomfort, both physiological and psychological, that inevitably sets in somewhere between miles 18 and 20? I argue that she could not, and that this fact has important implications for philosophy of mind. Philosophy of mind is the branch of philosophy that deals with the nature of consciousness and its place in the physical world. One question that philosophers of mind must answer is whether the "what-it's-like" aspect of consciousness can be accounted for in exclusively physical terms. For example, are the marathoner's feelings of joy and pride when she realizes that she has achieved a personal record simply a matter of neurophysiology, or are they something over and above brain states?

Materialists hold that mental states are either identical to brain states or realized (brought into existence) by them, so that a creature's state of mind can be accounted for purely in terms of its neurophysiology. Dualists, on the other hand, maintain that an individual's mental states and brain states are somehow distinct, so that the marathoner's desire to run the race is something over and above brain chemistry and the firing of neurons. David Chalmers is a contemporary philosopher of mind who argues for a form of dualism and maintains that materialism is mistaken. According to Chalmers,[1] the fact that "phenomenal zombies" are possible illustrates that the phenomenal features of consciousness (such as what it is like to cross the finish-line) are something over and above its physical features (such as the release of certain chemicals in the brain). Two individuals that have the very same neurophysiology need not have the very same mental life.

As Chalmers describes things, a zombie is a molecule-for-molecule duplicate of me that enters into the same causal relations that I do

---

[1] David Chalmers, *The Conscious Mind: In Search of a Fundamental Theory* (New York: Oxford University Press, 1996), chapter three, pp. 93–122. Note that in this book, Chalmers offers numerous arguments in support of his view that materialism is mistaken. Here I wish to focus on the zombie argument.

Michelle Maiese

and yet lacks phenomenal experience. Phenomenal experience is the unique felt character associated with each individual's mental life and is a matter of what emotions, perceptions, beliefs, and desires *feel like from the inside*. Chalmers wishes to make a distinction between the causal face of consciousness (such as information processing and action) and the phenomenal face of consciousness (the qualitative, "what-it's-like" aspect of subjective experience). Along these lines, he distinguishes between the "easy" and "hard" problems of consciousness. According to Chalmers, accounting for the marathoner's ability to calculate her splits and lengthen her stride is the "easy" problem because this can be explained simply in terms of brain mechanisms. For example, one might view the brain as a sophisticated computer that can process information and perform various forms of computation.

The "hard" problem, on the other hand, is to account for phenomenal consciousness and explain why in addition to this constant processing of information, there is a subjective aspect to our mental states. Phenomenal consciousness is the private, directly experienced, felt side of mental life. Just as there is something that it is like to remember something, see the color red, and experience a stream of thought, there is something that it is like to experience "runner's high." Why is it that beginning a marathon, reaching mile 20, and bumping into other runners at water stations are all accompanied by phenomenal experience (i.e. experience with a distinct subjective, inner feel)? Chalmers argues that because these qualitative conscious experiences cannot be accounted for simply in terms of neurophysiology, materialism cannot be true. A creature's phenomenal consciousness is something over and above its physical make-up.

The notion that zombies are possible suggests that two creatures that are physically identical and perform the very same actions could be radically different in terms of their phenomenal experiences. In brief, one of these individuals could have a life rich with phenomenal experience, while the other individual could lack these experiences and yet do the very same things. Such an argument, if sound, would show that phenomenal consciousness and neurophysiology are distinct[2] and thereby demonstrate that materialism is mistaken (a conclusion which many readers may find appealing). Note that I believe

---

[2] In Chalmers' language, it would show that phenomenal consciousness does not logically supervene on (i.e. is not logically necessitated by) underlying physical features.

that zombies are conceivable and logically possible. After all, the notion of such a creature is not logically incoherent in the same way that a round square is logically incoherent. However, if we were to accept that zombies are possible in the actual world or in worlds similar to ours,[3] we would also have to accept that phenomenal consciousness makes no causal difference to our lives. For example, whether or not an individual experienced excitement, "runner's high," or pride would make no difference in his or her efforts to complete a race. However, is it true that the qualitative aspect (the "what-it's-like") of subjective experience plays no causal role in bringing about and sustaining action?

I believe that subjective experience does make a significant causal contribution to our lives and that a creature that was devoid of such experience would behave quite differently from an ordinary human being. Because phenomenal consciousness has tremendous motivational power, a zombie could not run a marathon. In fact, I think that one could make an even stronger claim to the effect that zombies are *incapable of genuine agency* because they lack the requisite passion and motivation. In short, a physical duplicate of me who is utterly feeling-less and yet performs the same actions I do is *metaphysically impossible*.

Breaking Through "the Wall": Overcoming Motivational Gaps

If zombies are metaphysically possible, then it is possible for there to be a world very similar to ours in which the causal processes of conscious agents exist without subjective experience. One might then regard this phenomenal aspect of consciousness as totally distinct from the causal and behavioral functions of consciousness, which include speech and action. This would mean that the qualitative aspect of subjective experience contributes nothing to these causal processes. It would then be what philosophers of mind call an

---

[3] In other words, while Chalmers may be right that zombies are *logically* possible, they are not *metaphysically* possible (in the sense that they exist in some possible world) or *nomologically* possible (in the sense that they are consistent with natural laws of our actual world). Thus, even if his zombie argument succeeds in demonstrating that logical supervenience is mistaken, this does not prove that all forms of materialism are mistaken.

Michelle Maiese

epiphenomenon, a feature of the world that is utterly lacking in causal power.[4] However, I believe that instances of mental and physical effort provide strong evidence that qualitative experience plays an important causal role in motivating action. How consciousness seems is linked to what consciousness does.

To see the causal power of phenomenal consciousness, consider the case of the marathon runner. Her attention is focused on how her legs are feeling, what strategy to adopt for the miles ahead, and how best to tackle the hill that is coming up. In addition to feeling many bodily sensations and hearing the cheering of the crowd, she experiences various emotions: excitement, pride, and hope. What it is like to experience these sensations and emotions seems to play a direct causal role in sustaining the marathoner's efforts. For example, there is something that it is like to feel a flood of anticipation as she begins the last mile of the race, and this phenomenal quality is part of what causes her to sprint toward the finish-line. If she did not feel exhilarated and determined, she would have little reason to try to move her legs faster. I believe that such instances of effort illustrate the causal power of phenomenal consciousness.

At this point, of course, many philosophers of mind will suggest that it is the surge of adrenaline that causes the runner to sprint, and that the subjective experiences of the runner play no integral role here at all. On this view, the case of the marathon runner will not demand that we take phenomenal consciousness seriously. It will simply be another example of how brain chemistry and the firing of neurons bring about action. If it is merely adrenaline that leads her to sprint, the case gives us no reason to endorse the notion that phenomenal experience has causal power.

Because it would be difficult to deny that adrenaline and various brain processes do play an integral role in causing the runner to sprint, I do not wish to suggest that action is the result of causes that are wholly non-physical. However, I believe that cases in which initiating or sustaining action is particularly difficult demonstrate that brain activity on its own is insufficient to cause action. For example, suppose that you have a long run scheduled for today and you find yourself wanting to skip it and go out for happy hour instead. In order to accomplish your running goals for the day and overcome

---

[4] Chalmers describes an epiphenomenon as a feature "hanging off the engine of physical causation, but making no difference in the physical world" (Chalmers, p. 150).

this motivational hurdle, you will have to give yourself an extra push. One strategy frequently suggested in running magazines is to try to imagine how energized and happy you will feel after going for your scheduled run. The promise of future pleasure and emotional contentment helps you to overcome your lack of motivation, and before you know it, you are lacing up your running shoes.

No doubt similar motivational obstacles arise during a marathon. Suppose that both Alexandra and her zombie counterpart have reached mile 22 of the race.[5] They have been running for several hours and their physiology reflects this fact: their heart rates are up; they are becoming dehydrated; their lungs are working overtime; and their bodies are starting to run out of stored carbohydrates. Suddenly they begin to ascend a rather steep and steady incline and their bodies think that it is time to stop running and call it a day. It takes every ounce of effort that they have to continue running, and both of them know that they have "hit the wall." How do they keep themselves motivated to continue running and finish the race? What is it that fills the runner's motivational gap and allows her to continue running well after her body and physiology tell her it is time to stop?

Note that while Alexandra is experiencing feelings of pain and discomfort, her zombie counterpart feels none of this. At first this might appear to give the zombie an advantage. After all, without undergoing any pain, wouldn't it be easier to complete a marathon? However, it is important to note that in addition to being devoid of pain, her zombie counterpart is devoid of the emotional experiences of hope, pride, and excitement that motivate Alexandra and lead her to continue running well after the pain sets in. Even though Alexandra and her counterpart both undergo a surge of adrenaline, only Alexandra experiences the corresponding feelings of excitement and exhilaration. Only Alexandra understands what it's like to hear the cheering of the crowd and hear music at mile-marker 19. Despite some uncomfortable bodily sensations, the "what-it's-like" of nearing the finish-line helps to keep Alexandra's legs moving. Her zombie counterpart, on the other hand, receives no such phenomenal or emotional rewards.

If a surge of adrenaline did not feel like anything, would it have enough motivational power to keep a marathoner going? If, on the

---

[5] Of course, it is also unclear whether a zombie would ever even *begin* to run a marathon or be capable of reaching mile 22. I assume it is possible at this point simply for the sake of argument.

other hand, this surge of adrenaline felt painful rather than pleasurable, might it lead an individual to stop running? The notion that phenomenal experience has no link to motivation runs contrary to common sense. After all, action is largely a matter of will and desire, and what feels good in a physiological and emotional sense strongly influences what we strive toward and want. If a surge of adrenaline did not feel like anything, it would not have enough motivational power to keep the marathoner going. In short, what it's like to hear people cheering for you has motivational power not simply because of the brain chemistry involved, but also because of the qualitative feel of such experiences. If the marathoner's brain activity is to sustain action and keep her legs moving, it must be accompanied by various emotional experiences. On their own, a creature's neurophysiology and brain chemistry are not enough to bridge these types of motivational gaps and sustain a runner's efforts for 26 miles.

Therefore, while Alexandra is able to break through "the wall" and finish the race, her zombie counterpart is likely to stop as soon as soon as her body and physiology determine that it is time to do so. I have suggested that what fill the marathoner's "motivational gap" are her feelings of excitement, pride, and hope. Thus, I argue that it is only as felt and *infused with emotion* that many of our desires have the strength or impetus to sustain our efforts.[6] *Conscious emotional experiences and feelings play an indispensable causal role in bringing about action.* Because a zombie lacks all such experiences and does not have any such passion for the activities she undertakes, it is difficult to imagine that she could break through "the wall."

Knowing When to Stop and Overcoming Inertia

If it is true that phenomenal consciousness plays an important causal role in bringing about action, then the fact that my zombie twin is utterly devoid of phenomenal consciousness would make her future behavior radically different from mine.[7] This is because what it's like

[6] Of course, to really make sense of this, we need to supplement these reflections with metaphysical arguments about the relation between affect, motivation, and the production of behavior. The argument I present here is meant simply to show that commonsense observation provides strong grounds for such a thesis.

[7] Note that it is crucial for my thought experiment that the comparison/contrast in action occurs temporally downstream. The thought experiment as formulated by Chalmers does not include future times, whereas my own thought experiment does.

to experience various sensations, emotions, and moods would not shape or help to motivate my zombie twin's behavior. For example, the fact that volunteering at races made her feel happy would not draw her towards that activity, nor would the fact that energy bars made her feel nauseous cause her to avoid them. The way that it feels to be sad or depressed would not affect her beliefs or color her perceptions, and whether she feels bored, annoyed, amused, or terrified will not shape the course of her activities. Unaffected by the emotional experience or the feeling of "what-it's-like," her behavior would be mechanical and improperly motivated and would fail to qualify as genuine action.

Any attempt to imagine that my zombie counterpart is capable of volition and action leads to absurdities. First, it is unlikely that my zombie twin will persist at various tasks, so any activity that requires sustained effort and continues over a period of time will be unlikely. As discussed previously, this is because oftentimes it is only in virtue of our feelings of excitement, anxiety, and hope that we are sufficiently motivated to reach our goals.

On the other hand, one might imagine that as a result of being devoid of emotional experience, my zombie twin has an uncanny ability to spend large amounts of time doing those activities that most other people find painful or boring. For example, she is able to spend many hours doing hill repeats. Suppose that I begin the very same workout as my zombie counterpart and that initially our behavior is very similar. Both of us lace up our shoes, stretch, run up the hill, and then jog down the hill. Given our shared knee problems, we both notice some wobbling on the way down, and it occurs to both of us that maybe it is time to buy some new shoes. Suddenly my knee begins to throb and I begin to feel anxious. I am fearful of sustaining long-term injury, and this fear motivates me to walk down the hill to my car, drive home, and put an ice pack on my knee. My emotional experiences and sensations of discomfort thus help me to redirect or modify my training regimen when it no longer feels appropriate.

My zombie counterpart, on the other hand, never feels pained, anxious, or afraid. Because these qualitative experiences are absent for her, she may lack the motivation to stop doing hill repeats. At first, one might view my zombie counterpart as persistent and stoical. However, there is a point at which forbearance and endurance is no longer appropriate and may even become harmful. For me, as for all ordinary human beings, phenomenal experience often serves as an alert that something is wrong. The experience of pain and discomfort, in particular, helps to steer me away from scenarios that are harmful or dangerous. Because my zombie counterpart lacks phenomenal consciousness, what it's like to feel her knee throbbing cannot help alert her to the possibility that she will injure her knee. Likewise, feelings of nausea cannot help alert her to the fact that her blood sugar level is dropping and that she needs to eat. As a result, she has an impaired sense of when to call it quits.

So far I have suggested that emotional experience plays an integral role in helping to sustain and redirect our activities and efforts. My examples have relied upon the supposition that zombies are in fact capable of undertaking activities and projects. But is this true? Without emotional experience, *could a creature even begin* a training regimen, enter a race, or run a marathon? Perhaps for a time, we might we might be fooled into thinking that a zombie could do these things and that its behavior was an example of genuine effort and action. However, because the zombie utterly lacks any phenomenal experiences and emotional feelings, these behaviors will result simply from brain mechanisms. Everyday observation, on the other hand, suggests that people do things for reasons and that phenomenal consciousness often provides the impetus for action. A creature with no passion for anything, not even life, *has no reason* to try to become a better runner, achieve a personal record, or even get off the couch.

Indeed, insofar as my zombie duplicate lacks a capacity for emotional experience and feeling, circumstances simply lack importance or significance from her personal point of view. If she performs well in the marathon, she will not feel proud or happy. If she performs badly, she will not feel ashamed or disappointed. It seems that her accomplishments will simply have no meaning for her, and that as a result, her behavior will be stereotyped, unimaginative, and lacking in creativity and initiative. She is likely to appear indifferent, resigned, and apathetic, and any movements that look as if they belong to her are likely to seem mechanical. Rather than being repelled or attracted to activities or scenarios, she is likely to exhibit utter indifference. Because feelings of hope, pride, and yearning are not present to generate new desires, it is reasonable to conclude that she will not be motivated to do anything.

We have seen that phenomenal experience is central not only to redirecting our action and sustaining our efforts, but also to initiating these efforts. Thus, the fact that phenomenal consciousness played no causal role in my zombie twin's actions would make her future behavior different from mine. Emotions and mood would not shape or help to motivate her behavior. Desire, pleasure, and the avoidance of pain would not figure into her actions and she could not be drawn toward activities that she felt passionate about, such as running. Because her experiences lack a qualitative feel altogether, "what it's like" to be running a race, getting a muscle cramp, or crossing a finish-line cannot alter the course of her activity. Once we have traced conscious effort and desire to emotions and feelings, it seems clear that zombie behavior would be vastly different from the actions of ordinary human agents.

The Impossibility of Zombies

If emotional experience and its associated desires have causal power, the existence of a creature physically and causally identical to me that performs the very same actions I do, and yet lacks phenomenal experience, turns out to be impossible. There is no possible world in which my zombie, marathon-running duplicate suddenly begins to sprint due to feelings of pride and excitement. After all, if there is nothing that it is like for this creature to exist, it has no reason to do anything. In other words, because the subjective experience and the feelings associated with emotions are strongly linked to desire and motivation, there can be no such thing as a being, considered from my present vantage point on my own future, that performs the same actions that I do (i.e. is causally identical) and yet lacks phenomenal consciousness. This is because without phenomenal experience and feelings, the drive and passion needed to initiate and sustain efforts of will such as marathon running would be missing. In all possible worlds that contain creatures such as us, there is a tight causal connection between phenomenal consciousness and agency.

If zombies are metaphysically impossible, then Chalmers' argument fails to demonstrate that materialism is mistaken. Note that the discussion here is meant to demonstrate simply that while there may be very strong arguments against materialism, Chalmers' zombie argument is not one of them. Thus, these observations do not rule out either materialism or dualism, nor do they suggest that either of these positions is more plausible. What the above discussion *does* indicate is that there is tight connection between mind and body, as

Michelle Maiese

well as a causal link between how consciousness seems and what consciousness does. Any adequate theory of mind must explain the metaphysical and causal relationship between phenomenal consciousness, desire, and action. I believe that marathon running, with all its mental and physical demands, serves as a powerful example of the sorts of links that require explanation.

Chapter 19
The Soul of the Runner

Charles Taliaferro and Rachel Traughber

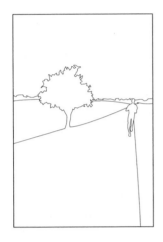

Ancient Greek and Roman philosophers commonly promoted athletics and physical exercise as part of the good life, often using athletic examples to exhort their students to pursue virtue. Just as an athlete must use his mind to control and subdue his body in the Olympic Games, so must the aspirant to a life of virtue control and discipline the disordered passions and desires that stem from our bodily appetites. This link between athletics and ethics may have been amplified because two of the main centers for philosophy (the Academy and Lyceum) were located by gymnasiums, places for athletic training and practice. From the work of Dio Chrysostom, Epictetus, Cicero, Lucian of Samosata, the Emperor Julian, Musonius Rufus, and others, there emerges a philosophical portrait of coordinated mind-body integration as key to achieving both athletic and ethical excellence. Traces of this portrait may also be seen in the New Testament (1 Tim. 4:7–8, for example).

Often this exhortation to virtue involved an explicit teaching that the mind and body are different, a position that has come to be called *dualism*. Probably the most famous case for a dualism of mind and body in ancient philosophy is Plato's dialogue the *Phaedo* in which the soul is depicted as a substantial reality distinct from the body and capable of surviving bodily death. This dualism was not unchallenged among the ancients – Democritus and Epicurus were early advocates of a fundamentally materialist view of the world – and today a range of philosophers would claim that the mind and body are one or, putting it differently, "the mind" is the body.[1]

In this chapter we consider the case for and against a dualist view of running and of human nature in general. We propose that while an extreme form of dualism is implausible, it is also implausible to collapse completely the difference between the mind and the body. Our essay, then, is a modest defense of the Greco-Roman philosophical tradition that maintains that the soul or mind is distinct from the body. But while they are different, they are also profoundly interwoven. The health of the body and the soul are mutually supportive, and fulfillment lies in achieving soul-body integration. Our positive case for our position will be built, in part, on the experience of what it is like to be a runner.

A few observations on terminology and on the importance of the issues before getting underway: In this chapter, the word "dualism" refers to the view that the mental life of a person that is traditionally attributed to the soul – her desires, thoughts, sensations, emotions, intentions, and so on – are distinct from physical things and events such as a human brain, central state nervous system, or one's body as a whole. Dualism is often taken to involve other claims as well, such as the view that only human beings have souls and the view that the mind is good while the body is evil. Most dualists today reject both assumptions, acknowledging that non-human animals have souls (the dogs we run with are fully conscious) and they reject any dualism of values in which the body is considered degenerate or base compared to the mind. We propose to use the term "holism" to stand for the view that the person is her body. According to holism, it is not the case that a person's desires, thoughts, sensations, etc. are distinct from her body; they are either brain or other bodily states or ways in which the person's physical body behaves in the world. On this view, the soul is the body. Aristotle held a position like this, and today this view is held by materialists, behaviorists, and others. The chief representative of holism we will consider is the British philosopher Gilbert Ryle (1900–1976). We believe his critique of dualism

---

[1] For an overview of Greek and Roman philosophical uses of athletics and other practices such as medicine in the pursuit of soul–body integration and virtue, see A. J. Malherbe, *Moral Exhortation: A Greco-Roman Source Book* (Philadelphia: Westminster, 1986) and Martha C. Nussbaum, *The Therapy of Desire* (Princeton: Princeton University Press, 1994).

has not been surpassed in content or credibility; he has the respect of one of the most prominent advocates of materialism today, Daniel Dennett, and, unlike virtually all contemporary philosophers, his case for holism involves an appeal to skilled practices like running. We also believe that Ryle's depiction of what it is like to engage in skilled practices provides an excellent case for the view which we will come to articulate and defend.[2]

Why should it matter which view is correct? We believe that extreme forms of holism and dualism lead to an imbalanced treatment of our minds and bodies. Holism rightly gives center stage to our bodily life, but, taken to an extreme, it threatens to diminish or even eliminate our mental life. Extreme holism can cover up or completely ignore the subjective inwardness of our lives. Dualism, taken to an extreme, can diminish our bodily life or treat it as irrelevant. An unhealthy dualism would see the body as a mere vehicle for the soul. Both views are, to put it mildly, unhealthy. And, following some of the older Greco-Roman moralists, we believe that coordinating the mind and body in an integrated fashion can provide a stable framework for the pursuit of virtue.

There is another reason why it matters which view is correct. Due to limitations of space, this factor cannot be discussed at length. We suspect Plato is right in the *Phaedo*: if the soul is distinct from the body, it is possible that the soul can survive the death of the body. But if the soul is the body, as Democritus thought, then the annihilation of the body amounts to the annihilation of the soul. Consider this analogy: If Bennie the Jet is the Speedster (in fact, these are the nicknames of the same person, Bennie Brazell, who was a 2004 Olympic team member for the US), then the annihilation of Bennie the Jet amounts to the annihilation of the Speedster. If we are our bodies, there might still somehow be an afterlife.[3] Perhaps there is a God who will resurrect our bodies or recreate them, but we think that the prospects of an afterlife look much grimmer given holism rather than dualism. The implications of whether one adopts dualism or holism or a combination of the two can have an impact on one's view of death.

---

[2] Dennett was a student of Ryle's and often sings his praises. See, for example, Daniel Dennett, *The Intentional Stance* (Cambridge: MIT Press, 1987). Ryle is widely credited with spearheading the attack on dualism in post-World War II philosophy. There is some resemblance between his critique of dualism and the arguments of Ludwig Wittgenstein.
[3] Taliaferro has pursued such issues in Charles Taliaferro, *Consciousness and the Mind of God* (Cambridge: Cambridge University Press, 1994).

A Holistic Account of Running

One of the reasons the holistic account is attractive is that dualism seems intolerable. To believe that persons consist of a soul and body involves intractable problems concerning how the two are related, all of which may be avoided if you believe that a person is just one thing.

Dualism seems to introduce a radical division in which a person may be seen as having two lives: a physical, public one, and another one which is private and invisible. In *The Concept of Mind*, Ryle describes what he sees as the damaging consequences of dualism.[4]

> A person . . . lives through two collateral histories, one consisting of what happens in and to his body, the other consisting of what happens in and to his mind. The first is public, the second private. The events in the first history are events in the physical world; those in the second are events in the mental world. (Ryle, pp. 11–12)

One of the main problems that result from this division is that it invites an entrenched skepticism about the mental lives of other people. If you never see (literally, observe) another person's mental life, how do you know that the thing you see is actually a person? Perhaps it is a zombie-goblin, some soulless being with similar anatomy to human beings but without any consciousness whatsoever. As Ryle puts the problem:

> Even if he [the dualist] prefers to believe that to other human bodies there are harnessed minds similar to his own, he cannot claim to be able to discover their individual characteristics, or the particular things that they undergo and do. Absolute solitude is on this showing the ineluctable destiny of the soul. Only our bodies can meet. (Ryle, p. 15)

This is what some philosophers call *the problem of other minds*.

The problem of other minds is one that is easily illustrated in a comparatively modest case: How do you know that what you see and describe as the color "blue" is the same as what another person sees and describes as "blue"? Could it be that your brain is so peculiar that actually the same object in a box of crayons causes you to have

---

[4] Gilbert Ryle, *The Concept of Mind* (New York: Barnes and Noble, 1949). Hereafter, "Ryle."

different sensations than someone else? We describe this case as "modest" for surely there must be *some* natural disparity between the ways each of us experiences the world, but when you take it to an extreme, matters seem to become incoherent. How do you know that there is anyone else in the world if you cannot literally observe them (their thoughts, intentions, motives) but only their bodies? Do you simply form a hypothesis that other people exist or, rather, don't you (as Ryle suggests) actually observe the people you meet?

One way to get at the driving force behind Ryle's position is to consider this question: Do legs run or do people run? Arguably, it would be very odd indeed to say that your legs do the running, rather than the person as a whole being. Holism has the virtue of making sense of the way in which we naturally think of *the whole person* as engaged in running rather than, say, think that the soul runs by virtue of making the body move. Dualism threatens to treat running the way we treat driving a car. A contemporary dualist, Richard Swinburne, seems in danger of adopting this instrumental, vehicular model. "An agent has a body if there is a chunk of matter through which alone he or she can learn about the world."[5] Dualism can wind up equating the body as an organic vehicle in which the soul is mobilized (Swinburne's depiction of having a body might fit a description of what it is like to have exclusive control of a car) or, as Ryle thought, dualists treat the soul as a ghost inhabiting a body which functions as a machine.

Dualism not only faces the problem of knowing and experiencing other people and treating the person as a ghost in a mechanical body, but it also suffers from the burden of explaining the causal link between the soul and the body. How can something non-physical interact with something physical? Physical events cause other physical events in a world of space and time. If the soul is non-physical, presumably it would not be in physical space, with a given mass, volume, weight, and electric charge. But if the soul lacks all these properties, how can the soul make a difference to physical objects like your legs or body as a whole?

Although Ryle did not directly discuss running, much of what he has to say about the nature of skills and practices make running an

---

[5] Richard Swinburne, *Providence and the Problem of Evil* (Oxford: Oxford University Press, 1998), p. 98. While we are critical of Swinburne's presentation of dualism here, we highly commend his work in general. See Richard Swinburne, *Evolution of the Soul* (Oxford: Clarendon, 1997).

excellent example to support his position. What do people admire when they admire a superb runner? Ryle would say that they admire a public performance. "It is the visible performance that they admire, but they admire it not for being an effect of any hidden internal causes but for being an exercise of a skill" (Ryle, p. 33). Ryle claims that his non-dualist, essentially holist view of the person is much better equipped to appreciate how we acquire and judge skills. Dualists tend to give pride of place to a kind of theoretical knowledge – what Ryle called "knowledge *that.*" Descartes (1596–1650), the best-known advocate of dualism since Plato, believed that one must *know that* you have a body in order to *know how to act*. If Descartes is right, you cannot know how to run unless you know that you have a body, and so on. Ryle proposed, instead, that *the knowledge of how to do something* like running is more fundamental than an abstract claim about knowing that the world is the way it is, you have a body, and so on. *Know-how* involves learning public practices in a way that is prior to theoretical inspection and formulation. Did one learn how to run or walk through the practice of running and walking, or did one first have to learn the theory of these two movements?

> We learn *how* by practice, schooled indeed by criticism and example, but *often quite unaided by any lessons in the theory* . . . [A chess-player's] knowledge *how* is exercised primarily in the moves that he makes, or concedes, and in the moves that he avoids or vetoes. So long as he can observe the rules, we do not care if he cannot also formulate them. It is not what he does in his head or with his tongue, but what he does on the board [or, in our particular case, on the track] that shows whether or not he knows the rules in the executive way of being able to apply them. (Ryle, p. 41) [Emphasis added].

A holist view is therefore not to be preferred because the dualist view has problems, but because the holist view does the most justice to our experience. In the very practice of running, we are engaged in a fully observable, public action.

A Defense of Dualistic Runners

Despite this impressive set of reasons for adopting holism, dualism is not without its merits. We will in fact argue that some form of dualism is even required to make sense of the experience and practices of activities such as running.

Let's first consider Ryle's portrayal of dualism. In many respects Ryle exaggerates the way in which dualism is hamstrung by a fragmented, splintered view of embodied persons. Ryle is, in other words, attacking an extreme form of dualism. If the soul is non-physical, as dualism supposes, must the soul be thought of as non-spatial? Yes and no.

Yes. Dualists make a plausible claim in holding that thoughts, emotions, feelings, and other mental states and activities are not in space in the sense that they can be perceived to have weight, color, electric charge, and so on, the way one can perceive the weight, color, electric charge and so on of the brain or the body as a whole. When you are angry, this affects your adrenaline, heart rate, perspiration, brainwaves, and so on, but is the emotion (and the relevant feelings, thoughts, and desires) itself the very same thing as the adrenaline, heart rate, perspiration, brainwaves, and so on? Presumably you could know all there is to know about the physiology and location of the causes of anger (or fatigue, exhilaration, competitiveness, and all the other feelings bound up with running) without being able to pinpoint anger as possessing a given size, shape, and the like. Two leading contemporary philosophers of mind who are not dualists, Colin McGinn and John Searle, have recently conceded that consciousness is not itself experienced as a spatial object or process.[6] McGinn offers this plausible depiction of the difference between consciousness (as well as other mental phenomena) and bodily states:

> The property of consciousness itself (or specific conscious states) is not an observable or perceptible property of the brain. You can stare into a living conscious brain, your own or someone else's, and see there a wide variety of instantiated properties – its shape, color, texture, etc.

[6] John Searle: "We are not aware in conscious experience of . . . the dimensions of our conscious experience. Although we experience objects and events as both spatially extended and of temporal duration, our consciousness itself is not experienced as spatial, though it is experienced as temporally extended" (Searle, *The Rediscovery of Mind*, Cambridge, MA: MIT Press, 1992), pp. 113, 115. Colin McGinn: "It is precisely [spatially defined properties] that seem inherently incapable of resolving the mind-brain problem: we cannot link consciousness to the brain in virtue of spatial properties of the brain – consciousness defies explanation in such terms. Consciousness does not seem made up out of smaller spatial processes . . . our faculties bias us towards understanding matter in motion, but it is precisely this kind of understanding that is inapplicable to the mind-body problem" (Colin McGinn, *The Problem of Consciousness*, Oxford: Blackwell, 1990, pp. 11, 18).

– but you will not thereby see what the subject is experiencing, the conscious state itself.[7]

So, we think there is nothing intrinsically absurd about recognizing *a non-spatial dimension to human nature*, but for all that, dualism can recognize that, in a sense, the person and her body are both in the same place and share the same history *because the person (or soul) and body function as a unity*. In a case of healthy movement and activity, to see and listen to another person's body is to see and listen to her soul or, putting it differently, it is to see and listen to the person as a whole, integrated being. Our point is that while an extreme form of dualism can completely split the soul and define the body as a vehicle for the soul, dualists can also affirm the integrated, interwoven character of the soul and body. While there is a genuine distinction between the mental and physical, these can be so bound together that they function as a whole.

Let's return to the depiction of the mind-body relationship. It is true that if one is severely damaged, one's body might well feel like a remote "chunk of matter through which alone he or she can make a difference to the world, and through which alone he or she can learn about the world." But unlike any other chunk of matter (or bundle of mass energy) to touch your body is to touch *you* because you have all the relevant sensations including the inner awareness of your bodily movements (you can tell whether your legs are crossed without looking). A more modified form of dualism needs to appreciate how we think, move, and act as embodied beings. When we line up at the starting line in a recreation of the *dolichos* (a long-distance race in the ancient Olympics), we do so as the embodied beings that you see, not as ghosts in running machines.[8] Dualism can capture the experience of why, sometimes, we do think of our bodies as machines or we even try to shut out feelings of pain and exhaustion as we run mechanically, resembling what must seem to non-runners as robots. But dualism is also able to capture the experience of mind-body coordinated functioning and integration.

[7] McGinn, *The Problem of Consciousness*, pp. 10–11.
[8] For the development of a form of dualism that underscores the unified nature of embodied life, see Charles Taliaferro, "The Virtues of Embodiment," *Philosophy* 76/1, 2001, pp. 111–25. For other arguments for dualism, see William Hasker, *The Emergent Self* (Ithaca: Cornell University Press, 1999).

Ryle suggests that dualism is profoundly at odds with our everyday descriptions and intuitions about ourselves, but note how running manuals routinely distinguish as well as interrelate (without identifying) the physical and the psychological. *Running for Dummies* is representative. In the chapter "What Running Can Do For You," (chapter 2) there are two subtitles: "Physical benefits from running" and "Mental rewards from running".[9] Authors Florence "Flo-Jo" Griffith Joyner and John Hanc are not advancing high-powered philosophical theories of human nature, but their helpful discussion of running benefits implies that running involves something more than muscles, bones, brain, blood, heart, and sweat. In addition to the physical dimensions of running there is the mental world of intentions, resolutions, sensations, plans, and so on.

Does dualism still leave one with a completely unexplainable gap in accounting for how the soul and body interact? The philosophy of causation is complex, and tackling this question fully would require a book of its own. A succinct reply can be made, however, in three brief points.

First, the charge that dualism is incoherent because it allows for causal interaction between radically different kinds of things is based on a narrow, perhaps even archaic concept of causal interaction. If we assume Newtonian mechanics, action between spatial objects from a distance is problematic, but now quantum theory seems to require a wholly different picture of interaction, including the causal interaction between non-contiguous, remote objects. The prestigious *Oxford Companion to Philosophy* entry for "materialism" offers an implied criticism of philosophers who assume that physical interaction is a straightforward, non-puzzling relation between spatial objects:

> Photons and neutrons have little or no mass and neither do fields, while particles pop out of the void, destroy each other, and pop back again. All this, however, has had remarkably little effect on the various philosophical views that can be dubbed "materialism," though one might think it shows at least that materialism is not the simple no-nonsense, tough-minded alternative it might once have seemed to be.[10]

[9] Florence Griffith-Joyner and John Hanc, *Running for Dummies* (Foster City, CA: IDG Books Worldwide, 1999).
[10] Ted Honderich (ed.), *The Oxford Companion to Philosophy* (Oxford: Oxford University Press, 2005), p. 564.

In the evolving portrait of contemporary physics with dark matter, 12 variations of leptons and quarks, and four distinct force particles (photons, gravitons, gluons, and intermediate vector bisons), it is harder to rule out dualist interaction from the get-go.

Second, contemporary neurology has not demonstrated the identity of the mind and body. On the contrary, contemporary science establishes correlation and interaction between the mental and physical, demonstrating the ways in which neurological damage or health can define mental illness and health. But correlation and interaction are not identity. And, as McGinn has noted, no observation and analysis of the brain *as a physical object* amounts to observing and seeing a person's mental life. A neurologist can certainly claim to see the organic foundation and causal condition for thinking, but this is not the same as the observation, witnessing, or experiencing of the thinking itself.[11]

Third, the dualist has no more of an explanation gap between the mental and the physical than holism. Virtually all plausible accounts of physical causation eventually have to posit certain basic powers or causal properties of objects or micro-particles and events that are not further explained by deeper laws or powers. Ultimately, both dualists and holists must recognize that certain objects and events have basic causal powers. While holists do not posit a causal link between the physical and non-physical, most still recognize that there is some mystery as to when the brain, nervous system, and body constitute a conscious, mentally endowed person and when they do not. The emergence of consciousness (even if we imagine it is fully observable and physical) is not like any other emergent property. You do not see thoughts by seeing a brain event the way one would see the molecular constitution of water after immense magnification that displays the hydrogen and oxygen bonds. Jaegwon Kim, a well known contemporary philosopher who is not a dualist, puts the problem this way: "How could a series of physical events, little particles jostling against one another, electric current rushing to and fro . . . blossom into a conscious experience? . . . Why shouldn't pain and itch be switched around? . . . Why should any experience emerge when these neurons fire?"[12] No contemporary holist or materialist has (in our

[11] See M. R. Bennett and P. M. S. Hacker, *Philosophical Foundations of Neuroscience* (Oxford: Blackwell, 2003).
[12] Jaegwon Kim, *Philosophy of Mind* (Boulder: Westview Press, 1996), p. 8.

view) eliminated the mystery of the transformation and evolution from physical phenomena that have no consciousness to physical phenomena that are conscious. A leading philosopher, David Chalmers, comments on how the emergence of consciousness from non-conscious public substrata is basic and not explainable in deeper terms:

> It might be objected that [his theory of how the mental emerges from the non-mental, merely physical processes] does not tell us what the connection is, or how a physical configuration gives rise to experience. But the search for such a connection is misguided . . . [B]eyond a certain point, there is no asking "how."[13]

The problem of confidently knowing that other humans have minds is yet another major hurdle for dualists to jump. Is the dualist left only with solitude? In one sense, we think that there must be a kind of solitude that is possible and hard to avoid. It is possible (we think) for us to be systematically mistaken, caught in the Matrix as it were, so that everything we thought we observed is a systematic hallucination, coordinated by drugs and supercomputers. If Ryle is right, one simply cannot be mistaken in one's experience of meeting other people, but we think this goes too far against the possibility (however strange) of skepticism.

But abstract thought experiments and science fiction are unnecessary to reply to Ryle. How might one distinguish the following two states of affairs?

> Chris the Cheater: In a competitive run, Chris intentionally runs recklessly, thus bumping someone out of the race.

> Pat the Clumsy: In a competitive run, Pat unintentionally runs awkwardly, thus bumping someone out of the race.

Imagine neither has done the act before, neither confesses, and everything about both of them is meticulously observed. Even their brains are being monitored. Would we be able to distinguish between these two cases by only observing their bodies? We do not think so, and yet this is a clear example in which the first mishap was done on

[13] David Chalmers, *The Conscious Mind: In Search of a Fundamental Theory* (Oxford: Oxford University Press, 1997), p. 170.

purpose whereas the second was not. Holism cannot provide grounds for distinguishing the different cases.

Imagine this reply: But if you are observing the brain of each of them, would you not detect some slight difference between the cases? Perhaps Chris's mishap causes him/her to be happy because there is one less person in the race to compete against, whereas Pat is devastated because he/she may unintentionally have seriously injured someone. Surely this must be visible in their brainwaves – different parts of the brain react to the same situation – even if we cannot observe any difference between the two persons in terms of their behavior or what they tell us. Perhaps there is no outward, visible difference between Pat and Chris, but, given access to their brains, the two situations would be distinguishable.

While there are centers of the brain that can be well matched with differences in emotions – even emotions that seem rather similar such as feelings of guilt versus shame seem to involve different neurological events – there is nonetheless reason to believe that there is no evident *identity* between thoughts and brain states so that if the two people had the same thought (e.g. there is a marathon tomorrow), that thought would be grounded in the same brain state. Very different brain activity can sustain similar thoughts, and very different thoughts can accompany or match very similar brain activity. (Philosophers call this *the problem of multiple realizability*, referring to the way in which the same mental states can be realized in multiple ways.)[14] If this is so, then holism would still not have a way to distinguish the cases of Pat and Chris. But, rather than insist on this reply, consider the possibility that the holists *are* able to map out neuroanatomy completely in order to distinguish accidents from cheating. Would this in any way show that dualism is false and holism is true?

We do not think so. The achievement of such a complete neuroanatomy would, rather, make clear that holism is a theory of the *correlation between mental states* (e.g. attempting to cheat in a race) *and physical states, and correlations are not identities*. We certainly do not find in such an imagined complete neuroanatomy anything remotely like the identities in science, such as heat *is* mean kinetic energy. You look closely enough at hot metals and you measure molecular motion; the relation, like water and H_2O, is one of

---

[14] See Bennett and Hacker, *Philosophical Foundations of Neuroscience.*

constitution, but there is no analogous relation of constitution between the mental and the physical. More powerful magnifications of the structure of the brain will not bring to light and make observable a person's thinking, feeling, desires, and so on.

We conclude, then, that dualism deserves a serious hearing and rests on plausible intuitions and observations about human nature. For all that, however, we are also pulled in the direction of holism because of its highlighting of the profound unity of human experience. This comes to the fore in Ryle's depiction of know-how and the skill of running.

What It's Like to be a Runner

One of the most famous papers in contemporary philosophy of mind is Thomas Nagel's "What is it like to be a bat?"[15] Nagel argued that there are subjective mental states (including the feelings had by bats) that are not explained by current forms of materialism. In a related fashion, we think that the experience of what it's like to be a runner secures an important position in philosophy of mind; namely the thesis that, on the one hand, dualism needs to accommodate the holist thesis that we are integral beings and that holism, on the other hand, needs to make more room for subjective experience. We believe that Ryle has rightly given a central role to practical know-how and that this is an illuminating contribution to our thinking about human nature. We believe that this, in a way, exhibits why one needs a view of human persons that fully brings together the bodily and the mental as Ryle does, but without collapsing the mental and the physical into a single, homogenous thing. So, returning to Ryle's account of practice, we indicate in brackets where there needs to be an explicit recognition of the mental:

> We learn *how* by practice, schooled indeed by criticism [teaching and criticism involves intentional instruction] and example, but often quite unaided by any lessons in the theory [this depends what one means by "theory;" one cannot eliminate all *knowledge that*; in order to run intentionally, presumably we must know that there is a route ahead of us and so on] . . . His knowledge *how* is exercised primarily in the

[15] See Thomas Nagel, *Mortal Questions* (Cambridge: Cambridge University Press, 1979).

moves that he makes, or concedes, and in the moves that he avoids or vetoes [this seems to involve choices and intentions]. So long as he can observe the rules, we do not care if he cannot also formulate them [observing is mental]. It is not what he does in his head or with his tongue, but what he does on the board that shows whether or not he knows the rules in the executive way of being able to apply them [we may not care about an independent investigation of the head and tongue because we assume the person is healthy and trustworthy].

In this enlarged portrait of skilled activity – consider the case of running particularly – one may readily see how one needs to philosophically recognize an intimate interaction of the mental and physical. This seems to match in an ideal way our own experience of running, of working to control the breathing, to know when to sprint in a race, and so on. Running makes no sense if it is understood as primarily mental, but neither does it make sense if one thinks of it as primarily material. Pain and exhilaration are physiologically based but are not the same thing as physiology; to address pain and exhilaration we need to move beyond physiology to include psychology. This combination of holistic and dualistic insights we call holistic dualism.

Once one allows for both the mental and the physical in running, one may readily see the pursuit of excellence (or fun or exercise or therapy) in running as a coordination of the soul and body, the mental and physical. Holism, we believe, captures the genuine insight that we naturally pursue and understand our running and other practices as individuals in public, observable ways. Holistic dualism, then, can articulate when one is running in an integrated, healthy fashion, as well as articulate and explain when this integration is lost, as when one of us (Charles) had a hopeless knee injury that left him very much feeling like a ghost in a machine for three months. Back to Swinburne's bizarre picture of the soul inhabiting the body as if it were an organic car: the problem was not that this picture of the soul and body is always wrong. A person can suffer a massive breakdown and accurately think of his or her body as such a peculiar machine. But Swinburne's case is not a portrait of what it is to be integrated with soul and body, mind and matter, and running like the wind.

Back to Ryle's earlier charge that dualism is locked into viewing the soul and body as having two histories or that dualists treat the soul as solitary. We objected that the soul and body can share the same history and enjoy a public life, but we also want to allow that holistic dualism can recognize that sometimes, in great anxiety and focused activities, we can undergo two histories and experience immense isolation. A runner at the start of a race, spikes on, feet in blocks, at the moment before the pistol fires, can be living in a focused, nervous, adrenaline-driven, isolated, profoundly interior life. Later, she may have an altogether different, public life, enjoying the exhilaration of the crowd, embracing friends. Our point is that this portrait of shifting between the interior and the public does involve two, valid points of view. Holism as well as dualism is vindicated by the multi-dimensional mental/physical interaction, in integration as well as in breakdowns.

We suggest that the most promising account of human nature lies in combining holism with an appreciation of the dualist insight that there are distinctive, non-physical psychological states. Holistic dualism allows one to appreciate that in this life we function as an integration of mind and body, and to appreciate, too, that Plato in his dialogue the *Phaedo* might, after all, be right about life and death. Perhaps, and maybe just perhaps, the death of the body is not necessarily the end of the road for the soul of the runner.[16]

[16] We thank Mike Austin and Kristen Rauk for comments on earlier versions of this essay.

Notes on Contributors

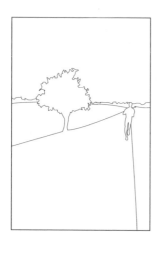

Michael W. Austin is assistant professor of philosophy at Eastern Kentucky University. He has published articles in ethics and philosophy of religion, and is the author of *Conceptions of Parenthood: Ethics and the Family* (Aldershot: Ashgate, 2007).

Gregory Bassham is professor of philosophy at King's College (Pennsylvania). He coedited *Basketball and Philosophy: Thinking Outside the Paint* (Lexington, KY: University Press of Kentucky, 2007) and *The Lord of the Rings and Philosophy: One Book to Rule Them All* (Chicago, IL: Open Court, 2003) and is coauthor of *Critical Thinking: A Student's Introduction* (Boston, MA: McGraw-Hill, 3rd edn., 2007).

Raymond Angelo Belliotti, distinguished teaching professor of philosophy at SUNY Fredonia, has published seven books on topics that include legal theory, sexual ethics, personal and ethnic identity, Nietzsche, the meaning of life, human happiness, and the philosophy of baseball. He is currently composing a book on Machiavelli and philosophy.

Amby Burfoot won the Boston Marathon in 1968, and has been executive editor of *Runner's World* magazine for the past 25 years.

Richard DeWitt is a professor of philosophy and chair of the department at Fairfield University. His main areas of research are logic and the history and philosophy of science, and he is the author of *Worldviews: An Introduction to the History and Philosophy of Science* (Malden, MA: Blackwell, 2004).

Jeffrey P. Fry is assistant professor in the department of philosophy and religious studies at Ball State University. His recent publications have focused on the intersection of sport, ethics, and religion. He is the author of "Pain, Suffering and Paradox in Sport and Religion," in *Pain and Injury in Sport: Social and Ethical Analysis*, ed. Sigmund Loland, Berit Skirstad, and Ivan Waddington (New York: Routledge, 2006).

Douglas R. Hochstetler is assistant professor of kinesiology at Penn State University, Lehigh Valley. His research areas of interest include sport ethics, meaning in physical activity, and the history of inter-collegiate football.

William P. Kabasenche is assistant professor of philosophy at Washington State University, and was Bell Fellow at the Center for Biomedical Ethics at the University of Virginia.

Sharon Kaye is associate professor of philosophy at John Carroll University in Cleveland, Ohio. She has published on a range of topics primarily connected with medieval philosophy and is the author of *Philosophy for Teens* (Waco, TX: Prufrock Press, 2006).

Chris Kelly is visiting assistant professor of philosophy at the University of Maryland. He specializes in value theory, moral psychology, and metaethics. In addition, he is working on a theory of international justice.

Kevin Kinghorn is philosophy tutor at Wycliffe Hall, University of Oxford, and assistant professor of philosophy at Asbury Theological Seminary. He has published articles in moral philosophy, metaphysics, and philosophy of religion, and is the author of *The Decision of Faith: Can Christian Beliefs be Freely Chosen?* (Edinburgh: T. & T. Clark, 2005).

Michelle Maiese is assistant professor of philosophy at Emmanuel College. She has published in the areas of conflict resolution and philosophy of mind, and is the coauthor of *Embodied Minds in Action* (New York: Oxford University Press, 2008).

Christopher Martin is a doctoral student at the Institute of Education, University of London. He has published in the areas of educational justice and philosophy of education.

J. P. Moreland is distinguished professor of philosophy at Talbot School of Theology, Biola University. He has authored, edited, or contributed to 35 books, including *Does God Exist?* (Amherst, NY: Prometheus, 1993); *Naturalism: A Critical Analysis* (New York: Routledge, 2000), *Body & Soul* (Downers Grove, IL: InterVarsity, 2000), and *The Blackwell Companion to Natural Theology* (forthcoming). He has also published over 60 articles in professional journals.

Martha C. Nussbaum is Ernst Freund distinguished service professor of law and ethics at the University of Chicago, appointed in the philosophy department, law school, and divinity school. Her most recent book is *Frontiers of Justice: Disability, Nationality, Species Membership* (Cambridge, MA: Harvard University Press, 2006).

Ross C. Reed is assistant professor of philosophy and interdisciplinary humanities at Rhodes College. He is also a philosophical counselor in private practice in Memphis, Tennessee. He is currently working on a book on philosophical counseling.

Heather L. Reid is associate professor of philosophy at Morningside College in Sioux City, Iowa, and current president of the International Association for the Philosophy of Sport. She has published in ancient Greek philosophy, philosophy of sport, and Olympic studies. Her book, *The Philosophical Athlete* was published by Carolina Academic Press (Durham, NC) in 2002.

Charles Taliaferro is professor of philosophy at St. Olaf College. He has published in philosophy of religion, ethics, and philosophy of mind, and is the author of *Consciousness and the Mind of God* (New York: Cambridge University Press, 1994) and *Evidence and Faith* (New York: Cambridge University Press, 2005).

Rachel Traughber has studied music and philosophy and done a great deal of running at St. Olaf College, the Institute for the Education of Students in Vienna, Austria, and Boston University. Her most recent publication is a contribution to *The Chronicles of Narnia and Philosophy* (Chicago, IL: Open Court, 2005).

Raymond J. VanArragon is assistant professor of philosophy at Bethel University in St. Paul, Minnesota. He has published in philosophy of religion and ethics, and is coeditor of *Contemporary Debates in Philosophy of Religion* (Malden, MA: Blackwell, 2004).

J. Jeremy Wisnewski is an assistant professor of philosophy at Hartwick College. He has authored many articles in moral and political philosophy, as well as *Wittgenstein and Ethical Inquiry* (London: Continuum, 2007) and *The Politics of Agency* (Aldershot: Ashgate, forthcoming). More importantly, he is the editor of *Family Guy and Philosophy* (Malden, MA: Blackwell, 2007) and *The Office and Philosophy* (Malden, MA: Blackwell, forthcoming).

Index